THE MAKING OF MODERN DRAMA

RICHARD GILMAN

THE MAKING OF
MODERN DRAMA

*A study of Büchner, Ibsen,
Strindberg, Chekhov, Pirandello,
Brecht, Beckett, Handke*

NEW YORK   *Farrar, Straus and Giroux*

Library of Congress Cataloging in Publication Data
Gilman, Richard.
    The making of modern drama.

    1. Drama—19th century—History and criticism.
    2. Drama—20th century—History and criticism.
    I. Title.
PN1851.G5   809.2   74-1171

For my son Nicholas,
and for Harold Brodkey

CONTENTS

FOREWORD

The origin of this book is in a course of lectures on "modern" drama I have been giving for several years at Yale. I put "modern" in quotation marks because its use here is something of a chronological absurdity. We speak, for example, of modern fiction or poetry and mean fiction beginning with the first works of Joyce, Mann, or Gide, say, and poetry that comes into being with Valéry, Eliot, Rilke, at the earliest Mallarmé. In other words, literature of the twentieth century or just before. And even so we are compelled by time and artistic change to adopt a new term, "post-modernist," to keep us abreast of what has happened. But there is no such term we can use for present drama, since in almost all the textbooks the modernity of the theater goes back in an unbroken line to Ibsen's *Brand* and *Peer Gynt*, written in the 1860's. And I have pushed the chronology even further back, to Georg Büchner, who died in 1837.

What this means is that the modern in drama is something considerably different from what it is in the purely literary arts. There is no great mystery about the matter. Drama, the compromised—or at least compromisable—art, the one that depends so heavily on physical factors and economic wherewithal, as well as on collaboration, has always lagged behind in innovation, internal transformation. When in the 1880's Strindberg complained that the theater discouraged new ideas and techniques, he simply gave utterance to what every great artist-playwright since Büchner has known. For the theater has for several centuries been primarily a bourgeois art or enterprise, and therefore a conservative one, and it is still so in its major sectors. The result of this is that the artist in the theater has had to work against the tide, perpetually trying to "catch up" to artistic developments elsewhere.

Another more hidden result is that modern drama has never held the kind of central position in educated consciousness that modern fiction and poetry have. We may admire Chekhov and find Strindberg perversely interesting, we may think Brecht important and Pirandello stimulating, but we do not accord to these writers the homage as shapers of our sensibility and awareness we give to novelists like Joyce, Proust, or Kafka, or poets like Eliot and Yeats. If, that is to say, we any longer give such homage at all. Still, even the revolt against literary models for consciousness—if such a thing is really as widespread as chic wisdom would have it— is itself a testament to some former sovereignty which the drama hasn't exercised since Shakespeare.

My assumptions in this book are that drama ought to matter to us as a source of consciousness, that great plays can be as revelatory of human existence as novels or poems, that such plays aren't discrete objects to which we "go" but analogues of our lives which we encounter, and that an account of how some of them came into being in the modern period, against heavy obstacles and on unpromising ground, can be an instructive—I hope fascinating—chapter of imaginative history.

It will be obvious to any reader that I have attempted no sort of comprehensive history, no "survey" of modern drama, not even a complete study of the playwrights I have chosen to write about. My principle of selection has simply been this: these are the playwrights of the past century or so I most love or admire, these are the plays of theirs I find most significant, either in themselves or in regard to the author's development. There are no eccentric choices here, nor are there any unknown masterpieces brought to light, although a word might be said about Peter Handke, a writer just out of his thirties, uncanonized as yet, the way the other seven, intelligently or not, have been. I include Handke because he seems to me to have written the most interesting plays since Beckett and, more than that, because he is carrying on more resolutely than anyone I know of that effort to renew drama, to combat its tendency to inertia and self-repetition, which is one of my book's implicit subjects.

The book is arranged chronologically because that seemed to me the simplest way of doing it, not because I see drama as obeying those strict laws of progression (or regression followed by juvenescence, etc.) whose identification makes up so much academic toil. On the contrary: my essay on Büchner, that scarcely accountable genius, makes it clear that I think artistic history is much more a matter of mysterious changes and sudden leaps than of steady movement, Hegelian fulfillments. Dramatists, like other artists, naturally learn from their predecessors, but even more perilously than novelists or poets or painters they find themselves thrown on their own inventiveness, having to "make it new" because the old so adamantly persists.

The book contains no footnotes, so I would like to acknowledge here my sources for factual material and the translations I've used. For Büchner, the translation of *Danton's Death* is by Carl Mueller and of *Woyzeck* by Henry J. Schmidt; the biographical data from Mueller, Herbert Lindenberger, and Michael Hamburger. The translation of Ibsen's *Peer Gynt* is by Rolf Fjelde, those of the other Ibsen plays by Michael Meyer; I have made extensive use of Mr. Meyer's splendid biography of Ibsen and have drawn on Evert Sprinchorn's *Letters and Speeches of Ibsen*. The translations of Strindberg's *The Father* and *Miss Julie* are by Meyer, that of *To Damascus* by Graham Rawson, of *A Dream Play* by Elizabeth Sprigge and of *The Pelican* by Sprinchorn. I have used Miss Sprigge's *The Strange Life of August Strindberg; Letters of Strindberg to Harriet*

Bosse, edited and translated by Arvid Paulson; and several volumes of Strindberg's autobiographical writings translated by Sprinchorn.

For Chekhov I have used David Magarshack's translation of *Platonov;* Ronald Hingley's of *Ivanov, The Wood Demon, Uncle Vanya,* and *The Seagull;* and Randall Jarrell's of *The Three Sisters.* Ernest Simmons's *Chekhov* and Magarshack's *Chekhov the Dramatist* were my chief sources of biographical information. The Pirandello translations (by far the least satisfactory; but they are the only English versions extant, a strange gap) are by Arthur Livingston for *Right You Are!* and Edward Storer for *Six Characters* and *Henry IV;* Walter Starkie's *Luigi Pirandello* was my main source for the life. The Brecht translations are all by Eric Bentley, and I have used David Ewen's biography and Martin Esslin's *Brecht: The Man and the Work,* and *Brecht on Theater,* edited by John Willet. The Handke translations are all by Michael Roloff.

The sources listed above have been my main ones. In addition, I have made good use of various issues of *The Drama Review* (and its predecessor, *The Tulane Drama Review*) and *Performance* magazine. Whatever else I have drawn upon is acknowledged in the text.

The chapters on Büchner and Pirandello were published in *Yale Theater,* on Handke in *American Review,* and on Beckett in *Partisan Review,* all in slightly different form. Thanks are due to the editors of these publications for permission to reprint.

THE MAKING OF MODERN DRAMA

BÜCHNER

A genius may be a century ahead of his time
and therefore appear to be a paradox, but ultimately the race will assimilate what was once a
paradox in such a way that it is no longer para-
doxical.

KIERKEGAARD, *Genius and Apostle*

There is a temptation to think of culture as continuous and
progressive, to see works of art, for example, succeeding one
another like animate bodies in the physical order, organically
breeding their own more or less predictable descendants. We
want to consider imaginative and intellectual works as elements in a purposeful scheme and find it hard to believe that
any significant artist or thinker would be without solid, identifiable forerunners. This is one reason we balk at the new,
which seems to lack connections and derivations; periods of
so-called experiment are regarded as the spawning time of
monsters—in the precise physical sense—which disgust or en-
rage us until time softens their alien features and they take
their place as docile components of a lineage. But then fresh
aberrations appear, which once more upset our careful organized histories of the arts and of creativity in general, until
these things, too, are domesticated and made subject to ongoing time.

3

There is another and reverse temptation, the comparatively recent one of spontaneous generation, by which works are regarded as emerging in absolute originality, productions of an avant-garde which, its definition having been undermined, is the entire army in itself. Tradition and the individual talent; Eliot's phrase tersely sums up the antinomies. And on his way to reaching a balance Eliot offered two judgments that have to be held in mind whenever we consider how artists are related to the past. He criticized the fact that "we insist, when praising a poet, upon those aspects of his work in which he least resembles anyone else" and "dwell with satisfaction upon [his] differences from his predecessors." But he also flatly declared: "Novelty is better than repetition."

Academic historians of the arts are hard put to keep this latter assertion in consciousness, even where the particular historian thinks himself well disposed to its argument. For the tendency in writing such histories is always to search for and find connections, unities; "development" is a key word in these chronicles. And this is why they also contain such phrases as "ahead of his time," "out of the main stream," "idiosyncratic talent," and the like, expressions that indicate something knotty and unplaceable having been encountered, something that interferes with chronology.

And yet if, as Eliot maintained, no artist springs out of a historyless present, there are artists whose work does stand at especially great removes from the past, so great in certain instances that there seems to be no way of bridging the gaps. These are the creators with whom the histories have difficulty, the ones who are either fitted into the central tradition by procrustean methods or left outside. But it may be that the central tradition is a myth and that the true tradition—the continuity that is made up of discontinuities—is a matter of many kinds of originality making themselves known in disorderly succession and with debts to the past that may be remote or unacknowledged but are always present. At the very least, originality is an implicit recognition of what has existed.

By all the presumed laws of cultural development the plays of Georg Büchner ought not to have been possible in his time and place—Germany of the early 1830's—in the same way that the poems of Rimbaud ought not to have been possible in France a few decades later. The train has sped forward along tracks we cannot see, a baffling circumstance until we understand that we have been thinking of art as obeying laws, the way mechanisms do. But Büchner and Rimbaud are writers in whom history is especially clearly seen to take a leap whose effect is to demonstrate that the imagination doesn't operate by laws at all but by precedents.

That both Büchner and Rimbaud were such extraordinarily young geniuses is one clue to their creation of such radically new styles and patterns of consciousness. Youth is no guarantor of originality, or even a sufficient cause; but it offers a ground. By keeping Büchner and Rimbaud free of an accumulated past, it enabled them to function to a high degree outside the grip of time, to proceed as though history—the history of the imagination—had just begun, in them. The truth is that in a way we haven't begun to understand they had actually absorbed it all with blinding speed, and this is in fact what made them ready to be original. These minds, so seemingly recalcitrant to what lay behind, so immersed in the verbally and psychologically *possible*, accomplished as one of their unconscious missions an overthrow of chronology, which is one of the means we have of ensuring against sudden unbearable alteration in the way we see ourselves and the world.

Rimbaud, the more mantic and seemingly self-generated, the *poète maudit* for whom nothing but extreme imagination was sacred (as long as he remained a poet; at a certain point he would succumb to the terrors of just such extremism), has usually been regarded as far surpassing Büchner in the radical originality of his work and in its influence on what came after him. But a case can be made out for Büchner, whom histories of drama continue to treat gingerly and as a paradox, as not only the greater writer but also the more profoundly original and, besides that, the more enduring. The value of the argument isn't for the erection of hierarchies but for the light it might throw on certain differences between the arts of poetry and drama, and for the awareness we ought to have that no medium ordinarily changes as slowly as the theater.

Living so completely as a function of language, its forms needing little justification by direct experience of the world, poetry much more readily than the stage shapes new structures for the mind and presents itself more willingly to change. The theater metamorphoses with painful slowness, and its vital history is marked by wide gaps, periods when its immersion in social contingency and physical obligation prevents it from assuming new and necessary forms. A communal art, an art subject to immediate pressures of taste and judgment—to *verdicts*—the stage has always found it especially expedient to mimic its own past and understands that it attains its chief revitalizations at great cost. In Georg Büchner's case the cost was that of having his plays remain unknown or unappreciated for almost half a century after his death.

The only major contemporary of Büchner who seems to have expressed admiration for his work was Friedrich Hebbel, who was born in the same year, 1813, and it was not until the heyday of the naturalist movement of the 1880's that Büchner's influence can be said to have begun. The first playwright of stature to speak of him then was Gerhart Hauptmann, whose consciousness of Büchner rested understandably enough on the ways the earlier writer could inspire and justify Hauptmann's own dramatic procedure. The chief element was Büchner's anti-aristocratic and anti-hierarchical temperament, which manifested itself in the plays, most thoroughly in *Woyzeck*, as a profound and unappeasable bias toward powerless and undefended men.

For Hauptmann, as for the lesser naturalists, Büchner could be seen as an early organizer of a kind of drama in which human fate broke through social hierarchies and class distinctions to display itself in the persons of the least distinguished, most denuded souls. More than that, Büchner's brilliant cold refusals of fantasy and myth-making, his clear, rational consideration of the physical world as both non-illusory and—if you went beyond its appearances—accountable, reinforced the naturalists' theories of reality and of reality's relation to the imagination. It was entirely understandable that a playwright who had seen ordinary life with remarkable steadiness and had refused to fantasize his way into anything "higher" should have been hailed as a spiritual father of the naturalist movement.

But accurate as it was from a certain vantage point in artistic morale—the repudiation of drama as a form of cultural consolation and a bourgeois ritual—such a response to Büchner was a narrow and shallow reading. As was to be true of Strindberg, who jumped to call himself a *nyanaturalist*, a new one, an artist at work beyond the limited concerns of the quasi-official movement, Büchner's commitment to such aims as the naturalists were later to articulate was at most a matter of tactics. His art was much more complex and, most significant for the future, embodies a far-wider revolution in dramatic technique and vision than any of the naturalists ever accomplished or conceived of. It was to be to playwrights like Frank Wedekind and, even more influentially, Bertolt Brecht, that the full astonishing implications of Büchner's genius would reveal themselves when the naturalist impulse was over.

I am alone as though in the grave: when will your message wake me? My friends desert me, we scream in one another's ears as if deaf; I wish we were dumb, then we could only look at one another.

Büchner to his fiancée

Such facts as we possess about Büchner's life leave his writings without any sort of basis in his biography. He was born October 17, 1813, in the small town of Goddelau near Darmstadt, the son of a doctor in government service, a free-thinker and ardent admirer of Napoleon. The oldest of six children, several others of whom would also achieve intellectual or political eminence, Georg was a precocious boy and seems at an early age to have decided on medicine as a career. Enrolling at the University of Strasbourg in France, he changed two years later to Giessen, a German university, in order to supplement his medical studies with work in history and philosophy.

At this time he became heavily involved in radical political activity and was forced to flee the country, making his way back to Strasbourg and then, a year and a half later, to Zurich, from whose university he had obtained his doctorate by mail and an appointment as a lecturer in natural history. Less than three months after taking up his academic duties he fell victim to an epidemic of typhoid fever and after a short illness died on February 18, 1837. He was only a few months past twenty-three.

From everything we know (a handful of his letters are almost the only source) he seems to have written his three plays during intervals in his studies and political activity, working in short furious bursts. (He also wrote a political tract, *The Hessian Courier*, and a section of a novel, *Lenz*.) Very little in his childhood or adolescence had indicated a desire for or likelihood of a future as a writer, although he had, at thirteen, composed a rather remarkable essay on suicide, in which he argued that life ought never to be regarded as a preparation for something higher. At his death he seems to have still thought of himself primarily as a scientist and educator.

Yet everything converged to make his dramas come into existence: a preternaturally swift acquisition of formal knowledge and technique; the early consolidation of a relentless critique of history; a political education that went very much deeper than the ordinary radical-student kind; an instruction in human pain and the disasters of the spirit going mysteriously far and plucked, it almost seemed, from the air around him; the possession of an extraordinarily accurate eye for the world's palpable realities and of an iron capacity, all but unprecedented in one so young, to withstand every temptation toward consoling fantasy and the pleasures of dreaming.

Büchner's studies in medicine and natural history were, as it turned out, the perfect complements of his investigations of political and social history and his direct experience of politics and society. They gave him a ground in what we recognize as an experimental and pragmatic method and habit of mind, which helped keep him free of prejudice and distorting idealism in his contemplation of the materials that were to go into the making of his art and into the choices he was to make for its realization. In a manner that went far beyond what the self-declared naturalists were later to attempt, he drew on his scientific training, and scientific attitudes in general, as both an informing presence in his art and a non-transcendent principle of its justification.

In his inaugural lecture at the University of Zurich, a talk on cranial nerves, Büchner made an observation that directly exhibits the links between his scientific training and his art. "Nature," he wrote, "does not exhaust itself through an infinite chain of causes, each determined by the last, but is in all its manifestations sufficient unto itself." Such an observation is an anticipation of what is still a very new and radical way of regarding the physical world, but it is also a perception with pertinence in the realm of the aesthetic, and so is enormously important to any consideration of Büchner as an imaginative writer.

In its refusals of a prioris and strict causal relationships and in its acceptance of the physical world as existing straightforwardly and hiding nothing, the statement puts one in mind of a remark by another prophetic writer, Coleridge, who once wrote that "matter has no inward. We remove the surface but to meet with another." It also has affinities with certain notions of contemporary writers like Alain Robbe-Grillet and might in fact be acceptable as a motto for any number of artistic movements or impulses which have in common a rejection of linear construction, logical development, and causal connectedness.

Such a rejection will be at the heart of Büchner's revolutionary conception of dramaturgy. A function of his repudiation of all idealistic, tightly structured, and self-validating philosophical systems—he was a declared and vigorously hostile critic of Kant, Fichte, and especially Hegel, who reigned intellectually supreme during Büchner's student days—it was also the corollary of his affirmation of experience as sovereign over pure intellection and of sensual data over the abstractions by which the mind is continually tempted. We shall see that Büchner was able to bring new dramatic forms into being because they were themselves kinds of experience, because, in other words, he did not move from a theory of drama to a practice; he had failed to be taught what drama abstractly and ideally was supposed to be.

By a process we naturally cannot trace, Büchner modulated from a scientific outlook that was highly imaginative and open to an artistic procedure that obtained its data and worked out its methods through a pragmatic freedom from preconceptions, a liberation from the expectations and mechanical traditions of literature. As is always the case, such freedom meant that literature might therefore be renewed, made possible again through an act of life-giving heresy.

The literary atmosphere which Büchner entered when he began writing was of course that of Romanticism. Nothing could have been further from his temperament and dawning artistic concerns, and his letters contain a number of disparaging references to contemporary writers and to such earlier but still-dominant figures as Schiller, whose idealism and frequently inflated rhetoric he particularly despised. Whether or not he ever read anything by the two great contemporaries who stood outside the Romantic movement, Hölderlin and Kleist, is not known, but in any case he left no comment on them.

What Büchner must have disliked most about Romantic writing was its impulse to construct hierarchies out of experience—the ugly, the beautiful, the most beautiful—and to pursue transcendence on the one hand and pure sensation on the other. Even before he began writing he had thrown off the prevailing literary temptation to seek salvation in beauty conceived of as higher than ordinary phenomena, to achieve deliverance through a Faustian assertion of the self-in-despite-of-the-world.

Beyond this, he strongly believed that "the poet is not a teacher of morality." This was a much bolder and more rebellious position to have taken at that time than it would be now. What is even more impressive for us is the following dictum, which could only have been composed out of the widest absorption in the most diverse human phenomena and out of a sympathy such as only the greatest imaginations have possessed: "One can understand everything only when one allows no one to be too ugly or too trivial. The most insignificant fact makes a deeper impression than the mere sensation of the beautiful."

He seems to have had some enthusiasm for the early

Goethe and for the *Sturm und Drang* period of the 1770's in general. One writer of that time particularly interested him. This was the strange, half-mad minor poet and dramatist Jakob Michael Reinhold Lenz. Basing his work on a diary kept by a pastor who had befriended Lenz, Büchner wrote a prose work, probably a section of what was to be a novel—although the piece stands by itself—with certain crucial episodes in the writer's life as its subject.

The work was as advanced in its way as the plays were to be in theirs. Eccentric, in places dream-like and in others brilliantly hard and specific, full of strange compressions and repetitions, *Lenz* stands, as the critic Herbert Lindenberger has said, "as one of the first examples in European narrative fiction to demonstrate a method for the portrayal of introspective experience." Although "internal" experience might be a better term for what Büchner dealt with, for there is little that is ruminative or consciously considered in what his protagonist undergoes. A crisis of the mind and spirit, an ordeal in which sanity and the very capacity to live are being tested, Lenz's fictional destiny is of that order of psychic extremity and existential violence that will become the normative subject of imagination in Baudelaire, Rimbaud, Dostoevsky, and, in fact, the entire central tradition of what we call modern literature.

From Lenz's own writings for the stage, which suggested more than they were able physically to accomplish, Büchner appears to have gained a sense of new dramaturgical possibilities and a new artistic vantage point. In tentative, clumsy ways Lenz had moved toward a drama in which comic and tragic modes would enter an amalgamation, ordinary life would be validated as subject, and the hero would be depicted as a passive sufferer. Büchner was to carry these things immensely further, as he was to return, in that simultaneous act of invention and rediscovery that characterizes all innovating art, to Shakespeare, the only playwright besides

Lenz whom he seems to have admired and to have learned from; he read Shakespeare in translation and wrote once that, compared to him, "all poets confront nature like schoolboys."

Büchner will begin writing his plays, then, at a juncture of present dissatisfaction and remote literary indebtedness. There are no firm precedents for what he is about to do, no sustaining atmosphere to work in. There are only the hints of possibility that drama might be rejuvenated through a chastening of its traditional heroic impulse, its desire to make life more "meaningful" than it is, and through a repudiation of all narrow pedagogic functions. Like Joyce later on, Büchner is prepared to create the hitherto uncreated, to forge a conscience by forging a new speech.

> As for me, my life is not heavy enough, it flies and floats far above action, that dear mainstay of the world.
>
> Rimbaud, A *Season in Hell*

Late in 1833 or early in the following year, when Büchner was at Strasbourg for the second time, in flight and exile, he wrote to his fiancée, a Protestant minister's daughter named Minna Jaegle, that he had been doing a great deal of reading in the French Revolution. In this letter he had gone on to offer the most central revelation we possess of his conscious attitude toward history and experience and of the immediate sources of his forthcoming dramatic art:

> I have felt as though crushed beneath the fatalism of history. I find in human nature a terrifying sameness, and in the human condition an inexorable force, granted to all and to none. The individual is no more than foam on the wave, greatness mere chance, the mastery of genius a puppet-play, a ludicrous struggle against an iron-clad law, which to acknowledge is the highest achievement, which to master is impossible. I no longer intend to bow down to the parade-horses and bystanders of his-

tory. I have grown accustomed to the sight of blood. But I am no guillotine-blade. The word *must* is one of the curses with which Mankind is baptized. The saying that "it must needs be that the offenses come; but woe to him by whom the offense cometh" is terrifying. What is it in us that lies, murders, steals?

His plunge into history had left him without illusions of any kind. Writing was to be his means of opposing the world, true enough, but not in a Romantic mode; he would do it without egoism, without consolation. His strange, difficult task was to compel the world to yield up unheard-of and demoralizing truths. The imagination's triumph would lie in wresting such truths from the obduracy of mere events and the closed system of historical time. He would shape counter-truths to those of history and in this way establish a new morale and a new kind of hard-looking, unruly, unlofty "beauty." He would establish these things, that is to say, as the mode of other men's perception of them; his own purpose was simply to write as he knew how.

In this light *Danton's Death*, which is beyond question the most amazing first play ever written, is not a historical epic but a drama *about* history. Büchner was enraged when the play's first publisher (it was not to be produced on the stage until 1902) added the subtitle *Dramatic Images from France's Reign of Terror*. For apart from the completely uncharacteristic rhetoric, the letter which was quoted above makes it clear that the events of the French Revolution were not occurrences he wished to recover from the past in order to dramatize in the present—for reasons of one or another kind of perspective or instruction, let us say—but properties of an imaginative action that would rebuke history, turning it against itself and testifying to a new kind of freedom from its pitiless claims.

Büchner had been stricken by what we would now or lately have called an existential anguish or horror, he had seen vertiginously into the historical process the way the protagonist of Sartre's novel *Nausea* sees into physical matter. History—what men do in relation to one another and to time—marches as though it were a parade, an inexorable, intimidating display of physical force and moral compulsion. History in this sense is tyrannical beyond specific tyrannies; political freedom, which is largely an illusion, is no cure, even where it might exist, for the deep unfreedom of the historical process itself. As it works out its movement through time, not in the Hegelian sense of ideal or dialectic advance but through the blind wills of men, the physical and moral coercions of their communal existence, history, Büchner had seen, by being the sum of all that has happened leaves nothing to be done, leaves no loopholes.

This is the metaphysical basis of his vision and of *Danton's Death*. The moral and psychic basis is a perception of how history tramples on particular rights, how the urgency on the part of powerful men to fulfill their various destinies and the destinies of various ideas makes fate for the others a matter of chance, or, rather, leaves them with no fate that can properly be called personal.

Büchner would no longer bow down to the horses of history or be one of its paralyzed spectators. He would not simply "understand," as Spinoza had advised the historian and by implication all men to do. History coerced; he would exert a counterpressure to it in the form of a creation. In a drama seized from what had happened and been recorded, he would give form and expression to what had not been allowed to happen, what had not been recorded, what *still remained to be said*.

There is nothing fantastic in what he proceeds to write (the play is completed in a matter of weeks), he makes no exotic factual additions, lays on no "color." The French Revolution remains as it was, reordered, edited so to speak— Robespierre's public speeches, for example, are quoted directly, somewhat rearranged, from the histories Büchner consulted—but not revamped or heightened. The time and place are accurate; what happens publicly in the play, happened. Covering a period of twelve days in 1794, almost five years after the fall of the Bastille, the external action, the ostensible plot, describes the warring factions within the Revolutionary forces moving toward their struggle's denouement. Georges Danton, the most important of the moderates, is going to "lose" as a result of what takes place; Robespierre and Saint-Just, his chief adversaries, are, provisionally, going to "win." To a critic looking for the truth of the play on the level of actual history, everything appears in place and acquiescent, and so the Marxist writer Georg Lukács can comfortably think of the work simply as a drama of the clash between progressive and regressive ideologies and historical forces.

At first glance the play does indeed appear to embody a central fatal contention between Danton and Robespierre, the former a rallying point for humane values and a politics of skepticism, the latter the representative of ferocious sociopolitical abstractions and an idealism that leads to death as a form of its perfection. Robespierre and, in an even purer although less influential way, Saint-Just incarnate history and politics in their most ruthless ontological aspects. Robespierre, like all political men, is history itself; he *knows* himself justified in imposing the Terror, he fills the air with bullying mottos like "the will of the people" and "in the name of the law," he compares himself to Christ. Against this, Danton, sickened and dismayed, charges Robespierre with being "disgustingly virtuous," asks him if there isn't anything in him "that whispers sometimes . . . you lie, Robespierre, you lie," and tells his own friends that "I'd rather suffer the guillotine myself than make others suffer it."

Such a declaration is a statement in the moral order but

much more than that, for it is a significant clue to the play's radical alteration of traditional consciousness and, in terms of the theater, to its establishment of an anti-heroic mode. For Danton has resigned from the struggle as Robespierre has defined it. He is never to do battle with Robespierre except on the level of mutual awareness and questioning; the play is not going to be the story of their political or moral conflict, their dispute over means or goals; there are to be no victories and defeats in the conventional sense and no spiritual denouement advising the spectator of light at the end of a tunnel. The entire course of the drama will unfold along nearly unprecedented lines: the struggle will be between action and a refusal of action, between decisiveness and doubt, confidence in history and despairing disbelief, absolutism and a profound sense of the partial and incomplete.

If there is an ancestor in drama for this play of consciousness about human action, it is surely *Hamlet*. Yet while Shakespeare is concerned throughout with the difficulties and costs of action, his central character does act in the end; Büchner, in greater extremity, lays bare the deep malaise at the heart of the human (in its most virulent form, Western) compulsion toward action as a good in itself, action in the face of moral doubt (like Hamlet's), or worse, of knowledge that evil will be immediately forthcoming as the result of what one does, however "justified." To act efficaciously is the condition of remaining within history, is in fact the very definition of history, and Büchner makes the refusal to be made use of in this way the final ground of his vision.

Danton's Death is a play of unfulfilled expectations on more than one level. To begin with its "story," the spectator or reader is prepared by culture and education—which transmit the tradition of action in both life and dramatic art—for Danton to lead the opposition to Robespierre's reign of terror, to become the hero of the kind of moral and physical drama such a clash of temperaments, ideologies, and value systems as theirs ordinarily suggests. "You must lead the attack at the next Convention!" Danton's friend and supporter Camille Desmoulins tells him. "*I* must, *you* must, *he* must," Danton replies in a speech that echoes Büchner's remark in the letter to his fiancée about the word "must" being one of mankind's original curses. Danton will not be compelled into political or physical action against Robespierre's murderous abstractions, the slogans for the sake of which, as another character says, he would "sacrifice everything, himself, his sons, his brothers, his friends." To which Danton adds, "[He] is the dogma of the Revolution that can't be stricken."

The obligation to take action, the moral imperative held up to Danton by his followers, reaches him in the first place as a dogma in itself; it is not the wrong kind of values as enunciated by Robespierre and Saint-Just that dismays him as much as it is the human need to erect values into absolutes, abstractions which suppress sensual life, truth, idiosyncrasy, and all beautiful forgivable error, and which therefore exercise the most far-reaching tyranny over the self. The understanding comes at this point that the age-old dichotomy or opposition between action and contemplation—or, more accurately, intellection—the split that *Danton's Death* might seem to be about, is false; the opposition is really between action as the putting into effect of *ideas*, the cold, narrow, ruthless implementation of values, and action as the physical and moral mode of the entire self.

In a premonition of what will become the full spirit of the modern age, Büchner has Danton curse what we might call the "technicalization" of experience, the conversion of intellect and passion and instinct into modes of efficacy. "How I wish it *were* a fight," he tells Camille, "with arms and teeth tearing and clutching! But it's as if I'd fallen into a mill shaft, and my arms and legs were slowly and systematically being wrenched off by cold physical force. Imagine being killed mechanically!"

This is precisely what Büchner does imagine: death as the outcome not of organic life, the ordinary biological process, but of that most terrible man-made compulsion, "historical necessity." And the play proceeds to shape alternatives to such coercion. On the political level Danton's refusal to participate in this power struggle being carried on in the name of values is a negative action designed to break the chain of force and oppression; on the spiritual level it is a grave and bitter testament to a narrow and "illicit" freedom. For in a world wrongly fashioned, a universe in which human beings are swept aside by abstractions hurrying to fulfill their destinies, the only free act is non-compliance. You will be trampled and destroyed, your arms and legs will be wrenched off, but your consent, your very self, will have been withheld.

A world wrongly fashioned. In this perspective *Danton's Death* moves beyond the merely exemplary, beyond being a drama from which one might draw a political or philosophical argument. At an immeasurably greater depth than political or social or even moral insight can reach, or, to put it another way, from a vantage point impossible to those who are carrying on the world's business, Büchner sees into existence and finds it perverse, unfathomably misconstructed, a mockery of our self-proclaimed dignity. Like Shakespeare's vision in *Lear*, the world is revealed as dark and agonized; and it is the very nature of reality that brings into being its particular evils. For this reason it isn't Robespierre and the Terror that instigate in Danton his loathing and disgust, as much as it is the Revolution's cruel events which confirm his pre-existing sense of why one ought to despair.

"What is this in us that lies, steals, whores and murders?" he asks in the exact words Büchner had used to his fiancée. "I think there was a mistake in our creation; there's something missing in us that I haven't a name for—but we'll never find it by burrowing in one another's entrails . . . we're thick-skinned creatures who reach out our hands toward one another, but it means nothing—leather rubbing against leather—we're very lonely." And in an image that wonderfully fuses the drama's existential despair and its specific mood of horror in the face of life maimed by ideality and incorporeal values he says: "We are the swords that spirits fight with . . ."

With such knowledge as this Danton has chosen to live without plans or hope, in an ambience of sensuality and erotic abandon directly counter to Robespierre's and Saint-Just's wholly intellectualized, politicized, and puritan world. Yet he is anything but a conventional debauchee or common-place exponent of the flesh's glories. His sensuality is real and affords momentary pleasure, but at every point it presses against its own bitterly perceived limits and becomes the substance for metaphors in which existence itself takes on the attributes of a brutal and indiscriminate carnality. "A woman's thighs will be your guillotine," Danton is told, and he himself observes that "life's a whore; she fornicates with the whole world."

Büchner has no "solution" to Robespierre's inhuman-ity, and most certainly no remedy based on the erotic. Sen-suality has to be allowed to live, but Büchner is no prophet of the innocence of the body. In general, he is the furthest possible distance from a thinker like Rousseau, for one burden of his theater is that of an imaginative corrective to the naïve advocates of one or another psychic or social program or monistic theory of human distress. Humanity is tense with oppositions, and Büchner's task as a playwright is not to dissolve them but to articulate an experience in which they are displayed and yet simultaneously to fashion, as the very function of the imagination, the atmosphere of his characters' deliverance from what life has already proposed as solutions.

The play makes clear that Danton's profligacy and wan-tonness, although not his simple pleasure in sex, are despair-ing tactics in the void. Beneath their masks he remains moved by a spirit of inconsolable love and friendship in the face of a world whose god is "nothingness." As his execution draws near, he invokes his wife: "Oh, Julie! What if I go alone? What if I must leave her behind?—And even if I fell to pieces utterly, completely dissolved: I would always be a handful of tormented dust, no single atom of me could find rest except in her." And his last words at the guillotine are to the executioner who has stopped one of his fellow victims from embracing him: "Are you trying to be crueler than death? Do you think you can prevent our heads from kissing down there in the basket?" In a simple image, without hope or any trace of affirmation, above all without any implication of its being a solution, Büchner proposes such love and friendship as the only reply to historical necessity that ordinary life can make.

They forget God because of his bad imitators.

Danton's Death

In the opening moments of the play, during a scene which takes place in an elegant gambling salon and brothel, a character called simply a Lady has several short witty speeches and then disappears entirely from the drama. What she says has nothing to do with the plot, doesn't advance the action, contributes no pertinent information about any of the other characters, and, in short, appears to be wholly without thematic connection to the work. The Lady's departure from the action is unaccountable from the standpoint of classical dramatic construction. She has not been a "minor" character, as we know them in traditional drama, or even a functionary whose presence is of an instrumental kind—the bringing of messages, the making of announcements, and so on. She is there, Büchner meant it to be known, as a momentary presence in her own right, to participate in the exhibition of a world rather than in the unfolding of a tale. Since this is so, nothing required her creator to bring her back or to account in any way for her disappearance. But for Büchner to have reached this freedom in the disposition of his characters meant that a technical revolution had had to take place.

We accept as a commonplace by now that technique—the process of form—is inseparable from what we think of as values or meanings in works of art. We ought also to accept that substance, or, as we more commonly call it, "content," has no existence except that which is conferred on it by form. The crucial thing to understand about *Danton's Death* is that in order to bring into being his new subject Büchner had to *reinvent* dramatic form. What he accomplished was the greatest expansion of the procedural possibilities of drama, the widest accession of flexibility and diversity since the theater of Shakespeare.

Büchner was in the purest position of the artist who has to discover new means in order to come to grips with new experience, and who in fact makes his discovery as an aspect of undergoing precisely that experience. He was unhampered by rules or sanctified definitions of what constituted the art of drama—principles of conflict, development, resolution, and the like. Above all, he felt under no obligation to make his play satisfy considerations of verisimilitude, to write it as though he were composing a series of portraits from life.

His sense of experience was marked by an acute awareness of disconnection and particularly of the gulf between truth and behavior. Men and women acted *as they could* and not in coherence with either their beliefs or their self-images. He was convinced, too, that the chain-like succession of human events was an artifice, a construction of the mind. History was discontinuous, fragmented, and chaotic; the self was "foam on the wave." In an opposing act of the mind, the drama he was writing would reflect and incarnate what he had intuited about the ways in which the worlds of behavior and events were really organized. His dramaturgy would have its own order, but it would not stretch out compliantly, a roadway to a theatrical climax, his play wouldn't serve the spectator as a vehicle, rolling or bouncing along to a destination all the intermediary stations to which had been charted.

Büchner was fully aware of the radical nature of his dramatic construction and of the disturbance it would bring to the settled notions people had of theatrical art. In a speech of Camille Desmoulins he declares—as an event within his own play—his antipathy for the theatrical conventions of his day and enunciates an allegiance to an idea and practice of drama, and of art in general, whose central element, whose only stated condition, is fidelity to nature, that is to say to experience undistorted by idealism or artifice of the kind that results in "likenesses" or "beauty" or monolithic meanings.

This realism was the furthest thing from imitation. Büchner understood what was only much later to be generally grasped and is even now an insecurely held principle of cultural understanding: that an art which imitates life mimics an imitation, because life, without true imagination, is derivative and received. He also understood that one true function of any art, a function that has grown in importance ever since the bourgeois epoch began, is to repel and displace the false images of existence, the dead "likenesses" we construct out of a fear of seeing what we are really like. The imagination, a two-edged sword, hides the world from us and may bring it back. The speech of Camille's deserves to be quoted nearly in its entirety:

I tell you that unless they have wooden copies of everything, scattered about in theatres, concert halls, and art exhibits, people have neither eyes nor ears for it. Let someone carve out a marionette so that they can see the strings that pull it up and down and with each awkward movement from its joints hear it roar out an iambic line; what a character, they'll cry out, what consistency! Take a minor sentiment, a maxim, a notion, and

dress it up in coat and trousers, make pairs of hands and feet
for it, color its face and permit the whole thing to moan and
agonize about for three whole acts until at last it has either
married or shot itself dead—and they will cry out that it was
ideal! . . . Take these same people from the theatre and put
them on the street and they'll grow pained with pitiful reality!—
They forget their Lord God because of His bad imitators. And
they see and hear nothing of the creation round about them
and in them that glows, and surges, and glitters, and is born
anew with every moment. All they do is go to the theatre, read
poetry and novels, and grimace like the characters they find in
them, and then say to God's real creations: How commonplace! . . .

Büchner is the first "modern" playwright, and nothing is
more indicative of his modernity—the sense he gives of being
immersed in interests and conflicts that to some degree remain
our own—than his battle against the misuses of his chosen art.
The stage, he was perhaps the first playwright to see, can be an
especially virulent source of received ideas, clichéd perceptions, and unexamined pieties whose effect is to blind the
spectator to his own being or confirm him in an existing
blindness. Like the great original dramatists who came after
him, from Ibsen down to the present, he moved against his
art's codifications and mechanical pleasures—its "dressed-up
maxims and sentiments"—and fought the battle in the name
and interest of the hidden face of truth. Artistic creation at
Büchner's level is one of the chief instruments we have for
the recovery of consciousness from the sleep into which God's
bad imitators have led it.

Danton's Death is divided into four acts and thirty-two
scenes, some of them quite long, others lasting no more than a
minute. They alternate—with no sort of schematic regular-
ity—between private and public settings, soliloquies and the
expostulations of crowds, lyrical and declarative modes. These

alternations have the function of producing various types of perspective and of preventing the drama from assuming the steady uninterrupted course of a conventional theatrical tale. There is no traditional "development" and no observance of the Aristotelian unities of time and place. In lieu of the narrative compulsion which ordinarily drives dramas forward and sustains the viewer's interest, Büchner fashions a steadily expanding and deepening system of consciousness, a universe of feeling and expression whose internal arrangements are closer to the order of poetry and music than to the conventional linear and expository constructions of the theater.

In this dramatic system dialogue has the function of formulating insight, establishing perception, and exhibiting consciousness much more than of imparting information or building up a structure of plot. In a truly unprecedented stroke Büchner organizes his characters' exchanges so that they glide past or carom off or brutally collide with one another; a kind of speech which in German is called *aneinandervorbeisprechen*, it was to become, as a direct inheritance from Büchner or not, a major technical instrument in a later theater of incompletion and indirection.

What almost never happens in the play is that people talk directly to one another in that simulacrum of life outside the theater which had been and remains the stage's chief curse and chief self-justification. Along the same lines, images, comments, and reflections are thrown out which bear textural and poetic rather than thematic relations to what surrounds them, whole passages remain unassimilated to the drama's putative line of action.

In a long, beautiful monologue, for example, one of Danton's mistresses remembers her childhood and youth, recalling how desire awakened in her and how when her first lover drowned "it was the only time that my life ever stopped." Danton's response is to say, in obedience to his own painful ardency and Büchner's lyric purpose here, "Why can't I contain every part of your beauty inside me, hold it in my arms?" The woman replies, without having been coerced by his question, "Danton, your lips have eyes," to which with equal "irrelevance" he says, "I wish I were a part of air that I could bathe you all about in my flood, break myself on every cape of your . . . body." Nothing in the sequence contributes to the active plot or connects factually to anything else. The scene exists as an element—lovely, self-contained, and mysteriously resonant—in an imaginative terrain.

There is a sense in *Danton's Death* of expression hurling itself forward in the teeth of history's finality and sovereign conclusions. Not since Shakespeare had drama been the source of such splendid rhetoric, such fiercely seized verbal truths. The self, in the figures of Büchner's eloquent surrogates, throws out its psalms and laments, the language of its existence behind the back of necessity and on the far side of determined fate. Danton, his death near, holds out in the night beside his sleeping friends and fellow victims:

Will the clock never stop! Every tick pushes the walls closer around me, till they're narrow as a coffin.—I read a story like that once when I was a child, it made my hair stand on end. Yes, when I was a child! It wasn't worth the trouble to fatten me up and keep me warm . . . My dear body, I shall hold my nose closed and imagine that you are a lovely woman, sweating and stinking a bit after a dance, and pay you compliments. We've had better times than this with one another . . . Of course it's miserable having to die. What does death do but mimic birth? We die as helpless and naked as new-born babes . . . What good will it do! We can whimper just as well in the grave as in the cradle.—Camille! He's sleeping. (*While bending over him.*) There's a dream between his lashes. I mustn't wipe that golden dew of sleep from his eyes. (*He rises and goes to the window.*) I won't be going alone: thank you, Julie! Still, I wish I could have died differently, without effort, like a star

falling, or a note of music that breathes itself out, kissing itself
with its own lips, like a ray of light burying itself in a sea of
clear water. —The stars are scattered through the night like
glistening teardrops; what a terrible grief must be behind the
eyes that dropped them.

Lucille, Camille's wife, speaks to herself after his death:

There must be something serious in it somewhere. I must
think about that. I'm beginning to understand such things.—
Dying—dying!—But everything has the right to live, everything,
this little fly here, that bird. Why not he? The stream of life
would stop if even a drop were spilt. The earth would suffer a
wound from such a blow.—Everything moves on, clocks tick,
bells peal, people run, water flows, and so on and on to—no, it
mustn't happen, no, I'll sit on the ground and scream, that all
things stop, in fear, that nothing goes any more, that nothing
moves . . . It doesn't help, nothing at all has changed: the
houses, the streets, the wind blowing, the clouds passing.—I
suppose we must bear it.

Büchner's verbal resources seem inexhaustible. Lyrical,
witty, capable at times of the most brilliant exercises of reason
and at others of the most ferocious parodies of reasoning, lim-
ber, nervous, but on other occasions serene, full of energy that
at moments seems to overrun the limits of communicative expression to become a sort of joy in utterance itself, his verbal
power is on a level only just below that of Shakespeare among
dramatists, and reminds one even more directly of a modern
poet like Yeats or a novelist like Joyce. Throughout *Danton's
Death* we encounter language creating its own order of reality, making itself known as the originator of vision and not
its mere articulation.

In this supreme expressive power, which everywhere gives
the feeling of abundance and delight, lies something im-

mensely significant in regard to the question of Büchner's "pessimism," the despairing attitude toward history and therefore, presumably, toward human life that has been sketched out in this essay. To begin with, Büchner's theme may indeed be the hopelessness of social and political life and, even further—as we shall see in *Woyzeck*—the degradation of the self in a world of outrage, but the *action of his art* has nothing to do with categories like pessimism and optimism. His art is in fact a testament to an indestructible, if "impractical" and non-utilitarian, confidence.

The point is that to make imagination speak like this in the face of despair about life is to perform an action that is as much a part of life as any other, and is therefore, in the most paradoxical-seeming way, an act of faith. More than that, Büchner's alternative to history—which is what imaginative art might be thought of—constitutes his triumph over the very forces that on the level of sheer physical experience cause him to despair. In writing *Danton's Death* Büchner added to life a new fact which is both a recognition of disaster and a cure for thinking it all there is. Like the classic writers of tragedy, he leaves us not in despair but in possession of a means for confronting what would otherwise have killed us behind our backs.

There is something almost unbearably poignant about Büchner's reverence for creation when we consider how appalling he found the historical world of man's construction. At some points his work seems to be a sort of defense of God's universe against what men have made of it; this is another element in his rejection of the Romantic stance as defier of the heavens. But although there is some evidence that he might have been a believing Christian, his experience of the abyss was too profound to be meliorated by orthodox faith or hope. His fiancée put down in her diary a deathbed remark of his to the effect that "through our pain we are brought nearer to God," but in his work he dealt with the pain as though

there were no remission. At the same time, in that most para-
doxical way in which art may transform the grimmest material,
he produced something which was itself a species of remission.

D. H. Lawrence once wrote that an artist studies his great
predecessors in search not of technique but of spirit, an instruction in how to make himself ready for his encounter with
his own materials. This is largely true, but there are times
when the discovery of a previously hidden ancestor will also
appear to be a windfall of means and a bounty of ideas. It was
Büchner's large, open, aria-like manner of dramatic expression
that along with his plays' freedom from mechanical construction and their flexibility of tone was to be so instructive to the
young Bertolt Brecht nearly a century later. But this was inseparable from Brecht's response to Büchner's pioneering
immersion in previously suppressed realms of psychic truth.

The amazing relevance of Büchner's imagination to the
theater of our own day consists in the broadest sense in his
anticipation of our concern with self cut off from its human
ground and any sustaining milieu. But this is less a question of
a particular theme or subject than a reigning manner of
perception, a way of regarding experience as alienating and a
capacity to make the formal elements of drama serve changed
consciousness.

Büchner's second play, *Leonce and Lena*, his only work
in what because of the shortcomings of our vocabulary we
have to call a comedic and satiric mood, although it is much
darker than the words suggest, prefigures our theater of absurdity and verbal games. In this drama about an imaginary
kingdom in which the vices of real kingdoms are exposed,
Büchner extended his command over a theatrical universe of
deracination and estrangement from the self. But *Leonce and
Lena* is technically more derivative than *Danton's Death*, less
sure of its departures from the past. A year or so later he wrote
another play, *Woyzeck*, which picked up again his quest for

new forms and broke ground we haven't yet begun fully to occupy.

One thing after another.

Woyzeck

In so far as it bases itself on people who have actually existed and events that have really taken place, *Woyzeck* can be said to originate in the same realm of historical fact as *Danton's Death*. But to an even greater degree than in the earlier play, Büchner is concerned now with what has not yet been recorded about these people and occurrences, his attention fixed on the space that remains for the imagination to fill. And even more blackly than before, he is obsessed with the brutal indifference of history and society as they act on the individual and force him to obey the laws of *their* lives rather than his own. Yet unlike Danton, the dramatic figure who repudiates his expected heroic destiny, the new play's central character begins with nothing, as a man stripped of all the implications of value and significance with which protagonists had traditionally been invested. *Woyzeck* is the first play in German, and most likely in any language, to take as its motif the fate of a character without status, social weight, or any accepted kind of dignity.

The case of Johann Christian Woyzeck had caused considerable stir in the German state of Saxony during the early 1820's. A wanderer with almost no education and no fixed occupation since having been orphaned at the age of thirteen, Woyzeck had ended up in the army as a common soldier. When he was thirty he had fallen in with a woman who bore him a child, but had left her when he discovered that she had been betraying him with other soldiers. In 1818, out of the army and unable to find steady work, he had taken up with a widow named Woost, who in time also began cuckolding him. He was known to have beaten her a number of times for her infidelity. On the night of June 21, 1821, she failed to keep an appointment with him, having accepted an assignation with a soldier. Tracking her down, Woyzeck accosted her at her house and, after denouncing her, stabbed her to death with a knife blade attached to a wooden handle. He was seized almost immediately and is supposed to have said to his captors, "God hope she's dead. She's earned it."

A Saxon court physician named Clarus was appointed to examine the prisoner in his cell. On the basis of his investigation and report Woyzeck was found guilty of premeditated murder and on February 28, 1822, was sentenced to death. Shortly thereafter the court learned that he claimed to have been hearing voices and having visions. A new inquiry was ordered, the result of which was that the sentence was upheld. On August 27, 1824, Woyzeck was beheaded in the public square of Leipzig, before a crowd of festive and noisy spectators.

Clarus's report was entitled *The Soundness of Mind of the Murderer Johann Christian Woyzeck, Proven on the Basis of Documents According to the Principles of State Pharmaceutics*. The gist of the doctor's conclusions was that although Woyzeck was obviously a disturbed person, subject to jealous fits and on occasion a heavy drinker, he was not a pathologically violent man and there was no basis for declaring him legally insane. The report was heavy with moral bias: Woyzeck "in the course of an uncertain, desolate, thoughtless and indolent life [had sunk] from one level of . . . degeneration down to the next," until "in the dark tumult of primitive emotion" he had "destroyed a human life." He was therefore responsible for his crime and had to pay for it. The report became the subject of a great deal of controversy, at least one other physician arguing publicly that Clarus's findings precisely proved that Woyzeck *had* been insane, so that his execution had been a dismaying instance of judicial murder.

Although he nowhere makes any mention of it, Büchner

unquestionably read Clarus's report in the *Journal of State Pharmaceutics*, of which his father, a former staff member, had a complete set. He must have come across it on one of his secret flying visits home and he seems to have begun work on the play shortly after his arrival in Zurich. At his death two drafts were found, a sketchy first effort and a much fuller second one. The more complete yet probably unfinished version contained over twenty scenes in no specified order, a circumstance that made it possible for future editors and publishers to print the play in the most varied sequences. (It was not produced on the stage until 1913.) Recent scholarship has established an order as close to what Büchner might have intended as we are ever likely to get, yet the significant fact is that the work remarkably sustains itself as a supreme dramatic achievement in nearly any order in which its scenes are disposed.

The elements of the public debate that had swirled around the case a decade earlier were not the components of Büchner's fascination with it. For his imaginative purposes the questions of a possible miscarriage of justice or of Woyzeck's technical state of mind were wholly superficial and in fact served to mask the really important issues. Justice is a concept that can have meaning only in a universe where freedom is more than a concept, insanity is one that depends on the existence of an unassailable criterion—sanity—by which it can be measured. For Büchner the human world was irrational and unfree, cruel by nature and untransformable by abstract values, with the exception of the one value that judges and lays pressure on all the others: absolute honesty of feeling and perception. More than this, he was not interested in reconstructing, however "creatively," the biography of a person or the anatomy of an event; he would use the historical Woyzeck as a locus for perception, an incentive to dramatic imagination, making him the perfectly concrete, non-symbolic, mostly "invented" character who would embody Büchner's own apperceptions of the character of the world.

All these things are what go to make *Woyzeck* very much more than a social drama, though society figures in it, and more than a study in local persecution or injustice, though these are present. Woyzeck, technically a murderer, is in truth a man crazed by the conditions of existence, the victim and hence the violent indicter of the way things are. Dramatically he exists to bring into being a human environment in which nothing is contingent on anything else, which is to say that no discrete phenomenon, however complex, *causes*—and hence may be made not to cause, may be subject to correction—the sufferings of its inhabitants.

This is in fact the central difference between social or political or ideological drama and Büchner's kind of tragic theater. In the former, one or another choice is possible; the "wrong" choices bring about calamity, the right ones melioration or triumph. But for Büchner's theater, patently so much more hopeless or "pessimistic," calamity is inherent and the only choices are to turn one's eyes from it or face it, without weakening the gaze by explanations, in a confrontation that becomes the only true liberation.

Just as he had done in *Danton's Death*, Büchner drew from the historical record only what he needed in order to construct a new "fact," his imagination's rebuke to history's having finished off the case with such finality. He of course picked up the central act, the murder, and made use of the accounts of Woyzeck's visions and voices as well as of some of his purported remarks to Clarus and others, but he located the events at an earlier period of Woyzeck's life, placed him back in the army, converted the murdered woman into a more attractive and sensual creature than she had been described as being (one argument for Woyzeck's dementedness had been, incredibly enough, the fact that the woman whom he had loved had been rather fat and slovenly; it was impossible to understand "what he saw in her"), transferred to her the child Woyzeck's first paramour had borne him, and, most important of all, surrounded him with invented figures who incarnate, as the woman does, the forces that drive him to despair and are the true instigators of his madness and violent protest.

> Have you ever seen anything of double nature? When the sun's standing high at noon and the world seems to be going up in flames, I've heard a terrible voice talking to me.
>
> *Woyzeck*

At the center of a burned-out, morally desolate landscape—"it's as though the world's dead," Woyzeck tells his friend—the future murderer stands and waits for his destiny, a "naked thinking beast that makes no show." He is naked and he thinks; vulnerable to every aggression, the lowliest of the low, he nevertheless *thinks*, is aware of the most subtle calamities, knows that what he sees and undergoes is unfathomably wrong. A Hamlet without a mission, the prince's wretched antipodal brother, he is the incarnation of *what is done to man*, the infinitely passive sufferer, until through a single act of extreme violence, a knife thrust serving as an outcry, he makes public his outraged humanity. But all the while before that he has known.

What distinguishes Woyzeck's suffering from any kind known before in drama is that it is not the product of mischance, the vicissitudes of fate, or the working out of moral patterns. Nor is it the result of some particular defect of his own nature, pride, let us say, or spiritual blindness. The play is pitched outside both classic and Christian categories; neither villainous nor good, lacking the dignity of a fall from grace or of any kind of struggle against evil, Woyzeck is the victim because victimization exists, because, that is to say, the human world is so constructed.

Once again the nearest analogue in drama is the condition and fate of Lear. But the suffering king was mad, or at least went mad, or at the very least made an initial act of unreason from which the catastrophes inevitably followed.

This is not to make Lear's agony too easily explicable or to reduce the play to a case history. The point is that to a certain degree Lear brought on his own fate, however horrifyingly that fate exceeded the dimensions of his responsibility for it. In Woyzeck's case, however, nothing he does precipitates or speeds his fate, which is, in the drama although not in the historical life, to *testify to his status;* catastrophe has been established from the beginning as the modality of his existence among others.

In a far-reaching act of consciousness that was at the same time both a moral and an artistic decision, Büchner broke from the time-honored Western tradition of personal responsibility as a theme in art and as a principle of social coherence. It was not that he argued for any kind of irresponsibility or sought to explain Woyzeck, as a later sociological art might have attempted, as the product of a rapacious society which deprived him of any power of moral choice. That fact was true, but not the gravamen of the charge or the chief object of the play's consciousness. Büchner had moved to an ontological level on which Woyzeck's situation had passed beyond morality and personal fate to become representative of a condition: that of being acted upon, of being used.

More than anything else in Büchner's drama this was later to free the theater from its past by liberating it from the notion of the hero, tragic or otherwise, who incarnated the active principle, which in one way or another never failed to issue in an aggrandizement of mankind. *Woyzeck* chastens in a radically deeper way than by teaching us about pride or folly, from which instruction we emerge "purified" and more "human." What is on display here is a world from which values do not rise, denouements do not cure, personal fate does not teach others.

Woyzeck is abused in the most gross and subtle ways. The medical officer of his outfit (a figure loosely based on a pompous physics professor Büchner had once studied under) employs him as a guinea pig in an experiment which, if not as physically extreme as the Nazi doctors' laboratory uses of concentration-camp inmates were later to be, is in the same realm of dehumanization. For weeks he is kept on a diet of nothing but peas, in order for the effect on his urine to be ascertained. He is supposed to urinate only during scheduled visits to the Doctor, but on one occasion the latter catches him pissing, in desperation, against a wall.

In a brilliant, complex scene whose economy is representative of the play as a whole (the entire text is only about thirty pages long), Büchner exposes the Doctor's quackish and murderous theorizing, making it clear, however, that this is to be seen as only an extreme case of the general tendency of "pure" science toward inhuman and self-fulfilling systems of thinking. The Doctor berates Woyzeck for having been unable to defer answering a call of nature:

> Nature! Haven't I proved that the *musculus constrictor vesicae* is subject to the will? Nature! Woyzeck, man is free. In man alone is individuality exalted to freedom. Couldn't hold it in! . . . I'm revolutionizing science, I'll blow it sky-high. Urea ten per cent, ammonium chloride, hyperoxidic. Woyzeck, try pissing again.

The bitter irony of the Doctor's invocation of human freedom and superiority to nature is not lost on Woyzeck; nothing is lost on him. When the Doctor persists in his dithyramb about human character rising above physical nature, Woyzeck tells him, in a wonderful, stammering, unfinished insight (his perceptions are always incomplete; this is one way Büchner holds him to an injured condition and keeps him from becoming a figure of untroubled naïve profundity, a sentimentalized peasant philosopher), an insight into the true tension between human character and the physical world: "You see, Doctor, sometimes you've got a certain character, a certain structure. But with nature, that's something else, you see, with nature. (*He cracks his knuckles.*) That's like—how should I put it—for example . . . Doctor, have you ever seen anything of double nature? . . . I've heard a terrible voice talking to me."

His Captain exploits him more obliquely. A sentimental pedant, an "unintelligent Robespierre," as a critic has called him, the Captain uses Woyzeck's lowly status and radical lack of institutional strengths and graces as standards against which to erect his own aggrandizement. "Woyzeck, you've got no morality," he tells him. "Morality—that's when you are moral, you understand. It's a good word. You have a child without the blessing of the church, as our reverend Chaplain says, without the blessing of the church. *I* didn't make that up."

Woyzeck's reply is another of those unexpected pieces of broken wisdom with which his utterance, an amalgam of howls, mutterings, murmured aphorisms, anguished ruminations, and aggrieved retorts, is studded. "You see, Cap'n—money, money. If you don't have money . . . just try to raise your own kind on morality in this world. The likes of us are unhappy in this world and the next. I guess if we ever got to heaven, we'd have to help with the thunder." Remarks like this are tremendously disturbing to everyone who comes in contact with him. "You're running through the world like an open razor," the Captain tells him in an image that might serve for the entire play, and says to the Doctor that "I get dizzy around such people."

The vertigo stems in the first place from Woyzeck's presence as a stricken being, the kind of figure with the inexplicably cruel hand of God apparently on him—madman, great criminal, or victim of mysterious illness—who terrifies ordinary souls. But more subtly and in an aesthetic dimension, it is because he is a complete being, the only such one in the play. To argue as certain critics have done that the other characters are dramatically deficient because of this is to miss the point. For Büchner deliberately fashioned them this way in order that Woyzeck's agonized representative humanity might stand out and that he not be simply one particular kind of person among others.

The characters who surround him are in one way or another functional; he alone is not. They exist dramatically as narrow human faculties or impulses, or the distortions of these things, while Woyzeck lives on the stage without limitation or particular human role, as the entirely exposed, painfully sentient being in whom existence is summed up. The essence of his tragedy lies in his being continually used as an object of exploitation and solipsistic desires, manipulated by the needs of others. He is maddened by a world in which human beings fall drastically short even of the qualities that would make existence tolerable.

To have made the other characters "fuller" would have been to transpose the play to the psychological level Büchner was intent on transcending. Moreover, the criticism reflects an even broader notion of drama that he had set out energetically to overthrow: that a play is a construction like life, which is to say immediately recognizable as life and conceived in its terms, and therefore ought to be composed of characters as full and lifelike as possible. Camille's speech on the theater in *Danton's Death* is Büchner's explicit comment on that.

Woyzeck's only intimate connections, his bonds to life, have been with his paramour, a sensual woman "who could stare her way through seven pairs of leather pants," and their child. Physically ugly and graceless but faithful and generous to the limit of his capacity, he has represented security to her, while he in turn has rested his aggrieved, nearly annihilated sense of what being human is on her acceptance of his love and on her fidelity. Her betrayal is therefore the deepest aggression against his remaining dignity and selfhood.

In the world of motives, passions, and animal desires, she can be thought of as simply following the dictates of her nature—of nature itself—when she grows tired of Woyzeck and succumbs, although with twinges of remorse, to the temptation of the splendidly erotic—nothing-but-erotic—tall, long-striding Drum Major. But the betrayal is precisely in the realm of those questions about human nature which Woyzeck, the downtrodden, voice-haunted humanist, the philosopher *malgré lui*, exists to raise. On the immediate psychological level his reactions are of course jealousy, anger, and bereavement. Yet psychological realities, as everything ought to have made clear, are not enough. Woyzeck's truest experience is in a dimension of ontological truth; the universe itself has been split asunder by Maria's treachery. In this drama of elemental consciousness about oppression by the nature of things, Maria has already "murdered" Woyzeck by destroying their unity, so that his killing of her is both punishment and the only means he knows of bringing about the re-equilibrium of existence through a protest in the same terms as its own cruelty.

In one of those great darkly lyrical passages in which Büchner exhibits his Shakespeare-like capacity to fuse emotional and metaphysical significances, Woyzeck watches Maria dancing with the Drum Major and soliloquizes in anguish:

On and on! On and on! On and on! Spin around, roll around. Why doesn't God blow out the sun so that everything can roll around in lust, man and woman, man and beast. They'll do it in broad daylight, they'll do it in our hands, like flies. Woman! That woman is hot, hot. On and on, on and on.

The passage is reminiscent of Lear's outcry against woman's sexuality, his male vision of the dark swamp of carnality which he suspects is the truest origin of his suffering destiny. Woyzeck's experience, however, transcends gender; his protest is less against the particular nature of woman than against the blind, ruthlessly impersonal force of animal desire that grips men and women alike and that carries them past loyalties and into the destruction of all bonds forged by the spirit. In *Woyzeck* the juggernaut of sexual desire is an equivalent of the movement of power in *Danton's Death*; in both cases human beings are compelled to live by determinations made outside their wills, to live not as free agents of nature but as its helpless subjects.

In a scene laid in a tavern Woyzeck is beaten by the Drum Major. He has learned of the latter's liaison with Maria through cruel mocking hints by the Doctor and the Captain, and the beating is the final insult and injury on top of his intolerable loss. As he pulls himself to his feet he mutters, in what appears to be an astounding piece of understatement: "One thing after another." The phrase is of course one we use to describe the continuing knocks and crises of ordinary experience, a cliché expressing a sort of rueful acceptance. But for Woyzeck it is an exact description of his status as victim. At the same time, it can be read as a dramaturgical principle, a motto for Büchner's procedure. For *Woyzeck* is a play in which events occur—in the most literal sense and as a concession to theatrical duration—*after* one another and not through a chain of strict causality.

In an even more radical way than in *Danton's Death*, Büchner disposes his materials so as to fill an area, a field of action and perception, rather than forming them into a narrative line, a clear movement from outset to denouement. Woyzeck himself fills much of the space with his outcries and ruminations, his reports of "voices" that are really agencies of a reaction beyond the senses and serve as visionary equivalents of the physical calamities. But there are also the utterances, most often unconnected to any narrative progression, of the other characters who circle around him like satellites around a ruined star, and the action is further broken up by songs (many of them Alsatian ballads from a collection amassed by friends of Büchner) which are always metaphors and images in their own right.

In the light of all this, Maria's treachery may be seen as the act that instigates the murder, but the murder itself is not the mechanical result—along a trajectory of plot—of the act, nor are the preceding events steps in an inexorable process leading up to it. The murder takes place as simply one occurrence, highly "dramatic" as it might be, in the life of a created universe—the world of Woyzeck's oppression—and is less the narrative or thematic climax of the play than the central metaphor for Woyzeck's destiny and his ultimate protest against it.

This is why the order of scenes is so much less crucial than in traditional dramatic construction. Maria's encounter with the Drum Major and Woyzeck's discovery of her infidelity have naturally to take place before the murder, but apart from that there are very few scenes that cannot be shifted around with very little damage to the work's integrity. Even more securely than in *Danton's Death* Büchner had made good his escape from the dramatic logic that had based itself on the apparent logic of life outside the theater. A play is not a replica of the ways we ordinarily see and interpret experience, *Woyzeck* announces. There are no causes and results, no *reasons*. There is only the imagination filling its chosen space, bringing into being events that have never yet taken place and whose logic is grounded on a freedom from the merciless tyranny of the events that have.

Since *Woyzeck* is constructed throughout as a climate and field of expression, its movement is that of a steady accretion of feeling and revelation, rather than, as in conventional drama, of progress toward a culmination, a pinnacle of "meaning." Images and metaphors are therefore far less instrumental than expressive; the drama organizes itself according to the principles of a poetic exploration and discovery, and what is found takes its place within the ostensible "story" as tales in themselves, radiating meanings and imaginative intensities that contribute to the total work, it goes without saying, but are also their own justifications.

Two scenes in particular make themselves felt as this kind of autonomous but connected reality within the play as a whole. One is a scene at a fair which Woyzeck visits. There he and the other spectators, who include Maria and the Drum Major at their first meeting, are presented with a trained monkey and horse. The monkey is dressed in a soldier's uniform complete with sword. He does tricks, plays the trumpet, and is described by the barker as having a "beastly reason, or rather a very reasonable beastliness—he's no dumb individual like a lot of people . . . the monkey is already a soldier. That's not much—it's the lowest level of the human race." The horse, which is able to "add" by shaking its head, is "no dumb animal," but a "person, a human being, a beastly human being but still an animal, *une bête*," who puts "human society to shame" by his "learnedness."

The scene is self-contained; Büchner makes no preparations for it and no references to it once it is over. It functions metaphorically as a container for one of the play's central motifs: the brutalization of its protagonist. The horse and monkey are elevated to a "human" level at the same time Woyzeck is being debased to an animal one. What is in question is the idea of the human, the idea expressed in the German word "*Mensch*," which signifies both mere facticity—biological status—and the moral and spiritual qualities we think of as distinguishing us from the beasts. Herbert Lindenberger has remarked that "it is the burden of the play to break down and expose those meanings of the word which can no longer hold up in the world we see depicted here." This is true. What gives *Woyzeck* so much of its vertiginous horror is the way it exhibits the disintegration of the very notion of human existence as something unique and valuable and something in turn sustained by values.

Another wholly independent scene that is nevertheless as central to the play's reality as any other element is one of the children's games, at the end of which a character called the

Grandmother is asked to tell a story and relates the following tale:

> Once upon a time there was a poor little child with no father and no mother. Everything was dead, and no one was left in the whole world. Everything was dead, and the child went and cried day and night. And since nobody was left on the earth, he wanted to go up to the heavens, because the moon was looking at him so friendly, and when he finally got to the moon, the moon was a piece of rotten wood, and then he went to the sun, and when he got there, the sun was a wilted sun-flower, and when he got to the stars, they were little golden flies stuck up there like the shrike sticks them on the blackthorn; and when he wanted to go back down to the earth, the earth was an upset pot, and the child was all alone, and sat down and cried, and there he sits to this day, all alone.

Nothing better illustrates Büchner's poetic method, his freedom from the canons of dramatic plausibility, than the appearance without preamble or subsequent comment of this chilling little fiction. An anti-fairy tale, a narrative of the dead world which throws its icy light on Woyzeck's agony by recapitulating it in different terms, the Grandmother's story exists in the play as an image implacably summing up all others. That Büchner should have chosen to parody—in the most terrifyingly deadpan way—a child's medium of consciousness which is also an adult mode of imparting consciousness to children is one more example of his amazing intuition into the connections among things.

For beyond all social data and pathology, beyond his "adult" experience, Woyzeck stands before us as a child, the child we would all be—terrified, disconsolate, astounded by the treachery and cruelty of the world—were we not educated to acceptance and so blinded to the truth of what we feel. Woyzeck's lack of education, his failure to have been assimilated into the great conspiracy of silence and pretense, rationalization and vainglory, that the Doctor and the Captain and the Drum Major uphold, is of course the source of what he sees and of the ascription to him, as a consequence, of "madness."

It was Büchner's great sanity that he went beyond such an ascription, as he went beyond the corollary one of criminality, to create as a counterstatement to history's decisions his own infinitely forgiving and yet unappeasably painful vision. *Woyzeck*, a supreme risk in dramatic form, a liberation for future playwrights, is also, as such creations always are, a liberation precisely from appeasement, from the desperate untruths that cause life to bring about its only corrective: art such as this.

IBSEN

In the summer of 1885, when Henrik Ibsen, then fifty-seven, was vacationing with his wife at the pleasant Norwegian coastal town of Molde, a newspaper reporter wrote of seeing him every day on a jetty, looking down into the water: "He stands there most of the day." A few years later Ibsen told Henrik Jaeger, who was at work on a biography of the eminent playwright, of his feeling for the ocean: "There is something extraordinarily fascinating about the sea. When one stands and stares down into the water it is as though one sees that life which moves on earth, but in another form. Everything is connected; there are resemblances everywhere."

It is a surprising observation to have come from Ibsen, revealing an unexpected attentiveness in him. Despite the snows and ice mountains of *Brand* and *When We Dead Awaken*, the landscapes and deserts of *Peer Gynt*, and the sea's dominating presence or image in half a dozen plays, we are accustomed to thinking of him as intensely urban, a scrutinizer of society, the moral self, besieged domestic life, a dramatic poet (if we consider him one) par excellence of the indoors. We see him, as Henry James did, with his light burning "in tasteless parlors" that give off "an odor of spiritual paraffin." In these surroundings his notorious "ideas" and problems work themselves out, with only the most minimal apparent connections to physical nature, the life of bodily forms.

Yet Ibsen, who in his youth had been an accomplished painter and witty caricaturist, insisted throughout his life that the central faculty of literature was that of sight ("A writer's task," he once wrote Bjornsterne Bjornsen, "is to *see*") and meant it in more than an abstract intellectual sense, that of insight, for example, or perspicacity. Several times in his correspondence or conversation he drew attention to the meaning of the word "theater," which in Greek is "a place for seeing."

When we really look at his plays as sensuous objects instead of abstractly interpreting them, we know how accurately he himself had seen, how his portraits of the world are physically exact, truthful to the lineaments of phenomena and the relationships among forms. And we know that this is more than simply *mirroring*, something he had warned against in the same letter to Bjornsen; for to see is to relate, to make distinctions and connections. Even when he was most "indoors," most withdrawn from physical nature, Ibsen understood how the latter could provide him with analogues for interior terrains.

Ibsen. We have to overcome the narrow portraits and icy legends if we are to know him well. Begin with the person: dour, hard, wintry, adamant. In 1895 the British poet Richard Le Gallienne (whose daughter Eva was to do so much for Ibsen in America, as actress in and translator of his plays) met the sixty-seven-year-old writer in Munich and saw this: "A forbidding, disgruntled, tight-lipped presence, starchily dignified, straight as a ramrod; there he was . . . with a touch of grim dandyism about him, but with no touch of human kindness about his parchment skin or fierce badger eyes. He might have been a Scotch elder entering the kirk."

Perhaps. But others saw him differently. William Archer,

who along with Bernard Shaw was his chief evangelist in England, met him several times around the same period and found him "friendly" and even "charming." And Georg Brandes, the Danish critic who was his foremost champion in Scandinavia, wrote that while "it did not take much to put him out of humor or to arouse his suspiciousness . . . how many examples have I not had of his cordiality, his thoughtfulness, his gentleness?" It would seem that Ibsen, in his youth a rather ebullient, hard-drinking bohemian, had by middle age come to suffer from the institutionalization and exploitability of his fame, so that certain innate tendencies toward suspiciousness and prickly independence were encouraged. Still, to those with whom he felt comfortable, who were not intent on seizing him for ideological or sentimental purposes, he could be generous and affectionate, though holding his inner self rigidly shielded from their gaze.

Even so, his relationships with intimates were complicated and subject to violent alternations of feeling. This was especially true of his long friendship with Bjornsen, whose literary reputation actually surpassed Ibsen's during much of their careers, although there were always those who saw the large discrepancy of their talents. Ibsen's biographer, Michael Meyer, tells the possibly apocryphal story of the occasion in 1903 when Bjornsen, an inordinately vain man, went to Stockholm to receive the Nobel Prize (which Ibsen was never given). "He tried to enter the palace through a side door but found his way barred by a sentry. 'My good man,' Bjornsen informed him, 'I am Norway's greatest writer.' 'Oh,' said the sentry, making way. 'I beg your pardon, Herr Ibsen.' "

Bjornsen seems by turns to have helped Ibsen and either condescended to or reviled him. Several times he solicited financial support when Ibsen was in particularly great need, and he encouraged him with expressions of faith in his genius. But he also wrote to a mutual acquaintance when he and Ibsen were in their thirties that "as soon as Ibsen recognizes that he is a minor writer, he will at once become a charming poet," and he later said of A Doll's House that "it is technically excellent, but written by a vulgar and evil mind," an opinion which, it is true, was shared by many at the time. Still, Ibsen seems to have depended on the friendship more than on any other, initiating several reconciliations after fallings-out and accepting, if without overt enthusiasm, the marriage of his only child Sigurd to Bjornsen's daughter.

A man complicated beyond our usual biographical methods, Ibsen seems to have united many contrarieties in his being. He was known (and known to himself) as something of a physical coward and exhibited extreme diffidence—possibly amounting to periodic impotence—in sexual matters. Yet he possessed intellectual valor of the highest kind: courage in the face of derision and attack. He was absolutely indifferent to ordinary literary politics, yet had a hunger for ceremonial recognition; he was a great medal chaser, pursuing decorations like any official hack, at one time writing to a court functionary about a decoration he was in line for in Egypt: "This honor is highly flattering to me, and it would also be of the greatest possible advantage in establishing my literary position in Norway."

In his defense we ought to know that for years his countrymen mostly ignored him, so that among other oppressions his financial situation was for a long time nearly desperate. And in his wider defense we should know that when his fame did mount, when he became world-renowned, he was always aware of the fickleness of public taste and, more important, how little he was actually understood, how little he could count on understanding. The medals and honors (for which he sacrificed nothing in his art) then became, perversely if we need to think so, emblems of acceptance, protections against his works and name falling into oblivion.

Whatever the truth of that, he was a hero, a knight of the

imagination, and not least for having tested his own honor in his works. It is another thing we find hard to connect with him, thinking him so objective, so coldly analytical and aloof, a playwriting machine. Yet late in his career he wrote that "everything that I have created has had its origin in a frame of mind and in a situation in my life. I never wrote because I had, as they say, 'found a good subject.' Everything that I have written has the closest possible connection with what I have lived through inwardly . . . In every new poem or play I have aimed at my own spiritual emancipation and purification."

His "subjects" were discovered by an extension of himself into the speech and gestures of possible surrogates. He embodied himself in his characters, as any true playwright does, except that in his case it is especially difficult to see because of those dramas—A Doll's House, Ghosts, An Enemy of the People, Hedda Gabler, The Wild Duck—which seem so descriptive of "others" and are the plays by which he is chiefly known.

In 1898, seventy years old, at the height of his fame and, as it turned out, with only one more play to write, he was given a testimonial banquet by the Norwegian Society for Women's Rights. With characteristic understatement he told the assembled ladies, for whom of course A Doll's House was the Bible, the Iliad, and Paradise Regained in one, that "I have been more of a poet and less of a social philosopher than people have generally been inclined to believe. I thank you for your toast but I must decline the honor of consciously having worked for women's rights. I am not even quite sure what women's rights really are. To me it has been a question of human rights."

"I have been more of a poet and less of a social philosopher . . ." Several years after Ibsen's death in 1906 Rainer Maria Rilke, who was to become one of his most fervent admirers, wrote after seeing his first Ibsen play (The Wild

Duck) that he had discovered "a new poet, one to whom we will go by path after path, now that we know one." He saw further than Gabriele D'Annunzio, who complained to André Gide about Ibsen's "lack of beauty," or Paul Valéry, who found him "tiresome."

Rilke went on to say that Ibsen was "a man misunderstood in the midst of fame, an entirely different person from what one hears." He was obviously using the words "man" and "person" to mean artist and playwright. There is something extremely significant in this for our understanding of cultural process, specifically the manner in which works of art become anthropomorphized into extensions or equivalents of their creators. It is not a question of biography—the most abstract and impersonal works undergo the same process—but of the human need to grant personality to the inventions of the mind. For most of us Marx *is* Communism, Einstein relativity, Darwin evolution.

In the same way works of art take on their creators' names and souls. We speak of a Rembrandt and of Shakespeare when we mean either the man or the world of his plays. We talk about long-dead artists "doing" or "saying" something in their work as though they were as alive as we are, the imagination making contemporaries of us all. Most importantly, we think of the works, and even find ourselves responding to them, under the simplified distinctive sign of their genius, the emblem by which to know them. Rembrandt is chiaroscuro, El Greco lightning flashes; more subtly Baudelaire is decadence, Joyce experiment. Intellectual rumor: the art of the past, and even of the present, comes to us like gossip in a salon. Criticism is, or ought to be, the action of dispelling such rumors or making them into more than phrases.

To most of us now, Ibsen comes down as narrow, programmatic, the social philosopher he knew he had never been. And the name stands between our senses and the plays. Ibsen: cold light, problems, living rooms, instruction. We can't obliterate the name; there would be nothing left by which to *refer* to the work. And besides that, he *is* the man who wrote it, though the life and the dramas neither explain nor justify one another. But they went on together, the work not representing him but rather being brought into existence to fill the moral and psychic spaces, the poetic space, between what he was and what it was possible to be.

In 1901 the nineteen-year-old James Joyce wrote a letter to the man misunderstood in the midst of fame, sending him greetings on his seventy-third birthday, in Norwegian, which he had learned in order to read the plays in the original. After telling Ibsen how he had been shouting his praises in public, Joyce went on:

> I did not tell them what bound me closest to you. I did not say how what I could discern dimly of your life was my pride to see, how your battles inspired me—not the obvious material battles but those that were fought and won behind your forehead— how your willful resolution to wrest the secret of life gave me heart, and how in your absolute indifference to public canons of art, friends and shibboleths you walked in the light of your inward heroism.

The inwardness of Ibsen's heroism, the hiddenness of his valor, was largely a matter of a temperamental inability to make himself known otherwise than in his work. The tight lips were those of a man for whom what he had fashioned spoke for itself. It was protracted work—Ibsen's career as a playwright covered half a century—and it is likely that one of the reasons he insisted so strongly at the end of his life that his plays be looked upon as parts of a whole, a single enterprise, was that he knew how long it had taken him and the shifting nature of the ruses and strategies he had had to employ. He knew, too, as many "cultured" persons do not, that to keep on writing plays, to keep on making art of any kind, is to have to learn as one goes, to wrestle with newly intractable material, to develop new strengths and modesties, to fail in the very appearance of success, but to be always engaged in a long, unbroken action whose unforeseen end lies in its beginnings.

The roots of Ibsen's dramatic art were in an exceedingly unpromising soil. Born in 1828 in the coastal town of Skien to middle-class parents (his merchant father later got into legal difficulties and fell on hard times, a circumstance which seems to have greatly affected Ibsen and may help account for the peculiar intensity of his terror of poverty in later life), he went before he was sixteen as an apothecary's assistant to another small town, Grimstad, where he remained for over six years. During this period he began to write and publish poetry and completed his first play, a rather windy and amateurish drama on Roman themes called *Catiline*. In 1850 he went to the capital city of Christiania (the modern Oslo) to prepare for his matriculation examination at the university there (he apparently intended to study medicine), and upon failing the test seems to have given up all thought of further education in favor of devoting himself entirely to writing.

But his literary work brought him next to nothing, so in 1851 he accepted a low-paying position as "dramatic author" with the Norwegian Theater of Bergen, a post whose duties entailed writing for the resident company, directing plays, and consulting on a hundred and one theatrical matters. He stayed there for over five years, then moved back to Christiania to fill a similar position with a new theater that had opened there, remaining in this job for nearly six more years. This long period of apprenticeship and immersion in practical theater undoubtedly laid a rough foundation for his future art, but the education was one he would have later to repudiate in large part. It was a bitterly frustrating time, for reasons mostly having to do with his own growing imaginative size and aspirations in relation to the low, crimped state of theatrical knowledge and practice in Norway.

Michael Meyer has described the conditions Ibsen met on his arrival in Bergen. Productions, for example, were rehearsed no more than four or five times and in performance "the normal placing of actors . . . was in a horizontal bow, with its tips in the downstage corners and everyone facing the audience, even when they were meant to be speaking to one another." Ibsen tried to do away with this convention and to move the theater generally toward more professional and intelligent practices (he had learned something about stagecraft during a short trip to Germany and Denmark, where the art was rather more advanced), but he made little headway and, what was even more discouraging, could do almost nothing with the prevailing repertoire. This was composed of pseudo-rustic folk plays, banal melodramas, historical pageants, and the most trivial of farces. During his stint at Bergen, Ibsen directed nearly 150 plays, more than half of them adaptations of light French *drames des boulevards,* twenty-one of these by Eugène Scribe.

The theater in Norway was almost wholly cut off from the stage's past. There were no worthwhile or even complete translations of the Greeks, Shakespeare, and the Elizabethans, the French tragic playwrights, or indeed any classics whatever. (Ibsen was more than once to lament his failure ever to learn English, although the likelihood is that in later life he read Shakespeare in German translations.) And there was almost no native drama, or literature of any kind for that matter.

The only dramatic writers Ibsen ever acknowledged learning from were Danish, or wrote in that language. They included the very minor Johan Ludvig Heiberg (1791–1860), who was also a poet and philosopher; Adam Oehlenschläger, a nineteenth-century poet and author of Schiller-like poetic tragedies; and Baron Ludvig Holberg, an eighteenth-century Norwegian who had lived in Denmark and written broad comedies of contemporary life in Danish. Ibsen was notoriously unwilling to admit influence, and in his case there is almost no evidence of there having been anyone from whom he learned more than some broad principles of construction, no master from whom he would have had to dissociate himself in order to strengthen a claim on originality.

It fell to him, therefore, to create a Norwegian drama, although for a time he seemed to be sharing the task with Bjornsen. His countrymen's pride in having this accomplished, their satisfaction in being brought into the wider European culture, became a chief basis for the esteem in which he later came to be held. It was a regard unaccompanied by much understanding, and it was continually under siege by an opposing attitude of resentment against him for having, as it was thought, held his fellow Norwegians up to ridicule, particularly in works like *Peer Gynt* and some of the later domestic dramas.

But even the opprobrium, with its testimony to recognition, was late in coming. In 1864, at the age of thirty-six, feeling unappreciated at home—such reputation as he possessed derived more from his poetry than his plays—and needing a wider and warmer world (he was to speak often from abroad of his countrymen's provincialism, their "cold, uncomprehending eyes"), Ibsen left Norway to begin a self-imposed exile that was to last for twenty-seven years. He had written ten plays, all but one of them historical dramas, of which many were based on the Norwegian sagas, half of them in verse and several others in a mixture of verse and formal, elevated prose.

As distinctive as these plays were by the standards of the day and place, with one exception they would have very little interest for us now were it not for their being Ibsen's, the first segment of his career's arc. Their inspiriting force is most often a nationalistic fervor (something that was to characterize Ibsen for many years and be present, though with decreasing explicitness and ardor, in a number of his later plays) whose principles and particularities are almost wholly alien to us now. Worse than that, these plays were written in a language engaged in trying to throw off the conventional attributes of "high" expression but having little else to rely on. Here is a representative passage from *The Vikings at Helgeland* (1858):

> I will follow you, in battle array, wherever you may go. Not as your wife will I go—for I have belonged to another, and the woman still lives who has lain by your side. No, not as your wife, Sigurd, but as a Valkyrie is how I will come—firing your blood to battle and great deeds, standing by your side as the sword-blows fall, shoulder to shoulder with your fighting men in storm and tempest. And when your funeral song is sung, it shall tell of Sigurd and Hjordis together!

Yet verbally stilted and physically clumsy as these plays almost wholly are, we can detect in them some faint foreshadowings of what Ibsen will come to do. The nationalism will be modulated into a structure of values of a far less localized kind, the historical materials will give way to those of a present seen as having invisibly assimilated the past. And the language will win its freedom from culture, from what is expected of *seriousness* in literary expression, from the corrupted inheritance of a classic set of rubrics.

In this regard *The Pretenders*, the last play of Ibsen's Norwegian beginnings, has the most stature of all as prediction. Although it too is a historical drama, set in thirteenth-century Norway and concerned with a struggle for the throne which resulted in the nation's being unified for the first time, *The Pretenders* compels our attention precisely by its nearly modern sound, its being written in prose of a sometimes terse and colloquial kind, and its rough elements of psychological and spiritual investigation. In it Ibsen begins to reach toward his true ground. Still, there is a seemingly unaccountable leap from its many awkwardnesses and inconsistencies and its ultimate failure as original consciousness to the plays in which his genius fully manifests itself for the first time, the first he would write away from Norway.

With his wife and small son Ibsen went to Rome, a favorite city among Scandinavian expatriates. He lived there and in other places in Italy for four years, spent the next seven years in Dresden, and the following three in Munich, returned to Italy for five more years, then, in 1891, having paid only sporadic visits to his homeland during all this time, went back to Christiania for what proved to be the rest of his life.

In Italy, between 1865 and 1868, Ibsen wrote *Brand* and *Peer Gynt.* With the exception of the monumental *Emperor and Galilean,* which he began in Italy and finished nine years later in Dresden, they are physically his largest works. But while *Emperor and Galilean* is very seldom performed or read, *Brand* and *Peer Gynt* remain at the center of any consideration of Ibsen and are indispensable to a full encounter with his mind and art. Everything he would write after this would in one way or another issue from their soil.

Unlike each other in subject and tone as they are, the two plays are bound in the most intimate unity, seeming to have been written in an unbroken sequence ("After *Brand, Peer Gynt* followed almost of itself," Ibsen later remarked). Their composition thus reflects what must have been a spontaneous movement of his imagination between the polarities he had come to understand in his own nature.

Far more directly than will be true again until the last series of spiritually autobiographical plays, *Brand* and *Peer Gynt* give us Ibsen projected on stage. They wear disguises, *Brand*'s protagonist that of an evangelical preacher, *Peer*'s of a picaresque adventurer, but internally, as moral and spiritual metaphors, they are their author's clear surrogates. And it is this movement toward the self, toward making plays out of what the self has discovered about its hungers and injuries, that becomes the basis of Ibsen's originality in these works and helps account for, though scarcely explain, the abrupt growth of his imaginative powers.

If the protagonist of *Brand* has too narrow a self, that of *Peer Gynt* has too wide a one; if Brand is an absolutist of the ideal, Peer is the epitome of anti-transcendence. Brand is an apostle, a man trying to serve something other and "higher" than himself; Peer is egoism incarnate, the very figure of self-regard. While Brand hunts with the hound of heaven, Peer seeks out the gross and subtle pleasures of the world.

Brand feels himself set on a prophetic mission, "born into this world to heal its sickness and its weakness." His religion is a species of newly primitive Christianity, a return to origins and sources through a faith whose central dogma, however, is that of human will and not divine mercy, and whose ruling principle is a Kierkegaardian "all or nothing." The world's illness is its spirit of compromise, its trafficking between material pleasure and metaphysical value, with a consequent softness and debility of soul. "We shall wander through the land," Brand exhorts his followers, "freeing our souls, purifying our weakness. Be men, be priests, renew God's faded image."

In his merciless pursuit of the absolute, Brand runs up against the limits of human nature, its inherent relativism, and is himself trapped in a fateful contradiction between abstract values and palpable life. To fulfill what he thinks of as his duty, he is forced to sacrifice his wife and child (a theme reminiscent of Kierkegaard's *Fear and Trembling*, which Ibsen may well have read) and he dies under an avalanche, one of those symbolic events in Ibsen which his detractors find so hard to accept. On his lips is a question to God—"If not by Will, how can man be redeemed?" to which the reply, from a voice crying "through the thunder," is: "He is the God of Love!"

While Brand incarnates will and an ideal purity whose unexpected action in the world is the destruction of the impure but living self, Peer is the embodiment of unprincipled selfhood, a representative of the search for unbounded personal fulfillment at the expense of soul and of others. To the long Western tradition of the value of knowing oneself he opposes the idea of "choosing" one's own being over all other life. The alternatives are most explicitly stated during the key scene in the hall of the mountain king: the motto is not to be "to yourself be true" but "to yourself be enough." This kind of self-sufficiency, Ibsen makes clear, is the province of animals, who have no need to work at being "true," and of that lower or animal self in man which is represented in *Peer Gynt* by the trolls, which Ibsen drew from Norwegian folklore.

The results of choosing oneself are thus to fall under the sway of one's baser part, to gain immediate satisfactions at the cost of dignity and honor, to cut oneself off from friendship and love, and so, finally, having no anchor in community and no center, to be "no one." The exact metaphor of this is the onion Peer peels off layer by layer to reach no core. "The art of daring, of courage in action," Peer says, "is to move with uncommitted feet among the tricky snares of life." But it is just this refusal to commit himself to anything that makes Peer, despite his charm and vivacity (or perhaps because of them: seductiveness is an agency of corruption), material for the Button Molder, another creature drawn from folklore whose function is to melt down such anomalous souls into a non-human substance. For, as the Button Molder tells Peer, he has not been a "serious" enough sinner for hell or "buoyant" enough for heaven. He is only spared in the end—a denouement which with some justification has been criticized as rather arbitrary—by his reunion with and acceptance of Solveig, the woman who has loved him and waited patiently for his pilgrimage of appetite to end.

From their antipodal starting points both Brand and Peer Gynt arrive at love as the power that will judge them. Nothing is clearer than that the writing of the two plays was in part an act of Ibsen's own submission to such an examination. "To live," he once wrote, "is to battle with trolls in heart and mind; to write is to sit in judgment on oneself." Another time he said that his work was concerned with the "contradiction between word and deed, between will and duty, between life and theory in general."

He knew these contradictions and antinomies in his own nature, and this is why, given the definition of writing he upheld, his work is never impersonal or narrowly objective, even when it seems to be most directly "social." He is Brand and Peer, the tragic and comic sides of his own propensities, if we want to categorize them that way. At the time, though, the plays were widely taken to be about *others*, Norwegian types who embodied national characteristics seen by an aloof ironist. *Peer Gynt* was mostly interpreted as a topical satire ("Why can't people read the thing as a work of fiction?" Ibsen protested), and *Brand*, which quickly became a rallying point for radical youth throughout Scandinavia, was often misread as a straightforward call to order, its protagonist being thought of as a kind of Promethean figure instead of as his own victim and debacle.

Ibsen's consciousness would remain rooted in these plays, which were like accusatory and cautionary fables of his own being. But the forms of his theater were about to change drastically from theirs. Both plays were written in verse and rank among the greatest poetic dramas since the Elizabethan and French classical periods. *Brand* is terser, harder, more economical and bare; in *Peer Gynt* Ibsen's style opens out into an expansiveness, flexibility, and sumptuousness it will never again attain. In both plays, though in *Peer Gynt* more freely, the unconscious issues its own images to describe its previously unreported life; the play will be the ancestor of many dramas pitched beyond rationality, among them Strindberg's dream plays and Alfred Jarry's *Ubu Roi*. But with these poetic monuments accomplished, Ibsen will appear to turn back, to reduce himself, abdicating from those verbal heights in order to gain a different kind of freedom, one he sensed was to be forbidden him there.

When *Peer Gynt* was published in Scandinavia (in accordance with contemporary practice, Ibsen's plays were published before being produced; in some cases, that of a potentially scandalous work like *Ghosts*, for example, it would be years before they saw the stage), it was extravagantly praised by some perceptive readers but more widely condemned for being ugly and "unpoetic." Ibsen's response was one of those violent, seemingly vainglorious replies to criticism which can be found throughout his career. "If my play is not poetry," he wrote to a friend, "then it will be; the definition of poetry will have to be changed in Norway to conform to my play." By poetry Ibsen meant something more than a technical category, as he knew his opponents did. For what was at stake was the definition of art itself. In that perennial finding that a new form or style of art is not art at all, the critics were rebuking *Peer Gynt* for its rough, unfamiliar energy, its unprecedentedly earthy and even vulgar language, and its wayward, "illogical" shape.

It was out of anything but a spirit of meek obedience to such judgments, then, that Ibsen now abandoned formal verse as the mode of his dramatic writing. The matter has become historical, which is to say it reaches us now with the ponderous inevitability the past forces on all its events. Ibsen changed the course of drama, theater historians tell us, because the drama was ready to be changed; modern, prosaic life was making its claims on the theatrical imagination, as on the novelistic one, and Ibsen was the first fully to respond. In this view, which is wrong only in that it misses the spirit of his action, everything personal in it, the artist is the servant of cultural destiny and originality is a question simply of foresight: the original artist is the one who does what is *supposed to come next*.

Brand and *Peer Gynt*, for all their splendors, belong to

the pre-modern period, we argue now in retrospect. And whether or not we dislike this aspect of the modern in drama, whether we think that Ibsen's social period brought the theater into an ironic kind of decadence in which prosaic actuality supplanted high imagination, or that the social plays were a new species of imagination made sober and truthful, we all succumb to the sense that this was the way it had to be. Yet Ibsen was a temperament as well as a man worked on by the times; his change of tactics, so portentous for the future of the drama, was the result of a choice, which he did not have to make and which much later on he would to some degree regret.

Ibsen knew that the dispute about his art would go on to the end. But he had become aware that contemporary tastes and attitudes worked against the success on stage of verse drama, however much it might be admired as literature, as among a passionate minority *Brand* and *Peer Gynt* certainly were. The sweep and range of his imagination in these plays were obviously better served by poetry than by the narrowly colloquial language of a work like *The Pretenders*, which had in fact been mixed with a more inflated prose, a pseudo-poetry such as "serious" drama was supposed to employ. Poetry had allowed him a suppleness, a power of implication and of elision that gave the plays their literary strength but at the same time made them difficult to perform. "I don't think the play's for acting," Ibsen said to a friend about *Peer Gynt*, and in fact neither play was to be staged for many years after their publication and both remain excessively difficult to produce well today.

It was essential for Ibsen that his plays be performed or at least have the potential for being staged. More than most innovators, he felt a need to count, to be immediately effective, so that changes in the formal means of his art were seldom dissociated from his effort to win a place, a large high position within the main enterprises of European civilization in his time. And the theater was the arena where that place might be most swiftly and decisively seized. Out of this urgency and with an internal struggle to bring into coherence his public ambition and sense of aesthetic rightness, he moved after *Peer Gynt* to make his theater more available, if without illusions that it would be more truly understood.

Some time later he was to write that "I came to regard verse as wrong . . . verse has been most injurious to dramatic art. It is improbable that verse will be employed to any extent worth mentioning in the drama of the future; the aims of the dramatist of the future are almost certain to be incompatible with it." He was to be proven right, to be one of the chief agencies of the proof, but the remark about the injuriousness of verse has a ring of rationalization to it. Since nineteenth-century plays in prose had not been a bit more distinguished than those in verse, the latter could scarcely be assigned the blame for drama's low estate.

But being intent now on writing in prose, Ibsen may have feared that this would appear to be a diminution of his artistic voice, since the prestige of poetry as the proper vehicle of *important* drama was still high, if only as a shibboleth. He needed now what he felt to be the right voice, the necessary one for a type of drama that would move from the exterior spaciousness and the perennial, legendary considerations of *Brand* and *Peer Gynt* to society, cities, houses, and rooms, to men and women as they actually, recognizably lived. He needed prose, felt it to be the more "human" voice now, seeing poetry slipping away, becoming inappropriate, too grand, too lofty and literary for his purposes.

Ibsen is certainly a "realist" in the cycle of plays which begins somewhat tentatively with *The League of Youth* in 1869, is set fully going with *Pillars of Society* in 1875–7, and ends, although the dividing line is not as absolute as that, with *Hedda Gabler* in 1890. But dramatic realism is not synony-

mous with emphasis on social problems and Ibsen is not the
limited playwright of "ideas" whose dramas, in Walter Kerr's
most recent formulation of the uncomprehending critical
line, are ones in which "people are digits, adding up to the
correct ideological sum." Our habit of looking at Ibsen not as
an artist but as a sort of grim (or splendid) fulminator, an
ideologue, or, at the lowest, a designer of problematic living
rooms, a theatrical upholsterer, has prevented us from seeing
how in his plays specific ideas or issues conceal truer, more
permanent subjects.

Ibsen's realism is in the first place a matter of having
chosen paradigmatic situations from the life of contemporary
society, from the newspapers in certain cases. He was a great
reader and creative user of newspapers (for much of his later
years he read very little else), and to this fact we owe a large
element of the renewed life of the theater, for the sources of
almost all other dramatic writing of the time were the artifi-
cialities and brittle inventions of the theater itself. Ibsen made
his social plays out of nothing other than *what might have
occurred* in what we call real life. It was a form of anti-
romanticism, an outward sobriety of imagination, but it was
also a specifically aesthetic repudiation of the stage as an arena
for fantasy.

This realism incorporated into its enterprise what might
be, and were, regarded as "issues." But it long ago became
clear that we have to distinguish Ibsen's thought from the
narrow and localized ideas for which he was at first wrongly
praised and then wrongly blamed, the former because he was
being so intellectually "advanced" and modern, the latter
because he was scanting feeling and sensuousness in his work.
As Eric Bentley has written, Ibsen "is far less interested in
'modern ideas' than in certain ideas that go behind them. In
Ibsen one must always look for the idea behind the idea."

One must also look for the poetry behind the prose. In
giving up formal verse Ibsen remained a poet in the sense in

which he had earlier defined it: as the man who sees. The apparent prosiness of the social plays was a mask for poetry of the most subtle, hitherto-unfamiliar kind. To achieve a drama of contemporary life, one whose language would be other than that of literature, conceived of as elevated expression, Ibsen rooted his methods in a lyricism that was informal, hidden, a matter of textures and relationships, implications and elisions, a prose-poetry which at first glance seemed only to be prose. Driven down into the depths, beyond the audience's immediate ear, it lay out of the grasp of paraphrase and socially exploitable meanings; the conscious, public, quickly assimilable events of the plays, their ostensible subjects, would make for those things.

What were those subjects, those purported themes which in Ibsen's own time caused so much scandal and uproar and in ours are grounds for thinking him invalidated by history? Consider the three plays for which he is probably best known. A Doll's House was and is held to be about women's rights; Ghosts about sexual morality and immorality or, more subtly, about moral continuity, how the sins of the parents are visited upon the children; Hedda Gabler about sexual frustration or neurosis among the upper class or the tensions of caste, or all three. We have seen how Ibsen repudiated that reading of A Doll's House; he never spoke about the widespread misinterpretations of the others, but if he had ever decided to, he surely would have issued the same sort of laconic, devastating corrections.

In his remarks to the feminists about A Doll's House Ibsen had said that to him it had been a question of "human rights." The clear implication is that the play is really about human appetites for power and exploitation and the corollary victimization of those who are not so driven. Beneath the appearances—a husband who patronizes, a wife who at first submits and then rebels—patronization, submission, and rebellion are themselves on exhibition; something more than sociological data is making itself known.

Historically, A *Doll's House* stirred or shocked most of its audiences or readers on circumscribed political or ethical grounds: married women ought not be the slaves of their husbands; married women ought to obey and defer to their husbands, etc. Yet the play's movement goes well past such limited meanings and arguments, so that when all the images and verbal intensities have crystallized in our memories, the work seems to point to something quite different from what we have supposed.

In its central movement A *Doll's House* is a drama of preparation, pitched beyond sexual difference, a play of encounter with the obstacles—in this exemplary case the institution of marriage—that act to prevent us from knowing ourselves and the world. "I must stand on my own feet if I am to find out the truth about myself and about life," Nora says, and when Thorwald replies that "first and foremost you are a wife and mother," her rejoinder—a statement that lifts the play wholly past ideology—is "I don't believe that any longer. I believe that I am a human being first and foremost . . . or . . . that I must try to become one."

Thorwald's very diction is that of someone for whom existence is organized into categories and whose feelings are shaped according to received ideas of fitness and acceptability. In Nora's speech we can detect the initial stages of a repudiation of such a "civilized" process, and this rejection, going so much deeper than a refusal of matrimonial responsibility, is what most profoundly, if subliminally, shocked the bourgeois audiences of the time. If A *Doll's House* now has a certain thinness, if it seems to us somewhat attenuated, this is not due to its being a play of narrow theoretical issues but to the thinness of the ice on which Ibsen was skating, to the fact that he did not yet quite have the artistic weapons to deal with so dangerous a subject.

The subject of *Ghosts* was also dangerous and so was partially concealed. It was surely not the "rigidity of middle-class Norwegian morality," as one recent critic has argued, but something far less fettered to a social proposition of that kind. *Ghosts* is "about" the rigidities, the fatal, blind movements of ideals and abstractions in a universe of fact, and about the status of the mind and will as prisoners of a tyrannical, invisibly operating past.

Morality, sexual or otherwise, is simply one strand of the web of self-deception and ignorance in which Mrs. Alving is caught. The "ghosts" that haunt her refer much more significantly to the complex of inherited, unexamined ideas and values which rule her as they do us all than to the specific forms of her moral and physical past. The evil she has done is ontological: she has failed to think for herself, to *be* herself. She has acted in bad faith, and the physical disaster that follows on this—Oswald's sickness and implied death—is a demonstration of her faithlessness, its "objective correlative." The reason why the discovery of penicillin did not invalidate *Ghosts,* as has so often and so seriously been argued, is that venereal disease was never the problem; it was simply an instance.

Hedda Gabler, the last and poetically richest of the social plays, is also the most mysterious. It was surely possible at the time and remains possible to think of Hedda as a decadent aristocrat chafing under the pettiness of her bourgeois marriage and surroundings, or as a deeply neurotic woman whose sexual aggressiveness masks a radical frigidity. When Bernard Shaw wrote that the trouble with such women is that they *don't* ordinarily kill themselves, he was of course partly subscribing to a view of the play as a sociological character study. Yet beneath its surface, under the mercilessly accurate portraits and the exact iconography of domestic crisis, Ibsen was trying to fashion something else: a new kind of tragicomedy, more metaphysical than it is comfortable for us to think, whose elements are energy turned in on itself and being wrestling with its tendency to dissolution.

On one level Hedda is indeed a frustrated woman and the play does offer a cold view of specifically bourgeois existence. Yet it is a mistake to stop there. For there is not the slightest indication in the play that a change of circumstances would have saved Hedda, that she is suffering a local, socially engendered fate. Her revenge upon Loevborg, the destruction of his manuscript (a murder of the "child" she cannot have) and then of herself, are actions in a dimension beyond technical or scientifically identifiable pathology. Hedda is unable *to live*. At the deepest level of Ibsen's vision she is caught not so much in a particular set of determining circumstances—these make up the dramatic occasion, providing the details by which the dramatic vision is made palpable—as in human circumstance itself. She is a victim of the way things are, a fish in Ibsen's great polluted boiling sea where ill-adapted creatures struggle to know what to do.

Loevborg swims alongside her, even blinder, more powerless and unhappy. He is the self-destructive creator, the one who, inadequate to the richness of his own intellect, turns his violence inward in an effort to escape responsibility. If he doesn't kill himself but dies in a ludicrous accident, it is because he is morally less than Hedda, not as brave; for her, suicide is an act out of a steely recognition that an intolerable point has been reached, that nothing outside herself will give way. Thus the sound of the pistol going off is an announcement that there is at least that strange sort of courage in the world which can cut through such impasses. It is left to the "dull" ordinary personages of the drama, Thea and Tesman, to go on, devoted, staying within human bounds, working away at Loevborg's manuscript, generous as Hedda in her anguish and deeper, fatal vision cannot be. *Hedda Gabler* is one of the greatest anti-romantic plays we possess, for its perception is of what remains possible after the outcries and seductive whispers of our own impossible cravings have faded.

It was Henry James who in Ibsen's lifetime saw most clearly the nature of his genius, grasping with great perspicacity the true imaginative action of the social plays. On the surface Ibsen was "massively common and middle-class," but James could see past that to his "independence, his intensity, his vividness, the hard compulsions of his strangely inscrutable art." That the art should be "strangely" inscrutable was due to just that discrepancy which was pointed out before between the plays' objective events, their stories or plots, and their hidden values or meanings. An art depicting society should be entirely available; if Ibsen's was all politics and moral study, if its energies were essentially forensic, why should it resist analysis so obdurately?

Ibsen's subject, James went on to say, "is always, like the subjects of all first-rate men, primarily an idea," and his chief idea is the "individual caught in the fact." The barest of propositions, the most abstract of critical formulations, but in its light everything puzzling and deceptive in Ibsen yields something to our understanding. Mysteries will remain, as they should. But we can see now what kind of dramas are being staged: enactments of the self versus the structure of experience, of personal being opposed by the hard details, outside and beyond the values we may place on them, of things as they are. Ibsen had spoken of his plays as dealing with contradictions, most widely that between "life and theory in general." One of his greatest artistic achievements was to have imagined the individual as a kind of theorem, something asserted but not proven; life, facticity, would provide the test, and the testing was the drama.

To accomplish this kind of philosophically oriented dramatic creation within the realistic mode he had chosen was Ibsen's unprecedented problem. In this regard nothing in the history of the modern theater has been more exhaustively studied than the question of his relationship to the French well-made play, the dominant theatrical genre during his apprenticeship and afterward.

The place to begin is in metaphysics, not stagecraft. For the well-made play was pre-eminently a bourgeois mode in having been designed for the amusement and edification of an affluent, newly cultured class and in reflecting that class's values and self-estimation, its sense of the world. The Russian theologian and critic Nicolas Berdyaev, citing the thought of Charles Péguy, once characterized what he called the "bourgeois mind" as "idolatrous" in so far as it invariably preferred the "visible to the invisible." Berdyaev was describing a predilection consistent with but going beyond economic materialism, and his terms are particularly applicable to matters of art.

The well-made play was one of almost entire visibility, which is to say it possessed almost no dimension beyond what was literally placed before the audience's eyes and ears; figures of inflated physical and deprived moral or spiritual status, at their extreme points the stock personages of melodrama and farce, its characters moved through dramas whose values were wholly corporeal, or else abstractions for corporeality—myths of love, power, social prowess, etc.—which its audiences uncritically accepted as the reflected truths of their own lives.

"The Ego against the Ego . . . the Soul against the Soul," James had said of the human encounters in Ibsen's plays and had gone on to describe them, in a wonderful and mysterious phrase, as "thinkable things." The very notions of ego—selfhood—and soul were what were missing from the French *pièces à bien faites*. Ibsen took over the apparatus of the genre and by infusing it with self and spirit put it to unheard-of intellectual and imaginative uses. By compelling the past to reveal its tyranny over the present and abstractions over palpable life, he gave to the well-made structure a depth of conflict that radically exposed the superficiality of the kinds of contests—immediate, mechanical, effortlessly assimilable—which were its stock in trade.

In doing this he changed the nature of dramatic plot, or at least the premises from which it proceeded in the well-made play. For the bourgeois audiences of the period (as for their counterparts today) plots were physically eventful stories mirroring the logical, unmysterious ways in which their own lives were presumed to move. Or else they were fanciful tales, logical and transparent in their own manner, that grafted comfortingly romantic inventions onto otherwise prosaic existence and provided it with solacing endings.

Ibsen's plots were instrumentalities of spiritual and moral revelation, seeking to work against the process of replication of ordinary life or that of its romantic enhancement. They did this through the presence of poetic implication and statement beneath the realistic surfaces and in the interstices of the story's physical events, constituting what we would now call the "subtext." Unlike the plots of Scribe, for example, to whom story was everything ("When my story is right, when I have the events of my play firmly in hand," he once said, "I could have my janitor write it"), Ibsen's plots were in part *pretexts,* traps for the attention of the audience, which was then led, if it was willing to follow, toward his deeper subject.

Yet as time went on Ibsen grew more and more aware of the constrictions on the imagination that lay in even a strategic obedience to the tenets of the well-constructed plot. Had he been a novelist he would have been able to make use of those integumentary and aesthetically environing elements, that atmosphere of reflection, opinion, point of view, and so on which the writer of fiction brings into being in order to give his characters richer and more complex destinies than their literal actions can amass. Under the surfaces of Ibsen's social plays are present elements of a far-reaching tragicomic vision, yet this vision is continually impeded by the literalness of the narrative. Moral quests spread past the incidents devised for their unfolding; metaphysical actions take place in imperfect collaboration, sometimes in acute disharmony, with the physical details of their stage life, obliged as the latter are to provide recognizable portraits.

Most noticeably in plays like *Pillars of Society, A Doll's*

House, and *Ghosts,* but also in more complex works like *Rosmersholm* and *Hedda Gabler,* the machinery of plot works logically to establish necessary physical connections, more or less narrow sequences of cause and effect which propel the action forward but at the expense of a fullness of poetic significance. The poetry survives—it is what keeps the plays alive for our pleasure—but it is hemmed in, cramped; the trouble we have with these plays is that their plots keep crowding out their perceptions.

In the end their denouements have issued from mechanical rather than organically imaginative progressions, from an inevitability of physical causation resembling that which we illusorily feel in "real" life. The famous letter in *A Doll's House,* the father's pipe in *Ghosts,* Loevborg's manuscript in *Hedda Gabler*—quintessential objects of the well-made plot—have the effect of imposing on the plays a stringency, an inevitability of a smaller, more limited kind than Ibsen's imagination had conceived.

There has been little room for choice, the movement by which a character is shown to elect his or her own fate, the way Oedipus and Macbeth do, as a consequence of his own nature and existential situation and as an image of these things, instead of having a destiny thrust on him by a logic of happenstance. However much these events strive to attain the condition of fatality, they remain incommensurable with the characters, too local, specific, and literal to contain all their meanings and significances or to support fully their stature as freely imagined beings. Thus once the letter is in the box Nora is compelled by the logic of the plot-as-fate to act on the coercive knowledge of the effect its discovery will have on her husband; once Rosmer has learned of Rebecca West's machinations he is propelled by that knowledge to a death intended partly to atone for her acts and on that account smaller in implication and metaphoric density than the one Ibsen was trying to create for him.

In the same way, once Hedda has destroyed Loevborg's

manuscript, which has itself come down to her through a chain of plotted, charted circumstances, she is led to destroy herself, having literally burned her bridges behind her. Or rather it is the plot that has burned them for her; and thus we feel a discrepancy, an uneasy space, between its inexorable physical action and the realities of her nature. The violent circumstances may be physical or objective indications of her moral and psychic being, but they are by no means equivalent to it, so that what she incarnates is reflected in the events of the play like a face overflowing a small mirror held too close. The miracle is that Ibsen has been able to make her fate, with its implications of a disorder at the heart of existence itself and not merely in a particular social or psychopathological modality, as convincing as he has.

With *The Master Builder* in 1892 Ibsen entered his last phase, the so-called "symbolic" period. At the age of sixty-four, unquestionably the world's most famous playwright, he set out once again to alter his methods, one result being to disconcert all those who thought that they had finally come to grasp what he was about. The undertaking is an exemplary instance of the subtle relationships between psychic reality and aesthetic forms. Pressures within his sense of self now compelled Ibsen toward the creation of new dramatic styles, new structures of consciousness, for the awarenesses he now possessed could no longer be contained within the forms he had been working with, the tightly organized, logically proceeding, objective-looking drama which he had strategically employed and compromised with for so long.

If psychological criticism scants formal values for the sake of clinical findings, pure textual criticism proceeds as though the art had been created in an inhuman zone of aesthetic autonomy. Much of the criticism of Ibsen's last plays is psychological rather than textual, and much of it has a negative cast. The plays are most often seen as problematic documents of embattled old age, with a subplot concerning the risks of being an artist; what is sometimes ignored is that they are also problematic exercises in dramatic technique, experiments in the working out of forms that will be the aesthetic equivalents of the playwright's experiences. Ibsen's internal life had entered a new, beleaguered stage. Realizations he had been holding at arm's length had come steadily closer, crowding his self-knowledge: he is growing old, the stern and amazingly disciplined practice of his art (for nearly thirty years he had written at the rate of a play every two years or so) has cost him human warmth, a fullness of actual life.

In the summer of 1889 at Gossensass in the Tyrol, he had met an eighteen-year-old girl, Emilie Bardach, who seems to have fallen in love with him, a feeling he reciprocated but kept severely under control, so that apparently nothing was consummated. In time he cut off their correspondence, but she, and several other young women he was to meet in the next few years, remained in his sentiments, poignant reminders of what he had missed and would not now have.

The question of Ibsen's emotional and sexual life, particularly as it concerns his wife of nearly fifty years, has been much debated. Michael Meyer's biography tries hard to do justice to the matter, in the face of the lack of any real evidence, and concludes that the marriage, while clearly lacking in passion, was solid and harmonious. Yet Meyer prints testimony of an opposite kind, excerpts from a diary (which was to remain unpublished for seventy-five years) kept by one Martin Schneekloth, a young Danish acquaintance of the Ibsens in Rome around the time of the writing of *Peer Gynt*:

Ibsen, Schneekloth wrote,

took [his wife] from her father's house, led her out into the strange world, and instead of devoting his life to finding some form of reconciliation he gives all his mind and passion to a demonic pursuit of literary fame. It is disturbing to hear him describe his plans to send his wife and child home so that he may work in peace abroad. He lacks the courage to pursue his career without abandoning his domestic responsibilities, to face up to the consequences of his ambition, to work incessantly to give her life fulfilment, to suffer and strive to educate his son. Thus he, who so loudly and brilliantly condemns the cravenness of our age, who in mighty poems proclaims the strength of human will, is himself a craven, a vacillating weakling.

We cannot know the truth of these charges. But what is important is that Ibsen came to convert into art the substance of the debate and the dilemma. By the time of *The Master Builder* he had become acutely aware of the dangerous ambiguities of consciousness itself, the relationship of artistic sensibility to wider human experience, to put it most flatly, the effect of being an artist on being a man. Once again we are reminded of Kierkegaard, in this case of *Either/Or* with its posing of the aesthetic/spiritual antithesis, and we think too of Yeats's dictum of the intellect having to choose "perfection of the life or of the work." In his last four plays Ibsen was to initiate, as nearly as such matters can be chronologically placed, the long contemporary process of the artist's questioning of his art.

His task in these plays was the nearly unprecedented one of making art out of the ambiguities and contradictions, the "inhumaneness" of the aesthetic mode of life itself. A half century later Thomas Mann would compose the definitive work of this kind, the novel *Doctor Faustus*, which a critic described as Mann's "eloquent compromise with silence." For Ibsen to speak or to be silent were never the alternatives; he would go on writing to the end. But from now on he would make the costs of writing, of living in and through language and ideality, his subject.

At first glance *The Master Builder*'s structure and procedures seem to be as before. Contemporary characters act in a sequential way within a recognizable social milieu, events concatenate and issue in a violent denouement. An aging architect or "builder," as he calls himself, forges a relationship with a young, intellectually and physically seductive girl (the original for whom was undoubtedly Emilie Bardach) who presses and inspires him to attempt a "dizzying" feat which brings about his death. In the course of this narrative, themes emerge which have to do with the pressure of youth upon age and the profound hostility between the life and commitments of art and the demands of the domestic and social. Yet we quickly become aware of a change in something beyond subject.

Ibsen's art has undergone a transformation into a suggestive indefiniteness, a mysterious transcendence of era and place. *The Master Builder* attains a more complete and self-contained metaphorical existence than has been possible for Ibsen to achieve as long as he was under the exigencies of his intricate entente with the realistic theater and its methods. His meanings and implications, the images and vocabularies from which they radiate, the objectifications of his intuitions, all exist now within an aesthetic environment less bound to historical time. His imagination functions more freely as a bestower of metaphor; he enters more completely into his creation, whose principles are now more consistent with his own nature and needs; and plot, the soul of the tragedy in Aristotle's definition, makes fewer concessions to the fixed, mechanical movements of a well-fashioned body.

As in the earlier social plays, the action begins in a long history anterior to the drama's physical events. Even more completely than is true of Ibsen's earlier protagonists, Solness, the master builder, is already almost wholly what he is going to be in the play, which is to say the latter's events do not so much create his character as reveal it.

This character, moreover, is not fixed, waiting to be exhibited through the stresses of the plot, nor is it representative of what we call "themes"; Solness is less an agent of meaning than a locus of ideas and intuitions brought together in an active, a dramatic *instancing*. The problem for Ibsen was how to make these ideas and intuitions, these experiences halfway between actuality and art, issue in a work that would transcend personal, limited fate to be exemplary of a condition of existence and not a mere career. It was the problem of how to make fate universal and perennial in an age in which the only publicly accepted fatalities were social and what we might call technical, questions of success or failure within a realm of palpable values.

In the way in which what is necessary and inevitable works itself out lies the subtly radical change from the previous plays. Nothing better illustrates this than the matter of the crack in the chimney. When Solness tells Hilde about the fire which had destroyed his house and led to the deaths of his children, he prepares the audience for causation within the canons of melodrama and the well-made play. Yet he quickly reveals that the crack he had failed to repair had had nothing whatever to do with the fire; it has continued to operate as an element in his awareness of mysterious spiritual connections among material phenomena, and his revelation of the part it did not play in the fire is an oblique declaration by Ibsen that there are going to be no more casual sequences of the earlier mechanical kind.

The Master Builder thus expands the space available to its protagonist for the discovery and assumption of his destiny by converting much of the machinery of plot from the order of physical contingency and necessity to that of ontological urgency and spiritual choice. Solness is not free to evade his fate—that he has one means that the work exists dramatically—but he is free within the dramatic narrative to choose the events that will reveal and constitute it. For the tyranny of the past is no longer absolute; it will not act now as a remorseless sequence of cause and effect. Nothing Solness does issues from the past like a time bomb going off; nothing has to happen simply because something else has happened earlier.

The "cause" of the culminating action of *The Master Builder* is an effect of choice, not the result of a coercion by a logic of physical event. When Solness climbs up the tower for the traditional wreathing ceremony, he has willed to do something he can repudiate at any time. That we feel his decision to be inevitable is not the result of his having been caught by circumstances, hooked in the mouth by plot, but of Ibsen's successful creation of a world of imaginative necessity. Solness is acting out of his creator's intuitions about the greatness and futility of art, about the terrible burdens it lays on the artist's ordinary life and the doubts it perpetually raises about its agency in the world.

Along with this awareness of art as the necessary but disastrous "dream of the impossible" is consciousness of another and related realm of besieged being: human existence in time, the tyranny of age and the loss of the self through the depletions brought about by the very choices we make in the belief they will carry us into "fullness." These two recognitions of finiteness work inexorably, as poetic potencies and dramatic energies, toward the tragic attempt at reversal, the leap to overcome the laws of time and physical being, by which Solness is made into a legend and the play crystallized into an irreducible image.

Unlike any of the social plays' protagonists, Solness has gone to the end of his possibilities with internal assent if not with full consciousness, and above all with freedom from mechanical pressure. His decision to climb the tower in the face of his tendency toward vertigo has arisen from his original promise to Hilde of a "kingdom," a promise which, since he had made it as nothing more than a flirtatious utterance to an enchanting child, puts him outside any rigorous moral or social obligation to fulfill. Yet he will give her her kingdom, for only this way can he assume his destiny.

Not since *Brand* and *Peer Gynt* has Ibsen made such complex and resourceful use of a controlling image. Beginning with its narrower function as a figure for romantic aspiration generally and for sexual promise, the notion of kingdom is steadily developed into a resonant metaphor for the life of art and, beyond that, for the ways in which existence presses toward its limits and discovers them in a dialectic of necessity and disaster. In the end the idea of kingdom has been modulated, after an intricate interchange in which Solness and Hilde swiftly uncover all the meanings and implications of their relationship, into that of "a castle in the air," one built, as Solness says, "on a true foundation." No more suggestive image for the nature and location of art in relation to life has ever been offered us.

When Hilde, in "quiet, crazed triumph," cries out at the moment of Solness's death that she has heard "harps in the air" and apostrophizes him as "*my—my* master builder!" she gives a home in consciousness to his lucid act of overreaching, one that contains all the splendor and dementedness of man's effort at transcendence. Solness has gone too far, which means he has reached a tragic condition, something that for a dozen plays Ibsen has been unable to achieve for his protagonists. But he has been able to achieve it for this one only as the outcome of a major shift in dramaturgical procedure and not as the simple result of a change of values or cultural ambition or experience.

Ibsen's last three plays are filled with even greater anguish than *The Master Builder*, yet they are even more minimal in style and architectonics, more sparing of means and less dependent on narrative structure and sequential action. Among them *Little Eyolf* stands somewhat apart, in its morale if not dramaturgically. In this play the extreme moral vision which it shares with the others is meliorated by an acceptance short of fatality, a narrow, immensely austere awareness of corrupted moral being which may still however be redeemed. But like the protagonists of the two plays to follow, as well as of *The Master Builder*, its central character is an artist, or artist-type, and its chief preoccupation is with the losses inflicted on others by the devotion to abstractions, to surrogate experience and ideal truth, which being an artist can entail and which by extension is a temptation in every life.

For *Little Eyolf* and even more for the plays which came after it, Ibsen reached a condition of lyric expressiveness that sharply reduced his reliance on linear movement, a progression of linked events. The great image of Borkman, the "sick wolf" perpetually pacing his room, is the type of Ibsen's utterance in these works. In all of them the decisive physical events issue from a generating environment of poetic feeling, not from a tightly knit narrative structure.

This is one of the reasons why so many critics have found the last plays inferior, thinking them, as Mary McCarthy once wrote, "inflated" and "grandiose." In this view Ibsen is supposed to have lost his way, gone artistically soft. The charge does gain a degree of plausibility from the fact that Ibsen was not able fully to solve the nearly unprecedented problem he faced: how to write directly about himself, about his moral and existential turbulence, within the rubrics and expectations of a dramatic method that contained no provision for this kind of writing to be conceived, let alone undertaken. As a result, the pure lyrical impulse is not always secure, assured of its rights. Still, the plays are not pretentious or self-indulgent or vague; incompletions, perhaps, partial failures at the extreme edge of ambition, they testify to the most unaccommodating and indestructible integrity.

John Gabriel Borkman and *When We Dead Awaken* are especially static creations, informed by the most radical moral and ontological perceptions and intuitions, and what is needed for their dramatic vitality is a form extensively different from anything Ibsen had thus far been able to control. He would not of course have called it "spatial form," that recent intellectual construct, but the term suggests what he was seeking. For the fact that almost all the crucial physical action of the plays has been completed before the stage life is set in motion, the two protagonists moving toward their deaths not as a result of traditional dramatic development but out of recognitions that have been almost wholly present throughout, means that development will have to take place in some other fashion. Something other than a chain of causally connected events will have to generate the ongoing movement, the suspensefulness without which no drama can be said to exist.

The suspensefulness is created by the poetry, by what we might call the gathering evidence of the condition of feeling in which the works will end, the almost intolerable recognitions the tension of whose presentation consists in our being led by them step by step past our ordinary vision and into a change of sight. It is a poetry of accumulating discovery and lamentation, of cold acceptance that the cost of wanting everything is everything, and of dark crystallizations of the sense and emotions of finality, of the irreversibility of the self's catastrophic ambitions. It has been argued that in these last plays Ibsen was repudiating his own career as an artist. This may be so, but it is important to remember that the repudiation took place within art itself; it is as if Ibsen was establishing once again that only the imagination can teach us about the imagination's own afflictions.

The two protagonists, Borkman and Rubek, have "sold" love and human connection for power over the earth and over experience, Rubek through art and Borkman through an aesthetically informed dream of an Alexander-like conquest of physical nature. They have thought of themselves as benefactors, but they have been monsters of self-regard. Their deaths, even more explicitly than that of Solness, are demonstrations of their having crossed a boundary line; they are punishments in the moral order, but beyond that are culminating actions in newly shaped artistic creations, legends of mortality as the process of discovering the ruin our ambitions will always incur.

Yet the poetry of this had still to have a base. For dramaturgical coherence and dramatic momentum, the problem was to make things "happen" within a structure of plausibility such as Ibsen's temperament and training as a playwright required but that could scarcely be sustained now by the replicas of stories from the self-dramatizing world outside the formal stage that he had been forced to devise and that had been barely adequate to his purposes even so. His main instrument, the past, is no longer a principle of active dramatic pressure, one that brings about revelations and denouements of the plays as physical consequences of moral realities or, as in *The Master Builder*, as spiritual ones in a sequential line. For both Borkman and Rubek already possess the attributes of their ultimate condition, and the plays, instead of being the unfolding processes by which that condition is reached, are its swift flowerings.

In a brilliant stroke Ibsen anticipated and partly inspired an entire genre of plays to come by describing his protagonists as already "dead," as they are told by others, already, that is to say, in the condition to which ordinary drama, and life of course as well, must lead with its parade of events. As far as he was able in these plays, Ibsen took the drama out of what Ionesco was fifty years later to call the line of the "detective story," the statement, development, and resolution or solution of one or another kind of human problem, tracked from beginning to end.

But he was unable to go the whole way. What marks *Borkman* and even more *When We Dead Awaken* as transitional plays (although no less wonderful for that; Joyce thought *When We Dead Awaken* Ibsen's greatest work) and brings down upon them the accusation of being damagingly "symbolic" are, even more than their language, their settings, the world of mysterious rooms, snow, storms, mountains, and avalanches, within which the true poetic bodies of the play form themselves. It may seem strange to say, but the real work of both plays is complete without those external elements, the consciousness is present apart from them.

Ibsen nevertheless brought into both plays this apparatus of external scene and suggestive setting partly in order physically to accomplish the deaths of his protagonists, but more subtly because he could not yet imagine how a play whose ambition was nothing less than to exist immediately, all at once, causing itself and not being instigated by anything outside itself, by anything from the world of "nature," and therefore existing as a poem does whose passage through time is a concession to physical laws but whose end is really in its beginning—how such a play could be written and staged.

And yet, great mind and tireless spirit that he was, he remarked after writing *When We Dead Awaken*, which he had called a "dramatic epilogue," that now that he was finished with this long segment of his career he might very well return to the "battlefields" but with "new weapons and new equipment." Not long after that he fell victim to a stroke. He lived on, increasingly debilitated, for five years, writing nothing more before his death in 1906. Passers-by and would-be visitors used to see him sitting stiffly in a chair by his window, gazing with his badger's eyes at the life of the streets, as he had once gazed at the living forms of the sea.

STRINDBERG

In his *Biographia Literaria* Coleridge wrote that "there have been men in all ages who have been impelled as by an instinct to propose their own natures as a problem, and who devote their efforts to its solution." Although he was not to "solve" anything, least of all the enigma of his nature, August Strindberg fiercely proposed himself as dilemma and laboratory, making his life a succession of attempts—blind or lucid, apocalyptic or sly—to get hold of his own truth, which he regarded as extreme but still humanly representative, the way all writers in some fashion must. What he succeeded in doing—no writer has ever done it more violently—was to place his nature on exhibition, objectifying its contradictions, confusions, and ambivalences in the most amazingly varied forms. Yet we have to remember that Strindberg was an artist, a being for whom "nature," his own or any other, is as much an invention as a given fact.

"You must have only one soul or you'll have no peace," the protagonist of his first important play, *The Father*, says. Having multiple souls of his own, Strindberg sought alternately to give reign to one of them at the expense of the others, to fix them all in equilibrium, and to escape from all of them at the same time. Like most imaginative writers, he no doubt did this last thing best in his plays and fiction. There is a classic simplicity to what he told his estranged third wife, Harriet Bosse, in a letter of 1903:

> I live and I live the manifold lives of all the people I describe, happy with those who are happy, evil with the evil ones, good with the good; I creep out of my own personality and speak with the mouths of children, of women, of old men: I am king and beggar, I have worldly power, I am the tyrant and the down-trodden hater of the tyrant; I hold all opinions and profess all religions; I live in all times and have myself ceased to be. This is a state which brings indescribable happiness.

Yet it was a state he seldom knew. Even when he was writing he seemed mostly to be tormented over his divided self, which was in fact one of his subjects. In one of his autobiographical novels he says of himself that he "was a quadroon, with romanticism, pietism, realism and naturalism in his blood. Therefore he never became anything but a patchwork." The epithet is far too demeaning. He was immensely complex, and trickier than we think, a site of warring faculties and impulses but no simple victim of them; he was tragedian and clown, insurrectionary and quietist, obscurantist and seer. No playwright ever contained in his private and public experience so much of the raw material we think of as "dramatic" and none was ever so histrionic outside the work.

Few can have spread their intellectual and creative energies as widely. Ibsen and Brecht wrote poetry; Chekhov, Pirandello, and Shaw fiction; and the last was of course a great essayist and critic. But along with his plays (more than sixty of them) Strindberg wrote novels and short stories; poetry; sociological and literary essays; art criticism; historical works; seven books of autobiography; scientific, quasi-scientific, and alchemical studies; and even treatises in such far-flung areas as Scandinavian folklore and Sinology, besides all this being a brilliant, innovative painter. The figure in cultural history he most resembles for the sheer magnitude and range of his productivity is Diderot, although in relation to the latter's orderly methods and eminent sanity he could not personally have resembled him less.

That Strindberg was in some manner not sane, certainly not mentally sound, is a commonplace observation now. He has been diagnosed (from afar, naturally) as a paranoid schizophrenic and as having suffered from a severe Oedipal conflict; none of these findings would be of very much importance to us were it not for their extension into criticism, where they continue to function (although with diminishing frequency) as grounds for a disqualification of his art or, perhaps even worse, as reductive explanations of it. The long-standing question of the connection of madness to art, pathology to creativity, has in Strindberg its *locus classicus*, just as has the related question of the connection of dreaming to formal imagination.

The clinical dossier in his case is a Gothic document. He was subject to violent alternations of mood, fits of murderous jealousy and hatred followed by demonstrations of tenderness that frequently verged on the pathetic. Several times in his life he went through periods, sometimes lasting for years, in which he knew himself to be at the edge of mental collapse, suffering delusions of persecution (he once thought that "enemies" were getting at him with electrical machines, felt the rays passing through the wall of his room and entering his chest) and believing once or twice that he had actually died. His megalomania was extreme and took the most bizarre forms. "I am the creator!" his alter ego in *To Damascus* cries, which is traditional enough. But in his mad alchemical pursuits he was convinced he had found the secret of making gold, spoke of having "eliminated the boundaries between matter and what was called the spirit," and wrote magisterially about being acquainted with the "psychology" of sulphur. Still, in his autobiographical *The Son of a Servant* he confesses that "he was born frightened and remained always afraid of life and of people."

Was he particularly afraid of women? He was especially agitated by them at any rate; his misogyny is the most notorious thing about him, almost his definition in popular culture. He had three marriages, the last two to women less than half his age; all three were filled with rancor, misunderstanding, impossibility. He railed against women in his books, depicting sexual love as a war and marriage as a hell, and made himself into the champion of husbands and all "downtrodden" males. He considered *A Doll's House* a "scandalous" work and seems seriously to have believed that Ibsen was the ringleader of a feminist conspiracy, one of whose objectives was his own downfall. There is scarcely a significant play of Strindberg's, to say nothing of most of his other writings, that doesn't bristle at some point with sexual hostility or reveal a strange, mystical bitterness toward women.

Yet there is a whole other side to the matter. We know, for one thing, that Strindberg's anti-feminism was in no sense political, that it was accompanied by a conviction, for which he publicly fought, that women had been the victims of legal injustice; in that sense he was at least as much a believer in women's rights as Ibsen. Moreover, we know how much he needed them. In an almost classic pattern, he had suffered from an early deprivation—real or imagined—of maternal love, spent his adult life searching for a mother substitute (even in the girl-wives who might have been his daughters), and held out motherhood and domestic nurture as his ideal of feminine being. He suffered too from doubts about his parentage, although the facts seem clear enough, and from shame over part of his social origins. His mother had been his middle-class father's second wife, a servant girl whom he had married after making her pregnant; Strindberg was one of twelve children. Throughout his life in his writings three themes recur:

hunger, the feeling of being both physically and emotionally starved; legitimacy, the question of who are one's parents; and inequality, the irrational differences arising from caste.

Yet none of these themes can be taken at face value as a reflection of the contents of his psyche. He once said of his anti-female biases that they were "the reverse side of my fearful attraction towards the other sex," and, even more significantly for an understanding of his writing than this confession of what is after all a phenomenon made familiar to us by psychoanalysis, he wrote to the critic Edvard Brandes that "my misogyny is only theoretical, and I can't live a day without supposing that I warm my soul at the flame of their unconscious, vegetable way of life."

That at bottom he shared a perennial view of women as more "natural," closer to biological sources, as well as the reverse of that clichéd stance—which is that they are potentially more spiritual, purer—is much less important than his avowal of the theoretical quality of his attitudes.

In the introduction to his translation of Strindberg's *A Madman's Defense,* a savage, thinly disguised autobiographical novel about the writer's first marriage (to Siri Von Essen) Evert Sprinchorn argues with originality and persuasiveness that Strindberg's anti-feminism was at least in part a matter of literary strategy. After pointing out the liberties Strindberg took with the facts of the marriage and how he used these distorted data for his forthcoming play *The Father,* Sprinchorn goes on to say that in this case (and by implication others) Strindberg "created his experiences in order to write about them. Interested in exploring the frontier where jealousy encroaches on madness, he set up a model of the terrain in his own home."

Further evidence of a related sort comes from Harriet Bosse: "I have a feeling that Strindberg revelled in meeting with opposition. One moment his wife had to be an angel, the next the very opposite. He was as changeable as a chameleon."

The inconstancy, however, like the ferocity (and self-pity) he displays in A *Madman's Defense*, was not simply one of the *données* of his temperament; he threw himself into violent states, changed dizzyingly, and demanded change in others, out of a requirement of his imagination, a writer's need to turn the world into usable data.

None of this means that Strindberg's mental and emotional disturbances were fictive, that he "made them up." They were real enough; but he used them, exaggerating them, trafficking with them, thrusting them against the world in order to break through the encrustations of habit and normality—his own and everyone else's—and making them into the energizing principles of his art. It was as if, knowing what he was like, he made himself *more like he was*, extending his self into a partially invented persona which could then be part of the subject of an art extreme and radical enough to satisfy the expectations he had of it. The awareness that he was doing this, that his art was in some way "fraudulent," was to remain with him always.

Strindberg was born in Stockholm in 1849, the year of Edgar Allan Poe's death. When in later life he fell under the influence of the American's writings and discovered the date they had in common, he is said to have wondered for a time whether he might not be Poe's incarnation. He shared the latter's Gothic cast of mind, his unstable personality, for a while his reliance on alcohol. For years he even felt destined to the same kind of literary obscurity Poe had suffered from in his lifetime.

His early career bore resemblances to Poe's but was even more diverse. After a lonely, bookish childhood, he went to the University of Uppsala at eighteen, became a medical student, dropped out to enter the Royal Academy of Acting, failed at that, and returned to Uppsala to pursue a liberal-arts program for a few more years before leaving without a degree.

After that he was successively a reporter for a radical Stockholm newspaper, the editor of a trade journal put out by a group of insurance companies, and an assistant librarian at the Royal Swedish Library.

His first play, *The Freethinker*, was written in 1869, when he was twenty; his second, and the first to be produced, *In Rome*, the next year. But these works and a third play, *The Outlaw*, while showing that he had energy and somewhat idiosyncratic taste, were youthfully derivative—of Shakespeare, Schiller, and Danish romantic tragedies among other sources —and won him mostly silence, so that his reputation was gained only later through his polemical writings and fiction, most of this autobiographical or in the mode of the *roman à clef*.

By the middle eighties Strindberg's fame, or notoriety in some minds, was secure in Sweden and throughout Scandinavia. He had as much as appointed himself the conscience of his country, a claim which was widely accepted in radical intellectual circles, but his campaign against social and cultural backwardness and political repression had earned him fierce enmity in powerful places. In 1884 he had been prosecuted for blasphemy on the basis of a few lines in a book of stories called *Getting Married*; a jury found him innocent, but the event seems to have had a permanent effect on his morale, frightening him but also instigating an intensification of what he thought of as social and psychic "truthfulness" in his writing.

In 1886 he sent to his publisher the manuscript of his autobiographical novel, *A Madman's Defense*, describing it as "an analysis of the soul, psychological anatomy." Early the next year he wrote to a friend that he had invented a new genre, "the battle of the brains." The genre he meant applied to the theater now, for he was working on a play that was to prove his first really original one. In the letter he said of it that "*The Father* is the realization of modern drama and as such is something very curious. Very curious because the struggle takes place between souls. It is . . . not a dagger fight or poisoning with raspberry juice, as in *The Robbers* [by Schiller]. The French of today are still seeking the formula, but I have found it."

For three or four years he had done no writing for the theater. The stage, he remarked during this period, was "reprehensible" in its impermeability by new consciousness, especially when compared to poetry or fiction, although he also excoriated traditional novels, which like the theater he thought of as fit only for "ladies," reserving his approbation for some scattered experiments such as Zola's. In 1886 he had been in one of his periodic rebellions from art in general. "It disgusts me to be nothing but an artist," he wrote to his publisher. "My intelligence has evolved from daydreaming to thinking. The deliberate summoning up of hallucinations at the writing desk seems like masturbation to me."

The connection of sex and writing, and the derogation of the latter as damaging fantasy, are recurrent motifs in Strindberg, indications, if we don't put too much on them, of how difficult he found it to keep separate what we ordinarily do so matter-of-factly; the carnal and the contemplative, daydreaming and formal imagination. In any case, *A Madman's Defense* had been written in a spirit of what he had convinced himself was scientific objectivity, though it was in fact as "literary" as anything he ever wrote. *The Father* appears to have emerged out of the same state of self-deception, although by now very much less complete.

The Father is enshrined now as Strindberg's first "naturalistic" play and, along with *Miss Julie*, the one he wrote soon after it, as one of the masterpieces of the genre. The vicissitudes of that genre come to our attention at this point. It is greatly significant that almost as soon as Strindberg had been identified as one of the leaders of naturalism he hastened to call himself a *nyanaturalist*, a "new" one. It was true that in

their contemporary subjects and colloquial manner, their dealing with problematic immediate life, Strindberg's plays (and
novels) of this period resembled those of the movement's
acknowledged leaders, Zola and Hauptmann chiefly; but the
differences were more important.

While the "old" naturalists were drawing upon sociological data and organizing their works according to principles of
fidelity to social reality and repudiation of gross theatrical
artifice, Strindberg, with a much more naturally histrionic
sensibility and a greater access to unconscious and irrational
sources, created plays of psychic and spiritual warfare which
went far deeper dramatically, at the same time as they were
more truly modern. For these reasons "naturalistic" is an
inadequate and misleading term to describe his plays of contemporary life.

Above all, what distinguishes Strindberg's effort and
achievement in *The Father*—and in *Miss Julie* even more—
from those of the naturalists is the presence in them of self,
personal existence. As different as their methods were from
one another's, Strindberg and Ibsen share the honor of having
brought drama back to individual being, to subjectivity and
human specificity, after nearly two centuries during which the
stage's uses had been almost wholly for the exhibition of
archetypes. In these plays of Strindberg's experience is no
longer codified, made into a system of emblematic gestures
within a universe of accepted, unexamined meanings, but is
allowed to issue forth in singular, unruly unexpectedness.

The Father can be said to be a domestic drama, but only
in the sense that it takes place within a home and concerns
family relationships. The first of Strindberg's plays of marital
and sexual torment (its specific characters and setting will be
used fifteen years later for his definitive work of this kind, *The
Dance of Death*), it exhibits a ferocious struggle for power
between a husband and wife, with their daughter as the prize.
"It isn't enough for me to have given the child life," the

Captain says, "I want to give it my soul, too." Against this paternal, masculine desire is pitted that of the mother, center of an inimical universe of women. On the surface as remote as it can be from Greek tragedy, *The Father* is informed in its depths by something close to an ancient spirit of blood-feud, a fatal enmity between closely related antagonists who incarnate an unbridgeable fissure in the world.

Yet the chasm isn't so neatly identified as being between husbands and wives, or even men and women. The wife's chief tactic is to plant doubt in the husband's mind as to whether or not he is actually the child's father. A theme rising directly from Strindberg's obsession with his own legitimacy, its presence in the play moves past that particularity to become a question—as it must have been for Strindberg all along—of what we might call the legitimacy of existence itself. For *The Father* gives off a sense of terror emanating from something wider and more mysterious than the details of the marital combat, from a region where the absence of any validation of our beings makes itself felt. In a speech extraordinarily reminiscent of one of Danton's in Büchner's play (which it is almost certain Strindberg did not know), the Captain says of the struggle that "it's like fighting with air, a mock battle with blank cartridges. A real betrayal would have acted as a challenge. But now my thoughts dissolve, my brain grinds emptiness."

The speech reveals Strindberg's deepest anxiety, the metaphysical anguish that lay beneath the clinical facts of his psyche and was the true source of his creative power. For, as is true of the protagonist in this play, it was the opacity of the world, its infliction of a mysterious suffering having to do with the uncertainty of our identities, the divisions in our nature, that so affected him, alternately plunging him into acute depression, inspiring him to demented alchemical raids on existence's secrets, and rousing him to furious megalomanic rebellion. And no suffering was more opaque and cruel to him than that imposed by sexual differentiation with its consequences in both masculine and feminine self-doubt, oppression by the "stranger." He once spoke of his "terrible fascination" as a boy with the "mystery of what lay under women's skirts."

The father's speech is thus not so much an outcry against women's dominance, or even their hostility, as against their unknowability and his consequent doubt about what stance to take toward them and, further, against the abstractness of the issue. He does not know how to fight. Brought down by a condition of doubtfulness, a loss of bearings in a sea of unanswerable questions—like Danton feeling himself the victim of abstract, uninterrogatable force—he finds his defeat fittingly crystallized in the image of the strait jacket in which he is put at the end.

Something of great significance for our understanding of Strindberg's dramatic art emerges from this: it is that the facts of sexual warfare so prominent in *The Father* are not causes but *instances,* so that the play's subject is something other than what appears. The excessiveness and inexplicability of the couple's hatred—qualities that have been used to question the play's validity on psychological grounds—are due precisely to Strindberg's not having written a psychological—and naturalistic—study at all but a modern legend of ancient despair whose subject is larger and more complex than the play's means of embodying it. The excessiveness is then the effect of a straining after an utterance and set of circumstances that will do justice to the magnitude of the theme.

This is not to say that *The Father* isn't "about" sexual and marital strife; Strindberg is not writing allegory. But it is about these things in much the same way *Hamlet* is about a familial and dynastic situation: these matters constitute the drama's occasion, its means of bodying forth something that will be palpable, actable, capable of being *seen*. Behind the details of event exists the play's true story, which is larger, less explicit, and more permanent than the physical life chosen for its exhibition. The invisible has always to be made known through the visible but is never conterminous with it, and the resulting gap between idea and incarnation is the theater's perennial problem.

Just as he exacerbated and exaggerated the facts of his life outside art in order to bring them closer to his imagination's needs, so Strindberg inflamed the details of his play so as to bring them nearer to the terrifying vision he had of something beyond. This kind of poetic or literary license is neither new nor culpable. What keeps *The Father* from full artistic realization, however, is that Strindberg's imagination is still too bound to his ego. The proximity of *A Madman's Defense*—a number of its lines and speeches are carried over into the play—with its aggressive defensiveness and deliberately shocking descriptions of a supposedly typical marriage, works to throw *The Father* into a reduced dimension and a mood of self-pity. For to be a husband, victim of an institution, is scarcely a tragic condition, much as Strindberg's overwrought self-regard might have wished it to be.

The Father's first production in Stockholm in 1888 was a disaster, one critic writing that the play "can be summed up in Hamlet's exclamation: 'O horrible, O horrible, most horrible!' Any other comment seems superfluous." Yet comments came from some impressive sources. Ibsen told a Swedish bookseller who had sent him the play that although Strindberg's "experience and observations" were not the same as his own he found it impossible to deny or resist "the author's violent force." Zola wrote to Strindberg that *The Father* was "one of the few dramatic works to have moved me profoundly" and praised its "philosophical idea" as "very daring" (although he was also to complain about an "obscure social milieu" and "incomplete characterization"). And Friedrich Nietzsche, whose writings had recently greatly stirred Strindberg ("My spirit has received in its uterus a tremendous outpouring of seed from

F. Nietzsche, so that I feel as full as a pregnant bitch"), wrote to him that he had been "astonished" to find "a work in which my own conception of love—with war as its means and the deathly hate of the sexes as its fundamental law . . . is expressed in such a splendid fashion."

Strindberg wrote *Miss Julie* at great speed a year or so after finishing *The Father*. We cannot know the sources of what he had learned about dramaturgy in the interim, or what acts of criticism he might have performed on his previous work, but a leap had taken place. For all its "violent power" and original perception, *The Father* had been structurally and procedurally a rather conventional play, one that adhered fairly closely to theatrical traditions of orderly, accumulating plot and straightforward dialogue. With *Miss Julie* Strindberg's technical means expand, the body of the work becomes more supple and elusive, the dialogue gains a capacity for dangerous surprises, not in terms of its "content" but in the sense of being unpredictably organized, of not following the established theatrical grammar of progressive exchange and interchange.

Few plays have come to us with so detailed an account of the thinking that went into their composition. From *Miss Julie* on, Strindberg would be most communicative about the principles of his dramatic art, far more so than any other of the great modern playwrights, with the later exception of Brecht. Out of his letters, his *obiter dicta*, and, most important of all, the prefaces he wrote for his own plays, a history of a revolution in stage theory takes shape, one that overthrew a wide range of sanctified ideas about the organization of experience into the formal patterns of drama. He had Ibsen as a predecessor—though he detested the Norwegian's ideas, he grudgingly admired and seems to have learned from his technical innovations—but he is not diminished by this; his important discoveries were his own.

In the preface to *Miss Julie* Strindberg composed a brilliant, elaborate justification for the dramatic practices of the play, its aesthetic choices; it was to be a manifesto for much future change on the stage. At the center of his argument was the recognition of what "character" had come to mean in the theater and of the way in which his own artistic urgencies could no longer be contained within that circumscribed, arrested theory and practice:

The word "character" has, over the years, frequently changed its meaning. Originally it meant the dominant feature in a person's psyche, and was synonymous with temperament. Then it became the middle-class euphemism for an automaton; so that an individual who had stopped developing . . . in other words, stopped growing, came to be called a "character," whereas the man who goes on developing, the skillful navigator of life's river, who does not sail with a fixed sheet but rides before the wind to luff again, was stigmatized as "characterless" (in of course a derogatory sense) because he was difficult to catch, classify and keep tabs on. This bourgeois conception of the immutability of the soul became transferred to the stage, which had always been bourgeois-dominated. A character, there, became a man fixed in a mold, who always appeared drunk, or comic, or pathetic, and to establish whom it was only necessary to equip with some physical defect . . . or else some oft-repeated phrase . . . This oversimplified view of people we find even in the great Molière. Harpagon is nothing but a miser, although Harpagon might have been not only a miser, but also a first-rate financier, an excellent father and a good citizen . . . So I do not believe in "theatrical characters." And these summary judgments that authors pronounce upon people—"He is stupid, he is brutal, he is jealous, he is mean," etc.—ought to be challenged by naturalists, who know how richly complex a human soul is . . .

The bourgeois conception of the immutability of the soul, of a permanent human "nature," to which Strindberg refers, was assaulted on every side during the late nineteenth century, Dostoevsky's underground man being the model of the slap in the face delivered to such complacency. But the theater, the bourgeois art par excellence, held out longest and in its widest sectors continues to hold out today. A few years ago Jean-Paul Sartre commented on this entropic tendency of the stage:

. . . the theater often does not portray the changes of man and the world but rather gives an image of an unchanging man in an unchanging universe. Yet we all know that the world changes, that it changes man and that man changes the world. And if this is not what ought to be the profound subject of any play, then the theater no longer has any subject.

Bourgeois life being itself one of more or less strict appearances, the life of the stage, whose art is wholly a matter of appearances, had been asked to provide the kind of reassurance that goes much beyond specific moral or social questions; reassurance lay in the manner in which things were done in the theater, in the perpetuation of dramatic forms that bodied forth human changelessness, coherence, consistency, in an exhibition and parade of the soul's categorical and unyielding identity. Strindberg had become possessed of a different awareness:

Since they are modern characters living in an age of transition more urgently hysterical at any rate than the age which preceded it, I have drawn my people as split and vacillating, a mixture of the old and new . . . My souls (or characters) are agglomerations of past and present cultures, scraps from books and newspapers, fragments of humanity, torn shreds of once-fine clothing that has become rags, in just the way that a human soul is patched together.

In regard to the related question of motivation and hence of one of the central elements of plot, he wrote:

> What will offend simple minds is that my plot is not simple, nor its point of view single. In real life an action—this, by the way, is a somewhat new discovery, is generally caused by a whole series of motives, more or less fundamental, but as a rule the spectator chooses just one of them—the one which his mind can most easily grasp or that does most credit to his intelligence . . . I congratulate myself on this multiplicity of motives, and if others have done the same thing before me, then I congratulate myself in not being alone in my "paradoxes," as all innovations are called.

Ibsen, particularly in *Peer Gynt*, had been one of his predecessors along this line. But the confusion or multiplicity of motives in that play was considerably more acceptable to audiences because of the structure of fantasy; the "realness" of *Miss Julie* ironically seemed to demand a narrower psychology.

Finally Strindberg spoke about the changes he had made in the structure and aesthetic intentions of dialogue:

> . . . I have departed somewhat from tradition by not making my characters catechists who ask stupid questions in order to elicit a smart reply. I have avoided the symmetrical, mathematical constructions of French dialogue, and let people's minds work irregularly, as they do in real life where, during a conversation, no topic is drained to the dregs, and one mind finds in another a chance cog to engage in. So too the dialogue wanders, gathering in the opening scenes material which is later picked up, worked over, repeated, expounded and developed like the theme in a musical composition.

Some of Strindberg's ideas in the preface were theoretically in coherence with the program of naturalism in so far as they consciously aimed at a faithfulness to observed life. It had been naturalism's accomplishment to have gone back to the sources of literature in actuality, as a repudiation of the stage's or fiction's self-generated and self-perpetuating arti- facts. Yet in what we might call official naturalism, the move- ment from which Strindberg had been so quick to dissociate himself, there had been little room for the imagination truly to operate, so intent was its gaze on the external or visible phenomena and its thinking on the theoretical aspects of the life of society it wished to reinstate as the proper subject of literary and dramatic art, and so rigid was its adherence to a putatively "scientific" method for that life's apprehension.

In *Miss Julie* Strindberg's inventive powers work to con- struct an imaginatively open, complex drama whose materials in lesser hands could be expected to have been employed for narrowly psychological or sociological purposes: male/female, master/servant; the process by which the play is lifted past such dichotomies throws the clearest light on the relationship of imagination to the formulations of the moralist or so- ciologue.

Strindberg appears to have based *Miss Julie* on a true story he had heard about a disastrous sexual encounter between an aristocratic young woman and one of her father's servants, a tale whose constituents highly recommended them- selves to several of his governing obsessions. In *A Madman's Defense* he had written in reference to his own marriage to a woman much above him in social station that "the son of the people had carried off the alabaster beauty, the commoner had won the aristocrat, the swineherd had mated with the prin- cess. But at what a cost!" *The Son of a Servant* reveals more details of his lifelong psychic split over the question of class:

The boy had seen the splendor of the upper classes from a distance. He longed for it as if it were his native home, but the slave blood he had inherited from his mother rebelled against it. He instinctively revered the upper classes, so much so he despaired of ever reaching them. He felt that he belonged neither to them nor to the slaves. Between the two he would be torn for the rest of his life.

In this space between aristocracy and servility, and the overlapping one between the feminine and the masculine, or rather in the space between ideas of these things, Strindberg situates himself as an artist, his imaginative sympathy and creative concern extending to either side so that he embraces the dilemma—the social and sexual antinomies—in a clasp of reconciliation, not factual or "real" but aesthetic. This is to say that while the sexes and the classes may war blindly in actuality and may do so forever, within the work of dramatic art they exist in interpenetration, necessary to each other, illuminating each other, arising as they do from the imagination, whose truths are indivisible.

Therefore, the first thing to see about Miss Julie is that the conventional description of it as a duel to the death between "objectively" irreconcilable opponents is false; the play's movement is instead that of a continual confrontation between aspects of the self. For it is Strindberg's own masculinity and femininity, his aristocratic yearnings and sense of social inferiority, that provide the materials of the drama. As we shall see, he will transpose these dualities to a level of the creative self on which there is no "winner" or "loser" but a poise of recognition.

What follows from this is that for all its accuracy as sociosexual portraiture, its firm grasp of the observable phenomena of the life of the period, Miss Julie is not finally a psychological or sociological document, not a tragedy of contemporary misalliance or inequality. It is not a tale of the wreck of passions and aspirations but an anatomy of them. For all Strindberg's interest in his characters as representatives of determinable social and sexual realms, he is more interested in them as figures in an internal landscape of doubt, ambivalence, insurrection, and submission; his characters confront one another with a despairing sense of otherness, as agents of his own self-division. Such a concern is of a more durable order than that of the clinical gaze upon what is not the self.

Strindberg's imagination had gone beyond all the particularities of feeling and behavior it had marshaled for the play, to a wider subject of which they became the demonstrable elements, the *evidence,* so to speak. Ibsen had called the poet (the writer generically) the man who sees, and the preface to *Miss Julie* tells us what Strindberg had noticed: that men and women had become—had perhaps always been, only now it could not be ignored—"split" and "vacillating," a "mixture of old and new"; that human souls are "fragments," "torn shreds . . . patched together." He was his own best specimen of this, the only one he could verify. But he was an artist and so (as he tells us in another section of the preface) could not "create a new drama by pouring new ideas into the old forms." He had to invent the kind of play for which his discoveries will not simply provide the substance but the very shape, the form.

Whether they were farces, melodramas, or naturalistic and sober tales, plays for a long time had been images of wholeness, continuity, and coherence, stable little models for the reinforcement of the audience's illusory sense of their own world's fixity. *Miss Julie* establishes a counterworld of discontinuity, fragmentation, and contradiction, not simply as its theme but as its manner. This is the true purpose of the breaking up of the logical patterns of stage dialogue and the introduction into plot of a multiplicity of motives that Strindberg talked about.

To look closely at his dramaturgy in *Miss Julie* is to be struck first by the remarkable compression he achieves in making the events of a single night issue in a grave denouement. In that era of the theater such compression would mostly have been employed for the purposes of a swift unfolding of melodramatic or farcical events, as in the rapid, circumstantially linked, "outer-directed" plays of Scribe, Sardou, and their students. In *Miss Julie* it is the effect of a cutting away of integumentary material, of all that explanation and exposition that had burdened the "serious" theater, making it into something very like a sermon on the logic and shapeliness of human experience, no matter how disastrous the action being portrayed might be. The connections Strindberg makes are inward for the most part, unstated, carried by implication in the gestures and reactions to one another of the two main characters, whose conversation, rather than being an exchange of information or a species of repartee, is mainly a series of instigations to internal activity, which then issues in speech as further instigation.

The play's action advances by fits and starts, by reversals, sudden leaps, and regroupings, although the dominant motif and impetus remains the movement toward Miss Julie's final loss of will and subsequent (implied) suicide. The crucial thing to notice is that this suicide is not brought about by anything inexorable in the working of the plot. Her death isn't even, properly speaking, a denouement at all (though it is an ending), for it is not the inevitable outcome of a logic of dramatic cause and effect. The play's central event has been Julie's seduction by Jean—or rather his forcing her own seductiveness to face its consequences—but even the fact that the news of their having slept together will become known is clearly no sufficient reason for killing herself; Strindberg makes no pretense of its being so, though a conventional playwright would have made a mainstay out of it. Nor is her shame a sufficient reason either.

Julie kills herself for much the same reason Ibsen's Hedda Gabler does (although in Ibsen's play the plot does much rationalizing work to keep up the appearance of realism): she cannot live. We do not die from our deaths, Charles Péguy wrote, but from our whole lives, and Julie has discovered the truth—or rather the play is the process of such discovery—that she lacks a principle of coherence, which is what self-esteem ultimately depends on; she is "split" and "vacillating." The plot is the story of her self-division, as it is also of Jean's, the image of it, not a vehicle in which she travels to her destruction. And its final action, her moving toward her death, is an aesthetic as well as spiritual recognition—of the possible "wholeness" of which she has not been able to partake—not a judgment in the moral or social order. Like Hedda's, her act, in the imaginative dimension it occupies, issues from a mysterious kind of valor: the courage to not be, if being is obstructed.

Julie is of course only half the play, one member of its *pas de deux*, but in being absorbed in her fate we tend to lose sight of that of her partner, the servant Jean. Nothing better demonstrates that Strindberg is not writing social analysis than that Jean is finally seen not as Julie's executioner but as the agency of her self-knowledge, as she is his. For he too is made aware of his unfreedom, his riven and incoherent self. He prods Julie to suicide but he cannot really live either, being still bound to his subservience, fear, and unaccountable guilt —his psychology—and, more deeply, to his invented and therefore sterile persona. They have fought each other to a standstill: "You take all my strength from me, you make me a coward," he tells her, his complementary semblance, his *frère*, at the end.

Miss Julie was followed over the next three or four years by a number of plays more or less in its vein of *nyanaturalism*, among which perhaps the most durable are *Creditors* and *Playing with Fire*. But then in the early 1890's Strindberg entered on what he called his "inferno" period, a time when he suffered his nearest approach to actual madness. During these three or four years, most of which were spent in Paris, he engaged in attempts to make gold and in other alchemical research, underwent profound if rather cloudy religious and mystical experiences, and wrote only one work of permanent interest—a far-seeing essay in aesthetics called "On the New Arts, or The Risk in Artistic Production"—and nothing whatsoever for the theater. Then in 1897 he emerged with his creative faculties seemingly intact, the first product of this restoration being a new play, To Damascus, which was as radical in its relation to the body of existing drama as Miss Julie had been ten years before.

As Evert Sprinchorn has remarked in his introduction to one edition of To Damascus, it is almost a "banality of modern criticism" to call the play one of the starting points and origins of the most interesting works of twentieth-century theater. "Expressionism, surrealism, and the theater of the absurd are all clearly adumbrated in this pioneering work," Sprinchorn, risking the banal, goes on to say. Yet in our own time this enormous play—some 250 pages of text, divided into three parts, the first two written in 1898, the third five years later—is steadily fading from the repertoire (Part III is almost never performed), and this is due as much to its thematic preoccupations as to its physical unwieldiness, its multiple sets and teeming accoutrements.

On the most immediate level To Damascus is a product of the religious experiences Strindberg had had during the inferno period, two chief elements of which had been his excited discovery of his countryman Swedenborg and his intense interest in the Catholic Church. The title refers of course to the journey Saul was making when he underwent the mystical visitation that turned him into Paul. A character known throughout as the Stranger travels the stages of a complicated pilgrimage in search, as he says, of "light." At various times he thinks of himself as a Cain-like figure, whose sin is that of having slain his brother, but at others he takes on a guise as Prometheus: "the crime I committed . . . is that I wanted to set men free." Before the play culminates in his arrival at and presumable spiritual rebirth in a Catholic monastery, every possible change has been rung on the themes of temptation, sin, guilt, repentance, and belief.

The Stranger is patently Strindberg's alter ego, for the play is full of the most undisguised references and allusions to events of his own life; there is even a summary and exact description of him (circa 1888) in the form of a police dossier: "Thirty-eight, brown hair, mustache, blue eyes; no settled employment, means unknown; married but has deserted his wife and children; well known for his revolutionary views on social questions: gives impression he is not in full possession of his senses." In short, *To Damascus* rises almost directly from Strindberg's consciousness of himself and his memory of what he has been and failed to be.

The Stranger is accompanied at various times by a woman who is called the Lady and who is clearly drawn after Strindberg's second wife, Frida Uhl, from whom he had recently been divorced. In the course of the pilgrimage he encounters paradigmatic figures such as the Confessor, the Beggar, the Mother, and the Tempter. Their speech is a peculiar mixture of the colloquial and the formal, even the high-flown, and, in the case of the protagonist and the religious personages especially, is heavy with Biblical quotations and occult verbiage. The latter isn't too strong a word to describe such talk; *To Damascus* is indeed a turning point in the history of the stage, but in many places its language exhibits qualities of strain, imprecision, and pomposity such as were wholly absent from *Miss Julie* and others of Strindberg's plays with contemporary settings. As a by-product of this, or more likely as its cause, the entire play suffers from what Bentley has called a mood of "unconvincing religiosity."

How then can we account for its importance to modern drama? To begin with, the influence it exerted was actually part of a broader one emanating from an entire genre of

Strindberg's late writing for the theater. *To Damascus* is the first of his "dream plays," of which the drama with that title, written in the same year as *To Damascus, Part III*, is the best known. From the works of this genre, which include, for all their special intentions, most of the later "chamber plays" and his last work for the stage, *The Great Highway*, arose a model of a new kind of dramatic procedure. It was not entirely without precedent, but it went beyond into a previously unoccupied imaginative zone.

During the 1890's, at intervals in his pursuit of the secret of making gold and between bouts of schizophrenic disorientation, Strindberg had done a great deal of thinking about artistic questions. His essay "On the New Arts" contains a radical call for risk taking in the making of art, its rallying cry being very much like that issued twenty years later by Ezra Pound. When Strindberg wrote, "It's got to be new. New and different!" he was calling for something close to the cubism and abstract art that were just over the cultural horizon. His own paintings, scarcely known until recent years, were themselves pioneeringly expressionistic and semiabstract, and he was also, in literary matters, under the purifying, dematerializing influence of Mallarmé and the symbolists. Out of this intellectual disposition the style and structure of *To Damascus* were shaped, the pressure of his recent spiritual inquiry and ordeal determining the not always appropriate materials.

Before going back to its text, it would be useful to attend for a moment to the author's note Strindberg wrote for *A Dream Play* a few months after he had completed its predecessor. A very brief statement, it ranks with the preface to *Miss Julie* as one of the key documents of modern thinking about the drama.

In this dream play [Strindberg wrote], as in his former dream play, *To Damascus*, the Author has sought to reproduce the disconnected but apparently logical form of a dream. Anything can happen; everything is possible and probable. Time and space do not exist; on a slight groundwork of reality, imagination spins and weaves new patterns made up of memories, experiences, unfettered fancies, absurdities and improvisations.

The characters are split, double and multiply; they evaporate, crystallize, scatter and converge. But a single consciousness holds sway over them all—that of the dreamer. For him there are no secrets, no incongruities, no scruples and no law. He neither condemns nor acquits, but only relates . . .

There are sentences in these two paragraphs (the note is only another half paragraph long) which describe nearly the whole of what we think of as avant-garde drama of the past fifty or more years. Words like "absurdity" and "improvisation" leap to our hearing with the sound of our own voices; the belief that "anything can happen" and is possible is one with which all our experiments begin, though they may go nowhere. The idea of characters dividing and multiplying, scattering and coalescing, stands behind the fluid stages of our theories and sometime practice. The note even seems to go beyond the theater to become a manifesto and operating manual for a more elastic art, that of the film.

What was Strindberg actually proposing, or rather telling us he had in hand? The dream plays have sometimes been interpreted as plays written *as though they were dreams,* as though they had been authored by the unconscious storytelling mind. Yet what Strindberg says is that his play attempts to "reproduce the disconnected but apparently logical *form* of a dream," a very different matter. It is the logic of disconnection, a logic operating outside wakefulness, beyond ordinary processes of intellection, that is decisive here.

It was an internal principle of dramatic construction that had almost no direct antecedents in the theater, although models for it existed in recent poetry and certain types of new fiction. There had of course been plays that had made use of dreams—Calderón's *La Vida es sueño*, Shakespeare's *The Tempest*—but these had not sought to imitate their very form. They had been *about* dreams or dreaming, but had retained their identities as constructions consistent with the operation of conscious logic, or with the conventions guarding the "reasonableness" of dramatic forms, even in works whose subjects were themselves irrational. Strindberg's only theatrical source would have been *Peer Gynt*, whose composition however was more like a fantasy than a dream.

The structures of the dream plays, while reasonable—logical—in themselves, were therefore not so by the criteria of accepted dramaturgy. Nothing was brought down with a louder crash than the Aristotelian unities of time and place, which had been broken before but not in such a thoroughgoing way. For time and space have disappeared as stable entities. "Where am I?" the Stranger asks at one point. "Where have I been? Is it spring, winter or summer? In what country am I living, in what hemisphere?" The world of *To Damascus* runs according to no known chronology; there are no fixed seasons, there is no sense of time passing at all, although abstractly the pilgrimage seems as if it ought to have taken a lifetime. And there is no fixed identity of place or places. In a stage direction that contains the essence of Strindberg's dream technology, his break with the theater's past is exhibited. We are at the end of a banquet scene:

The scene is changed without lowering the curtain. The stage is darkened and a medley of scenes, representing landscapes, palaces, rooms, is lowered and brought forward; so that the characters and furniture are no longer seen, but the Stranger alone remains visible and seems to be standing stiffly as though unconscious. At last even he disappears, and from the confusion a prison cell emerges.

Along with this dreamlike procedure of having one place give way to another without narrative preparation, Strindberg goes immeasurably further in breaking up the unity and stability of characters than he had done in *Miss Julie*. There his characters had been internally divided, but now they separate out into other characters: the Lady has several guises, none of them adopted as a matter of narrative tactics—she is not impersonating someone else—but in the manner of that dream mechanism whereby a single being is afforded diverse shapes. In the same way the Confessor is also the Beggar.

A *Dream Play* carries all this very much further. In it scenes dissolve into others without anything intervening, a most cinematic action. A forest of giant hollyhocks metamorphoses into a bare room, a doorkeeper's lodge into part of a lawyer's office, and the latter into the interior of a church; the play ends with a castle, which has appeared and disappeared many times before, catching on fire, with "the flower-bud on the roof burst[ing] into a giant chrysanthemum," a challenge to the inventiveness of directors and stage designers. Time moves backward and forward, characters change into their older or younger selves or take on wholly new incarnations.

A *Dream Play* comes out of much the same impulse of spiritual autobiography and quest as *To Damascus* and is suffused with a similar vague religiosity, its Christian and Catholic elements being replaced however by Eastern ones. The plot, such as it is, concerns the descent to earth of the daughter of the God Indra on a mission to determine the justice of human beings' complaints against existence. At the end of this investigation, whose data are taken in great part from Strindberg's own life—in fact and fantasy—she concludes that mankind is indeed "to be pitied" for a suffering that rises from its being caught between spirit and flesh. This motif, with its imagery of higher and lower, light and darkness, is the play's prevailing one, as it is in others of Strindberg's less technically radical plays.

Holding everything together in both works, as Strindberg says, is the "consciousness of the dreamer," the play's author, who determines what is to go into it with the continual power to choose, amend, delete, rearrange. This sovereign role of consciousness in producing the appearance of an unconsciously proceeding work is what profoundly distinguishes the dream plays from actual dreaming; in the latter it is of course the unconscious mind that decides the "play's" characters, actions, and motif, and so "writes" the work in the helpless theater of the sleeper's mind.

Strindberg demonstrated how to borrow the methods of dreaming while keeping authority over their uses. The effect was to release new parts of the self into availability for artistic acts. In one of those apparent cultural coincidences that are really signs of a change in the universal air, Strindberg was finishing *To Damascus* and writing *A Dream Play* at the same time that Sigmund Freud was working on *The Interpretation of Dreams*. Freud always considered that book the keystone of psychoanalytic theory, since, as he said, to possess the secrets of dreaming was to be on "the royal road to the unconscious." And in the unconscious Freud first explored through the investigation of his own dreams he discovered the same things Strindberg had: that there are no "secrets" there, no "incongruities," "no scruples," and no negatives—everything is possible.

The access Strindberg's dramaturgy gave to the unconscious meant that irrational material could now be presented throughout a play, as part of its very texture, instead of being confined as it had been in the past to *irrational characters*—madmen, say, or persons temporarily crazed by passion. Above all, it could be presented without comment or apology; it would not have to undergo a later "correction" into rationality through denouements, happy or not, which emphasized conscious, normative values. It isn't hard to see how from this accession rose the possibility of the surreal and the absurd in the drama of our era.

Strindberg wrote half a dozen works for the stage during the four or five years following *A Dream Play*, most of them historical dramas, none of them of much interest to us now. A point to be made about this is that Strindberg's career, which is often seen as having moved decisively from an apprenticeship in conventional romantic drama to a naturalistic period and then to a "symbolic" one—the dream plays—is in reality not at all so easily chronologized. Among the makers of modern drama he is the least consistent, the least sequential in the movements of his talent. Far-reaching innovations were followed by relapses into obsolete forms, efforts of genius by heavy-handedness. He made himself known as he could, and had varying degrees of inner light to work with.

He had long wanted a theater of his own, where his plays could be put on as he wished to see them done, for he had many ideas about acting (simplicity was his criterion) and stage design, as well as about the psychology and physiology of theatergoing. By 1907 this aspiration was being given new urgency by another of his technical advances in playwriting. In the summer of that year he and a young admirer, an actor-director named August Falck who had recently staged *Miss Julie*, took over a Stockholm store and rebuilt it into a theater which seated 161 persons. For this Intimate Theater, as they called it, Strindberg had ready a cycle of four plays, which he had written with amazing speed during the previous winter and spring, and which needed just such an "art" house for their presentation.

Strindberg called these works "chamber plays," with the analogy to music firmly in his thought. They are meant to be, and for the most part are, small, concise, swiftly and musically developed, perfectly self-contained. Just before writing them Strindberg elaborated their principles in a letter to a friend: "intimate in form; a simple theme treated with thoroughness; few characters; vast perspectives; freely imaginative, but built on observations, experiences, carefully studied . . . no huge apparatus . . . none of those 'old machines' [that are] built according to the rules; none of those drawn-out plays lasting all night."

The position of these plays in Strindberg's career has often been likened to that of the last quartets in Beethoven's: in both cases the works were produced in their authors' late fifties and proved to be their last significant accomplishment. But as Evert Sprinchorn has pointed out, the quartets are generally considered Beethoven's greatest achievement, whereas the chamber plays have most often been relegated to the status of eccentric pieces outside Strindberg's own main canon and that of the modern theater. In reality, they are central to both. More particularly, they represent Strindberg at his most complete, most unassailable; unlike the dream plays, there isn't the slightest space now between his materials and his technical means.

The first of the chamber plays, *Storm Weather*, is the one most rooted in the past, most naturalistic in appearance, and least intense in mood. *The Ghost Sonata*, the third play, is no doubt the best known, being both more widely read and more frequently performed than any of the others (as a student in Stockholm in 1941 Ingmar Bergman directed what is said to have been a spectacularly inventive production). *The Pelican*, the concluding work of the series, is probably the least known, although it deserves a much more prominent place, for nothing Strindberg ever wrote surpasses it in focused energy and brilliant, sure economy.

Like the three other plays, *The Pelican* may be said to be about death, in the sense that it arises from a desire for a cessation of being, for deliverance from life conceived of as radical suffering. A few years before he wrote the chamber plays Strindberg had delivered himself of perhaps his most extreme statement of that loathing for existence which was so prominent at various times in his life, its expression sometimes taking on the quality of a mannerism or pose or, least culpably, functioning as a catalyst for writing.

> Life is so horribly ugly [he wrote], we human beings so utterly evil, that, if a writer were to portray everything he saw

and heard no one could bear to read it. Breeding and education are only masks to hide our bestiality, and virtue is a sham. The best we can hope for is to conceal our wretchedness. Life is so cynical that only a swine can be happy in it; and any man who sees beauty in life's ugliness is a swine! Life is a punishment. A hell. For some a purgatory, for none a paradise. We are compelled to commit evil and to torment our fellow mortals.

The almost self-indulgent bitterness and indiscriminate horror of this outburst, reminiscent in some ways of Büchner's indictment of history in his letters to his fiancée, are now transformed the way the earlier writer's violent negation had been into the controlled specific vision of a work of dramatic art. What Strindberg had left unspoken in his diatribe was his unappeasable hatred of the family as the treacherous source of everything and the frustrator of so much. In the chamber plays as a whole, and in *The Pelican* most directly, this attitude returns to become an informing principle. Yet to call *The Pelican* a domestic drama is rather like thinking of *Oedipus* as one; its setting is a home and its ostensible subject is that of family relationships, but the anguished consciousness, like that of *The Father*, is of something much wider and more basic than those things.

The play's central situation is that of a mother and daughter in love with the same man, the girl's husband. The mother has recently been widowed and the couple has come to live with her and her other child, a law student (a maid completes the cast of characters). In the course of the swiftly unfolding drama—it should take no more than an hour and fifteen minutes in performance; as in the other chamber plays, there are no intermissions to disrupt the unity of mood— shattering revelations are made of the son-in-law's and mother's vicious greed and selfishness, the latter's being projected back into the past by the son, who accuses her, with the silent acquiescence of his sister, of having driven their father to his death and of having both literally and metaphorically starved them all their lives. The most telling image of this is of her having skimmed off the cream from the milk and given them the thin bluish remainder.

The play's title comes from a poem the son-in-law had written for the mother (on his wedding day) about the bird which mythically is supposed to give its own blood to its starving young. Nothing could be further from the mother's actuality, which the son underscores when he tells her that zoologists have thoroughly discredited the legend, so that even the forms of her self-deceit are wrongly founded. As the tension in the house grows, the division between the mother and son-in-law and son and daughter widens to become a chasm separating those in whom horror and loss of will are induced by the sight of limitless avarice and exploitation and those who persist in blind movements of appetite. The play culminates in the purgative flames of a fire set by the son; the mother jumps from a window to her presumable death, while her children, in each other's arms, crooning to one another of a lost and now transfigured childhood, sink to the floor as the "strong, vivid red" glow of the fire moves toward them.

Such a summary does no justice at all to *The Pelican*'s supremely concentrated force and queer, demoralizing beauty. As the play moves along with violent momentum, we become aware that we are being offered no explanations, or even discussions, on psychological or societal levels and that no traditional "development" is taking place. For Strindberg has created a perfectly autonomous and self-validating work of theater whose ferocious energy displays itself in the manner of a catherine wheel: spikes of brutal gesture and speech radiating from a center located and fixed in advance, implacably intuited.

In the most extraordinary way the house itself acts to become an inseparable element of the vision, not merely its physical container. Out of the life it has held and witnessed, it shakes, trembles, issues strange noises, and is swept by spectral winds before yielding itself to the flames which, the son prays, will destroy "everything old and mean and evil and ugly . . ." Every detail of the play bears on everything, nothing is wasted, nothing proffered for the sake of effect or aesthetic shapeliness. In this last work of his fully operating imagination Strindberg brought together all the disparate strands of his public and private existence, sealed up the spaces between his raw psychic energies and his creative ones, between what he craved and what he had seen. *The Pelican* emerges as the nearly unbearable crystallization of an entire era of consciousness—with its death of old pieties and advent of new awareness—to whose painful, liberating truths Strindberg had contributed as much as anyone.

He lived on for five more years after writing the chamber plays, producing a few more undistinguished theater pieces, including another dream play reminiscent of *To Damascus* called *The Great Highway*. At his death from cancer in 1912 he was living in virtual isolation, his misanthropy having fully blossomed, but his funeral, which he had wanted to be quiet and private, was attended by crowds of admirers—students, workers, literary and theater people.

Many years later, after there was no one left who could testify to what his presence had meant and he had been frozen into one of the narrow legends of modern literature, a countryman, the novelist Pär Lagerkvist, spoke of what had been done to him: "It has been Strindberg's fate, and probably will continue to be for a long time yet, that he is valued first and foremost for his bad qualities, both as a writer and a man. All of his repellent and morbid features were seized upon." Perhaps so; but there is a counterpressure to that fact, which comes from the continuing presence in living imaginations of the example he gave of creative unrestraint, visionary daring.

CHEKHOV

Among the most widely held views of the plays of Anton Chekhov is one that regards them as works of "mood" and "atmosphere," lacking in solid and well-defined structures, deficient in traditional theatrical action, inconclusive and relying heavily on that sort of emotional quality or nuance of feeling usually described as bittersweet. For the seventy-five years or so that they have been in the Western repertory these plays, particularly the last three masterpieces—*Uncle Vanya, The Three Sisters,* and *The Cherry Orchard*—have been thought of, positively or otherwise, as dramas of sensibility, muted and subtle compositions in which the great themes of human encounter and destiny have been transposed to the most minor of keys.

But the plays have also been seen, from a quite different perspective, as dramas of place and social process. In this view they are shrewd investigations and portraits of provincial upper-middle-class life in Russia at the turn of the century; more specifically they are prerevolutionary tales of the decline and forthcoming downfall of this *haute bourgeoisie* in the face of the onrush of the more energetic and capable, and so historically irresistible, lower middle classes and proletariat. Though it is scarcely confined to Chekhov's homeland, this naturally has been the quasi-official Soviet view, on occasion hardened into dogma, of Russia's greatest playwright.

These two readings of Chekhov, as a tender and melancholy lyricist of emotional states and as an unconsciously Marxist social observer, are not so far apart as it may seem. A poetry of loss and personal disaster is seen as the mode of Chekhov's observation of social change, so that to stress his atmosphere and manner is usually to imply his subject, and the other way around. In any case, although there are elements of truth in both positions, they meet in some common misunderstandings, chief among them that Chekhov has no subject beyond that of social existence and the psychic response to its vicissitudes and pressures, and that his work, however beautiful and "moving" it may be, lacks aesthetic size and intricacy.

In his extremely thorough and very valuable study, *Chekhov the Dramatist*, David Magarshack has ascribed the origin of this view of the plays as artistically small and transparent to Tolstoy, who seems to have greatly admired Chekhov as a man and a writer of short stories but not as a dramatist. And yet, as Magarshack points out, the very indictment which Tolstoy composed has been transformed by later opinion, in Russia and elsewhere, into the basis for favorable and even adulatory judgments. Chekhov is like life, these assessments mainly go; he is not so much a deliberate artist (with the implication in that of heavy matters for the mind) as a man with more sensitivity and eloquence than the rest of us, so that his works issue from his natural being: heartfelt, direct, relatively formless, and intuited rather than constructed. Exactly like life itself.

Tolstoy, a traditionalist in matters of the stage and a spokesman in his last years for the sober utility of art, considered Chekhov's lifelikeness, in this sense, to be unscientific and not useful, ground for his disqualification as a dramatist. "In a dramatic work," Magarshack quotes him as having told an interviewer a short time after Chekhov's death, "the author ought to deal with some problem that has yet to be solved and every character ought to solve it according to the idiosyncrasies of his own character. It is like a laboratory experiment. But you won't find anything of the kind in Chekhov."

Anton Chekhov, who had once written that "dissatisfaction with oneself is one of the foundation stones of every real talent," had made much the same reproach to himself. At a time when his reputation was at its height he had set down in his journal or notebook the following words, which referred to both his fiction and his plays: "I sometimes think that I have failed my readers because I have not answered the important questions." Thomas Mann, writing on Chekhov near the end of his own life and of a career in which he had not always resisted the temptation to pontificate, made the reply which the great modest Russian author could not have made to himself.

Chekhov's triumph, Mann said, lay precisely in his inability or refusal to answer any questions at all, whatever the pressure from the public. In a mood opposed to his self-doubt, Chekhov had once written that "the truth [about life] is by nature ironical and it can easily happen that a writer who puts the truth above everything else is reproached by the world with lack of conviction, indifference to good and evil, lack of ideals and ideas." Mann, to whom irony was second nature, could well appreciate this. Chekhov's ideals and ideas are there, he went on, but all unproclaimed. Perhaps more completely than any other writer who has ever lived, Chekhov rejected the roles of legislator, seer, or judge, working instead in an atmosphere of such extraordinary intellectual reticence and lack of artistic ego that we still have difficulty in appreciating his imaginative world's true size.

He disappeared into it, offering oblique hints of his presence from time to time, but leaving no track to follow. There are, for example, doctors in almost every one of his plays, but they are not like him; his imaginary medical men are not in the plays for autobiographical purposes and not even to be doctors in action, but because medicine was a social role whose definitions could be dramatically engaged; these physicians move in the space between what is expected of them and what they are.

In an even more complete obliteration of his personality, Chekhov will place in the mouth of a character a speech we might assume expresses his own considered thought on some subject or other, but then have us encounter, perhaps as the very next piece of dialogue, another speech arguing against the ideas of the first and with equal conviction and eloquence.

One point of this is that Chekhov cannot be deduced from his plays the way, for example, Strindberg or more indirectly Ibsen can. To an astonishing degree the plays are without an authorial voice, which is to say, at the very least, that they are untendentious and make no claim on any kind of personal territory, but more than this, that they appear to be natural objects, things come upon. These uncoerced dramas seem to issue from a distance in which a relinquishment has taken place: the characters have been placed on their own, there is no shaping and controlling creator arranging their movements and determining their fates. Or so it seems, and this appearance is one element making for the notion that Chekhov's plays lack dramatic architecture and are lifelike compositions without aesthetic magnitude or purpose.

One strand of Russian opinion during his life and afterward helped in a peculiar way to fix this notion in public consciousness. He was so admired as a man that it was difficult to credit him with being an imaginative genius of the kind who goes beyond immediate values and experience to grapple with something ultimate and devastating. Tolstoy called him "dear," "beautiful," and "wonderful," and Maxim Gorky, whose *Reminiscences of Tolstoy, Chekhov and Andreyev* provides perhaps the most intimate portrait we possess of him, spoke in reverent terms: "I think that in Anton Chekhov's presence every-one involuntarily felt in himself a desire to be simpler, more truthful, more one's self."

For his own part Chekhov once set down in a letter to a friend a spiritual and intellectual apologia which except for his characteristic underestimation of his talent nothing in his life would refute. In a negative way, as a warning about how not to approach him, the statement is a guide to his plays:

> I fear those who look for tendencies between the lines and want to regard me precisely as a liberal or a conservative. I am not a liberal or a conservative, an evolutionist, a monk, or indifferent to the world. I should like to be a free artist—and that is all—and I regret that God has not given me the strength to be one. I hate lies and violence in all their aspects . . . Pharisaism, stupidity and idle whims reign not only in the homes of the merchants and in prison. I see them in science, in literature and among young people. Therefore I cannot nurture any special feeling for policemen, butchers, learned men, writers or youth. I regard trademarks and labels as prejudices. My holy of holies are the human body, health, intelligence, talent, inspiration, love and the most absolute freedom—freedom from violence and falsehood in whatever forms these may be expressed. This is the program I would hold to if I were a great artist.

The personal modesty was reflected in a most modest art. One of the demands the plays make is that we go beneath their surfaces, not in order to discover some "true" core, the secret heart of Chekhov's matter, but to perceive how these surfaces themselves contain the depths, how modesty in Chekhov's case is a question of a respect for truth and of a refusal to make experience more "dramatic" than it really is or, as we shall see later, to construct his plays like mysteries. Which is to say that with perhaps greater clarity and resonance than any other playwright Chekhov discovered the drama of the undramatic, the uninflected and commonplace. In this sense his plays are opposed to the reigning tradition of overt passion and significant culmination, the tradition of Greek and French classical tragedy, of Shakespeare and the Jacobeans and indeed of all drama rising out of an impulse to organize the world in systematic, hyperbolic fictions, to magnify it and convert it into legend.

The very independence from dramatic and theatrical conventions on the part of the characters in his major plays, their seeming to have been transported to the stage as if from some scene of actual life—Chekhov's much misunderstood "realism"—was in a mysterious way a measure of his freedom from preconceptions and of his refusal as an artist to force existence into satisfying logical patterns. And the superficial quietness of his dramas, which has led to their being performed more often than not with a sort of hushed lugubriousness or delicate ennui, reflects his human voice, which seldom rose or broke.

Still, if it was Chekhov's own temperament, his restraint and gentleness (though not meekness; he could be roused to anger by stupidity or oppression) and dislike of systems and categorical procedures of any kind, that determined what his plays would look like, it was these things in conjunction with his attitude toward and critique of the theater as it existed in Russia when he was coming to artistic maturity that decided what they would actually be. Of course such convergences of inner being and objective cultural reality lie behind every transformation of the arts, but in the case of Chekhov the subtleties of the process are unprecedentedly complex and the ironies extreme. And the greatest of these is that Chekhov, to whom the thought of being a mighty innovator could not have occurred, fashioned, out of his reticence and uncertainty, one of the great revolutions of the stage and indeed of imaginative consciousness itself.

Tolstoy had accused Chekhov of not having solved any problems in his plays, or even posed any. One would like to think that by "problems" Tolstoy meant something less narrow and more ontological than a series of purely conscious issues, moral or social "questions," for example. Yet the evidence is that he meant exactly those things. His own plays, with one or two exceptions, were heavily didactic and moralistic, especially the adaptations of his own stories he wrote for a "people's" theater. Yet even giving Tolstoy the benefit of the doubt, his indictment reflected a conventional and increasingly outmoded notion of drama as narrative inquiry and, even more important, as provider of imaginary solutions to real dilemmas. The stage as a place where one learns how to live by precept or by analogy with the simulated life one encounters there: this is not the most foolish of ideas, but it is not what the great playwrights of the last hundred or so years have considered the central use of their art.

Fifty years after Chekhov's death Eugene Ionesco was to express in extreme terms a counterview of drama to Tolstoy's, one that had begun to be exemplified as far back as the 1830's, when Georg Büchner had composed his non-linear plays that built to no "solutions," and that had been most simply and directly articulated by Friedrich Hebbel, who in the 1850's had written in his journal that "drama should not present new stories but new relationships." The traditional theater from the Greeks to the present, Ionesco argued, followed the form of the detective story: in the first act a problem or mystery was set forth, in the middle act or acts it was developed, in the last it was solved. Ionesco wished to repudiate such structured, progressive, and narratively suspenseful theater and fashion one whose obedience would be to the way the world and experience really felt, whose "laws" would create themselves as the dramas unfolded and whose suspensefulness would be a function of aesthetic process, not of theme.

Anton Chekhov's repudiation of the detective-story tradition of drama was of a different order and was more subtle than that of Ionesco or of any of the playwrights whose work makes up what we have come to call the Theater of the

Absurd. At first glance his plays and theirs would seem to be worlds apart. Yet it is no mistake to see Chekhov as a precursor of theatrical absurdity, less obviously than Strindberg but with as much force; it isn't silly to regard *The Three Sisters*, for instance, as being very close in spirit and even in technique to a play like *Waiting for Godot*. For whatever the differences in their work of utterance, gesture, and *mise en scène*, the geniuses of Chekhov and Beckett share some common grounds and intentions: they will not make theater as they have seen it being made; they will present new relationships and not new tales; they will use the stage for the creation of consciousness and not for its reflection; and they will offer neither solutions nor prescriptions, not even heightened emotion, but mercilessly stripped artifacts of the imagination that will present our deepest "story."

The Russian theater which Chekhov knew when he began to write for it was in almost every respect an inferior and unoriginal enterprise, lacking in even those isolated but influential forces—playwrights like Ibsen and Strindberg, or even Hauptmann and Maeterlinck, directors such as André Antoine, *régisseurs* like the Duke of Saxe-Meiningen—who during the last decades of the nineteenth century were giving the stage elsewhere in Europe a new impetus and morale.

Theater as a formal and conscious art had come into being comparatively late in Russia, not having begun to metamorphose from its origins in folk drama and religious ritual until the second half of the seventeenth century. When it did, it was an activity carried on almost exclusively by imported Frenchmen, Germans, and, later, Italians. From the beginning it was attached to the court and the state, an obviously constricting condition, and from the start too it was subject to heavy and at times merciless censorship.

As time went on, something that could be called an indigenous theater developed, a few minor playwrights coming into view—Dmitri Fonvizin in the 1770's, Alexander Griboyedov in the early 1820's. But it was not until 1831, when Pushkin's *Boris Godunov* was published, and even more 1836, when Gogol's *The Inspector General* was produced in Moscow, that Russia could be said to possess a dramatist anywhere near the level of the great European artist-playwrights. But Pushkin wrote only that one full-length play and was better known as a poet, while Gogol's productive career was also thin and short-lived. By the time of Chekhov's youth the leading Russian playwright was Alexander Ostrovsky, whose somber dramas about provincial life and its sufferings were often marred by sentimentality and were seldom revelatory on an imaginative plane, but were highly regarded for their "truthfulness" and, an important consideration in the self-conscious culture of the period, their "Russianness."

Apart from works by these native authors, the Russian stage in the 1870's and 1880's presented an occasional foreign classic such as Shakespeare or Molière or Schiller, but was heavily occupied by melodrama and farce, either in translation or adaptation from the French or almost wholly derived from French models, and by light dramatic sketches and vaudevilles. Acting was on at least as low, which is to say as declamatory, a level as anywhere else in Europe, notions of directorial imagination were nearly nonexistent, and physical staging was generally crude or overblown. Historians of Russian theater tend to describe this period as having seen the arrival of a fully mature native practice (how else account for Chekhov?), but everything indicates that the theater Chekhov was nourished on and that continued to surround him even after his own plays ought to have shattered all complacencies was in almost every one of its sectors a place of banality and contrivance.

Chekhov was thoroughly aware of this state of affairs. His notebooks and correspondence are full of disparaging references to the stage in Russia. "The contemporary theater," he wrote to a friend, "is an eruption, a nasty disease of the cities."

On another occasion he wrote that the atmosphere of the stage in Russia is "leaden and oppressive. It is covered inches thick in dust and enveloped in fog and tedium. You go to the theater simply because you have nowhere else to go. You look at the stage, yawn and swear under your breath." And to another correspondent he wrote that "we must strive with all our power to see to it that the stage passes out of the hands of the grocers and into literary hands, otherwise the theater is doomed."

Those literary hands were chiefly to be his own, but to the end of his life Chekhov wavered between an acceptance of his role and pleasure in it and the most severe misgivings about his own artistic prowess. His informal writings are strewn with self-deprecatory remarks: "I'd say I'm an indifferent dramatist"; "as far as my dramaturgy is concerned, it seems to me that I was not destined to be a playwright"; "I do not intend to write dramas. I don't care for the work." Some of this may be set down to Chekhov's authentic modesty, but the complaint ultimately issued from a source beyond personality. The clue to what that was is to be found in two other remarks of his: "Writing plays has demoralized me," and "I swear fearfully at the conventions of the stage."

The two statements are intimately related. Chekhov's "demoralization" arose, it seems clear, precisely from his encounter with the conventions of the theater. These ranged from what we might call its sociology—the legitimized obtuseness of producers, critics, and entrepreneurs (the "grocers"), the time-honored insensitivity of actors—to its very artistic heart: the self-perpetuating mechanisms of dramatic procedure, the mindlessness of prevailing attitudes, all of them inherited, toward what constituted dramatic art and truth. In response to all this Chekhov resembled certain of his great contemporaries. Strindberg had given up writing for the stage for four or five years in the middle of his career, after having denounced the theater as "reprehensible" because it seemed to have no place for new ideas and techniques. And Ibsen had had to beat a strategic retreat from his earlier poetic plays and move into a more prosaic-looking and domestic drama in order to have his plays produced and considered at all.

To be an artist-playwright, in distinction to being a mere contriver of plays, a dramatizer of *incidents,* is to have to resist the process which Bertolt Brecht was to describe as the "theatering down" of dramatic art, and to force the reluctant theater and the world to accept new definitions of that art. This is what Chekhov, confident and beleaguered by turns, recognized that he would be called upon to do once he had become a serious dramatist, which is to say once he had gone past that condition of simple naïve love of theater as "magical" enterprise and ideal possibility in which all great playwrights are likely to begin.

Chekhov is sometimes assumed to have turned to the stage only after years of writing in other forms—humorous journalistic sketches, short stories, etc. The truth is that he seems to have been attracted to the theater after having seen his first play at around thirteen in his provincial village of Taganrog in the Ukraine, and to have written at least two full-length dramas (of which no traces remain) while still a high-school student. His first one-act plays or entertainments began to appear in the late 1880's, when he was drawing close to thirty, had been practicing medicine for some years, and had already been acclaimed for his fiction, and he continued to write these pleasant, unremarkable stage pieces well into the next decade.

His first major work, apparently written when he was about twenty-two or -three and scrapped by him without its having been publicly seen or read, wasn't discovered until many years after his death in 1904. When the manuscript came to light in the Soviet Union in 1923 it was published as *A Play without a Title,* and it has since been translated into

English as *Platonov*, the name of its central character. Two other full-length plays appeared in the late 1880's, *The Wood Demon* and, much more importantly, *Ivanov*.

A number of the one-act plays or sketches, such as "The Wedding" and "A Tragedian in Spite of Himself," were adaptations of Chekhov's own short stories, and all of them were influenced, technically, by the French-derived vaudevilles that were theatrical staples of the period and, in spirit, as far as that could be influenced at all, chiefly by Gogol, the Russian writer he most admired. They brought him almost immediate fame and a small steady income, but he invested little of his artistic morale in them and seems to have regarded them, wondering a little at their easy popularity, as insignificant *jeux d'esprit*, although he could at times become defensive about them. *Platonov*, about whose conception and writing we know nothing, since he never spoke about the play, was from its internal evidence another matter.

Chekhov was right in thinking *Platonov* a failure and an embarrassment, and therefore in keeping its very existence a secret. The play is confused, awkward, badly shaped, verbose, and tediously protracted (it is as long as all three of his last great plays put together). What's worse, it relies on a number of melodramatic incidents which are inappropriate to its presumed spirit and artistic intention and are almost wholly unconvincing in themselves. A tale of provincial life and a portrait of a tormented country intellectual, one of those "useless" men with whom Russian literary and educated consciousness were so concerned at the time, *Platonov* owes a crippling debt to theatrical conventions.

Yet the play is one of those artistic embarrassments in which the seeds of something previously unrealized and almost unimagined can be detected, the beginnings of an alteration in awareness. Nothing throws more light on what Chekhov, in the largest sense, tried and failed to do in *Platonov*, and for that matter on one of the central aspects of his final aesthetic achievement, than the following outcry and call to order, which had arisen from Gogol nearly fifty years earlier:

> Only a great, deep, rare genius can catch what surrounds us daily, what always accompanies us, what is ordinary—while mediocrity grabs with both hands at all that is out of rule, what happens but seldom and catches the eye by its ugliness and disharmony . . . The strange has become the subject matter of our drama. The whole point is to tell a new, strange, unheard of accident: murder, fires, wild passions, henchmen, poisons, effects, eternal effects.

It might be thought odd that Gogol, whose own writings after all were notable for their grotesque humors and extreme psychology, should have invoked an ideal of normality, ordinariness. Yet there is no real contradiction, for what Gogol was asking for was authenticity, truthfulness to existence. The quotidian reality he wanted the drama to deal with was independent of whatever might be perceived in it or imagined about it, so that it was the task of perception and creative vision to be as accurate as possible. It followed that to search for the exotic was to be blind to what surrounds you.

If reality is extreme and grotesque, as it surely was to Gogol, these qualities lie in the very texture of ordinary life and so ought to inform the drama; but they would be then, theoretically at least, universal and aesthetically inevitable. What was not universal or artistically necessary was the kind of melodramatic imagining which seized on the exceptional for its purportedly inherent dramatic substance, its *incidental* and bizarre flair. More than a hundred years later Ionesco would articulate much the same objection to fancy (in Coleridge's sense) in favor of imaginative perception when he remarked that formal surrealism was strained and merely eccentric since the surreal was what we experienced every day, what "lies at our feet."

Chekhov once wrote that a playwright was to be permitted the invention of any sort of reality whatsoever except one—the psychological; and this, if we broaden the definition of the word to mean, as Chekhov surely did, all realities of the mind and spirit, was what Gogol cared about. The "eternal effects" of which the earlier writer had spoken were the result in the theater of a failure of, or rather an incapacity for, psychological perception. What was substituted for dramatic visions based on psychological truth were systems of physical activities—acts of violence, simulations of passions, intrigues, disasters, all summed up under the rubric of "plot." And these gestures and movements passed themselves off as having been derived from experience, whereas in fact they were mostly appropriated from the history of the stage itself, from what had indeed once been expressions or dramatically objective correlatives of human truths, but were now clichés, conventions, and, worse, lies. Henry James once spoke of the public's inability to distinguish art from "sensation" in the theater, and in fact of its preference for sensation; what Chekhov was to bring about was something very much like the absolute triumph of art over sensation.

He was to become the genius who would answer Gogol's prayer, but in *Platonov* his powers were as yet greatly inadequate to even the circumscribed artistic ambitions he must have had at the time. He was not yet free from the "theatrical"; he had to pass through the school of conventional architecture before he could make his own designs. Yet *Platonov* gives the first faint indications of a future style and, even more, of a forthcoming choice of dramatic worlds. From the confused narrative accurate portraits emerge, and the narrative itself is interrupted on occasion for the kind of conversational "action," the revelation of character, and more than character—of thought and internal experience—that would be at the center of his mature works. Finally *Platonov* gives in a hectic and fragmentary way a hint of what is to be one of Chekhov's pervasive subjects: the way we construct our lives out of literature, so that we become abstract to ourselves and unreal.

Ivanov, written in 1887 and the first of his dramatic works of any description to be staged, carries these qualities and impulses much further, while remaining trapped to a degree in Chekhov's and the theater's past. Like the earlier work, *Ivanov* is set in the provinces, evokes much the same quality of upper-class uncommitted life as its predecessor, and has as its protagonist much the same sort of "superfluous" man, suffering from a similar kind of vague existential crisis and despair. The word "existential" here isn't an anachronism; for all its faults, the great interest of *Ivanov* is in its depiction—more accurately, establishment—of that sense of experience beneath moral or social categories and uncorrupted by theory that we mean when we use the word now.

"My plot is unprecedented," Chekhov wrote to his brother in a rare burst of exhilaration after finishing the play. Yet he was using the word "plot" in the loosest sense, to denote his dramatic subject and schema. For what was unprecedented was not his narrative, which is built along lines of marital and sexual entanglement and ends on a melodramatic and supererogatory note with the suicide of the central figure, but the play's artistic decisions and, as a function here of that, its moral ones.

A central instigation of *Ivanov* was Chekhov's desire to write a play which would say the last word on and so perhaps put to rest the theme of the superfluous man. He would anatomize this type of disconnected, solipsistic Russian whose nature and possible destiny were major issues of contemporary writing and speculation, and would do it chiefly by depriving it of its exotic quality. He wrote once in a letter that he had wanted to call his protagonist Ivan Ivanovich Ivanov to indicate his ordinariness, which is to say his unromantic, unliterary status as a dramatic character.

To his brother he wrote: "I wanted to be original. I did not portray a single villain nor a single angel . . . did not blame anyone or exculpate anyone." In the way such things sometimes happen, Chekhov's intention had altered in the course of writing the play, so that *Ivanov* emerges as a work whose vision and concerns go far beyond its origins in the external culture. By presenting no villains and no heroes, Chekhov introduced an almost wholly new non-judgmental note into the body of drama. More specifically, he broke with the literary conventions behind all systems, and beyond that struck a blow against the literariness of the way lives are organized.

The protagonist is a man whose erratic behavior, apparent cruelty, indecisiveness, and lack of clear self-definition inspire in others factitious interpretations and evaluations derived from literary and dramatic typologies. As one critic has described this process:

Sasha [Ivanov's wife], an impressionable young girl, and Dr. Lvov, a narrow, uncompromising man, both classify him according to literary conventions: Sasha sees him as a Hamlet, a superior man to be worshipped and redeemed, while Dr. Lvov regards him as an inhuman and selfish Tartuffe, to be punished and exposed. Chekhov's point, however, is that Ivanov is neither a hero nor a villain, but simply an ordinary weak man.

Actually, Dr. Lvov, who objects to Ivanov's treatment of his wife and pursues him like a nemesis, may be narrow and uncompromising, but he is not on that account contemptible. In a wonderfully interesting letter to his friend and publisher Suvorin, who had apparently suggested that Lvov be made broader and more blameworthy, Chekhov wrote that "Lvov is one of those honest, straightforward, frank but . . . rectilinear people . . . if necessary he will throw bombs under carriages, punch inspectors in the nose, and call a person a scoundrel . . . These people are necessary and quite nice for the most part . . . It is dishonest to caricature them." The breadth of acceptance this reveals, the refusal of the entire play to exalt or demean, would be a growing aspect of Chekhov's dramatic writing from now on.

The play had a mixed reception. Chekhov's brother Michael wrote that in general the public and the critics "did not understand *Ivanov* and for a long time the papers were explaining the personality and character of the hero." There is no doubt that the bafflement arose from the very elements that Chekhov had intuited as unprecedented: his play's moral neutrality and consequent abandonment of much of the ethical structure of bourgeois drama. The jettisoning was incomplete because Chekhov was not yet able to understand how the imaginative work of the play had been accomplished before its physical denouement and had therefore rushed one, borrowed from convention, into being. After an interval of several years and after one more large play that was in some respects a step backward from *Ivanov*, he would write a drama, *The Seagull*, from which almost all dramaturgical clichés or inherited gestures would have disappeared.

In his study of Chekhov as a dramatist, David Magarshack offers a theory that two great changes took place in his belief and work between the writing of *Ivanov* and *The Wood Demon*, which followed in 1889–90, and the creation of *The Seagull* in 1896, a period during which Chekhov wrote no major plays. The first change was from a conviction of the necessity of absolute objectivity on the part of a writer to a position of moral and spiritual commitment, and the second, a dramaturgical shift, was from what Magarshack calls plays of "direct action" to ones of indirection. Both observations have much truth in them, but they are subject to misinterpretation.

Chekhov apparently did come to think that pure objectivity was impossible for the artist, but this did not mean that his writing became tendentious or that it allied itself with any formal system of values; he did not become more "humane." Gorky and Stanislavsky were partly responsible, among others, for the idea that Chekhov's late plays are critiques of society and laments over the quality of life among the educated or, for that matter, among Russians generally. There is a famous passage in his *Reminiscences* in which Gorky speaks of Chekhov as though he were a sage or prophet:

> In front of that dreary, gray crowd of helpless people there passed a great, wise and observant man; he looked at all those dreary inhabitants of his country and, with a sad smile, with a tone of gentle but deep reproach, in a beautiful and sincere voice, he said to them: you live badly my friends. It is shameful to live like that.

It is true that Chekhov occasionally made this kind of observation about Russian life, in correspondence with friends and in his notebook. And the plays are certainly permeated with a rueful awareness of social malaise and of the peculiar unhappiness of people without ambitions or without the power to implement the ones they have. But as we shall see, the dramas do not originate in such perception and are very far from culminating in it. There is a profound gravity in Chekhov, but it is not at all the ponderousness and melancholy with which Stanislavsky was to invest his productions of the plays. What Chekhov's movement from a stance of quasi-scientific objectivity to one of commitment meant was that in the last plays he would identify more strongly than ever with his characters, would feel in himself more intensely the dilemmas and beleaguerments of existence they incarnated than he was able to with his first protagonists.

The more radical change from the standpoint of the history of the theater was the alteration in Chekhov's means of dramatic construction. Magarshack is right in using the terms "direct" and "indirect," as far as they go. For Chekhov did indeed reach a dramatic style, its major lineaments first fully if a little tentatively on display in *The Seagull*, in which crucial action of a physical kind takes place almost entirely offstage and in which the activities that do occur onstage are oblique, heavily verbal, and without resolution. But what lay behind this change, with its important consequences for the future practice of drama, was something well beyond narrow methodology; it sprang from an intuition into the very nature of action as it had almost universally been conceived throughout dramatic history. *The Seagull* puts this intuition to work.

As Robert Louis Jackson has written in an important essay, *The Seagull* is a play about art. In being about art, it is about the creative self and more specifically about the ways this self can sustain itself in relation to physical and social necessities and the contrary ways it can go under. The crux of the drama is in the opposing beings of Konstantin and Nina, the one enacting his career as a writer in a spirit of self-pity and romantic literary illusion, the other hers as an actress with devotion, clear-headedness, and, above all, stamina. Chekhov is saying that Konstantin goes down to defeat (his offstage suicide is simply the sign of his prior inadequacy) because he cannot accept his freedom and the responsibility that goes with it, wanting to be taken out of himself and to be nurtured by destiny, while Nina triumphs through a recognition that an artist survives neither by means of inspiration nor favorable circumstances but by persistence.

Such a truth is paradigmatic of life itself; like almost every modern writer who has made art one of his subjects, Chekhov uses the artist's fate as a perspective on wider existence. For in the artist's task and situation one can see in their purest, most conscious form the conditions of experience in which all are held. "The individual caught in the fact," Henry James described Ibsen's pervasive subject, and the observation illuminates a universal reality. Beneath our ideas and values, our ambitions and dreams, lies fact, the rock-hard actuality of what we are and must do. It is Nina's awareness of necessity that keeps her from self-pity and self-delusion, chief among the latter being a belief in love as an agency of salvation, a belief to which Konstantin and Masha, another character who exists in contrast with Nina, cling.

As Jackson points out, Nina has passed beyond such a demand that love give what it's unable to. She lives now in the recognition that nothing rescues and nothing ransoms, that she can expect no external force or human connection to embolden or give a warranty to her art, which will exist as the outcome of her acts of making it, of her free and responsible choice. What is true of her art is also true of her life; unlike Konstantin, she will not complain that "things aren't right" but will live open-eyed and disenchanted, working, *making* herself, being what she is. She is the first of Chekhov's heroines of existential sobriety, whose education is in discovering how to submit to limits and in learning about what cannot be, and her story is played out under the symbolic form of the seagull: free, vulnerable, an emblem of besieged destiny.

The Seagull demonstrates once again how form is a function of idea and perception and in turn modifies them. In placing offstage what might ordinarily be considered the play's major events, the happenings that ought to make for its "drama"—Nina's love affair with Trigorin, Konstantin's suicide—Chekhov accomplished a quiet revolution in our notions of action on the stage. For it was Chekhov's genius to see that those events, situated in the full light, would not have made for drama but for melodrama.

Melodrama, to approach it from another perspective, may be defined as physical or emotional action for its own sake, action without spiritual or moral consequence or whose consequences of those kinds have atrophied and turned into cliché precisely by having been the staples of previous "high" drama. Melodrama is in fact the periodic legacy of serious drama, Shakespeare being turned into bourgeois tragedy, Ibsen into

Arthur Miller. This is why a renewal of the stage is always partly a matter of a reinterrogation of the values of action and a revision of its definitions.

Chekhov once wrote that "men dine, just dine, and in this moment their fate is decided and their lives destroyed." But from within, not by a thunderbolt. In its recognition that existence makes its most significant statements to us behind our backs, so to speak, revealing us to ourselves and compelling our crucial decisions at the least "heightened" moments, Chekhov's remark can serve as a motto for the procedures of all his mature dramas. For the true revelations and significances of *The Seagull*, and even more those of the last three plays, are offered not through climactic encounters, clashes, and denouements, which would have contained their a priori assumptions—passionate love is fatal, murder is abominable, and the like—but in the subtle conversations and glancing meetings, the brushings against one another of these characters who are engaged with their opposites and counterparts at the least extravagant times, in the most ordinary of settings.

These flat, unexceptional *mise en scènes* ought not to be mistaken for traditional naturalism. It was not Chekhov's purpose to reproduce ordinary existence but to present its appearance, or certain aspects of its appearance, as a ground for his further-going exploration and to repudiate the exotic as a source of special significance or power. One of his quarrels with the Russian stage was in fact its deadly verisimilitude, its pretense of being lifelike when it wasn't being fanciful. Out of this critique was fashioned the following well-known speech of Konstantin's, which like that of Camille Desmoulins in Büchner's *Danton's Death*, is an expression, strategically placed near the center of his own anti-traditional work, of the author's contempt for the existing theater:

In my opinion the theater of today is in a rut and full of prejudices and conventions . . . When I watch these great and talented people, these high priests of a sacred art, depicting the way people eat, drink, make love, walk about and wear their clothes, when I hear them trying to squeeze a moral out of the tritest words and emptiest scenes, when I am presented with a thousand variations on the same old thing, the same thing again and again—well, I just have to escape, I run away.

In a lecture a few years ago the Polish director Jerzy Grotowski commented on the apparently ineradicable impulse in the theater to enact the obvious and banal, and the unaccountable pleasure numbers of people still take in seeing it done. Why should we go to the theater, he asked, to see men and women lighting cigarettes, answering the telephone, opening doors, and so on, things we can see a dozen times a day?

The point about Chekhov's "realism," his cigarette lightings and knocks on the door, is that its banality is completely understood and is used strategically to serve as an ironic base for truths beyond appearances, the "unreality" of invisible connections. When a Chekhov play is properly acted, we detect in that atmosphere of chatter, boiling samovars, and newspapers idly leafed through a mysterious kind of inattention to just those details whose exact reproduction in ordinary realism would be the very purpose of the performance. It is as though the characters understand, without explicit consciousness of it, that we secrete ourselves amid commonplace physicality, making our oblique communication to one another from behind sofas, over the rims of teacups, above the din of lunch being served. The "truths" of the plays are always in the relationships between a sense of self and of externality, and in the interstices of facts and values.

The basis for Chekhov's next play, *Uncle Vanya*, is *The Wood Demon*, which he had written in 1889–90. He always maintained that the plays were completely "independent," but the evidence is clear that he wished to dissociate the

immeasurably greater work, *Uncle Vanya*, from its predecessor, which in fact he allowed to fall into obscurity. In the
intervening years he had come into possession of his great and
final manner, which flowered for the first time in *The Seagull*,
and this threw a much harsher light on *The Wood Demon*
than the one in which he had originally viewed it. Not that he
had been satisfied with it at the time; he saw its weaknesses
and the way it even drew some of its strengths from dramatic
clichés, but lacking as yet the capacity for wholly new creation,
he was moved by his own attempt to discover what such new
creation might be like.

In 1888 he had written to Suvorin that "in the Crimea I
shall start writing a lyrical play." The word "lyrical" suggests a
changed aesthetic intention, but is easy to misunderstand.
What Chekhov meant was nothing rhapsodic or full of immediate emotional intensity but a quality of expressiveness as
opposed to straightforward physical action, the sign of a shift
from theatrical eventfulness to a more hidden dramatic poetry
of implication and subtle connections. *The Wood Demon*
does begin this process, but it is cluttered by characters present
for "color" or social verisimilitude, is given to the kind of
moralizing that had been mostly absent even from *Ivanov*, and
is severely injured by elements of almost pure melodrama.

While obviously not independent of the earlier work,
Uncle Vanya is profoundly different from it in ways that
testify to Chekhov's altered theory and vision of dramatic art.
He retained the major figures of *The Wood Demon*, some of
them under their original names, the main lines of the situation, most details of the setting, and even some large segments
of dialogue. But he radically simplified everything, eliminating
four of the original eleven substantial roles and severely limit-
ing the play's physical events, so that *Uncle Vanya* is less than
two thirds as long as *The Wood Demon*. It isn't too much to
say that the distance between the two plays is that between
drama as solicitation and as vision, between Gogol's lamented
"effects" and a theater of modest, austere truths.

The excisions and parings are the work of a transformed dramatic sensibility which has moved toward the creation of intense pressure in a small histrionic field. A sprawling, erratic play has been altered into a taut, obliquely proceeding drama without a clear denouement and without any quality of arbitrary color or seductiveness. Most revealing of what Chekhov is after is the radical change in the play's ending. In *The Wood Demon* lovers are united, families restored, a celebratory mood reigns over the tale. But in *Uncle Vanya* the distances between people remain, nothing has been bridged or filled in, nothing decided. Not only is the ending no longer "happy," it is *unfinished*; there is no resolution but only an implicit continuation: things will go on as they have.

A lesser but perhaps even more indicative change from the standpoint of dramaturgical choices concerns Vanya's violent relations with Serebryakov. In *The Wood Demon* he wishes to kill the professor but instead kills himself; in *Uncle Vanya*, out of what are ostensibly the same feelings of frustration and resentment, he shoots at Serebryakov . . . and misses. On one level the change is obviously from melodramatic heaviness to sharp, bitter humor, but it is more. For Vanya to kill the professor is a solution, a completion, a culminating act on his part. But as we shall see, Chekhov wishes no culminations, only extension; he wants Vanya and the others to be left with their lives and sense of self.

There is one more change that throws explicit light on Chekhov's new intentions, this one the creation of a character not present in *The Wood Demon* but one who functions in *Uncle Vanya* not as a complication but as a further element of reduction or "cooling." Like others of Chekhov's aged servants, Marina embodies the past, standing for nearly completed life. In doing this, she serves as a reminder of mortality, but also as a figure of one who has survived and knows, with almost unconscious folk wisdom, how one bears life. For Astrov she represents the undemanding conditions of affection he knew in childhood, for Sonya she is a counselor in patience and shrewd serenity. "It's all right, my child," she tells her during a scene of violent dispute and recriminations, "the geese will cackle for a while and then they'll stop. They'll cackle a bit and then they'll stop their cackling." You do not oppose them, you outlast their voices.

Mies van der Rohe's doctrine of more-is-less comes inevitably to mind in thinking about *Uncle Vanya*. Chekhov's central effort as a dramatist was always in the direction of the converse of Mies's principle, and nowhere in his career is the movement toward erecting "less as more" as evident as in the changes that made *Uncle Vanya* out of *The Wood Demon*. For to denude his dramaturgy, to strip it of spectacular, decisive events, of violent encounters, deaths, restorations, and resurrections, was to release a new sort of augmented consciousness, one which, we might say, placed itself in the neighborhood of all unspectacular events, facing all the gaps in our artificially "dramatic" lives, the mild, domestic, uncritical moments which determine our fate and define our being.

This is the origin of our habitual misreading of Chekhov; we want drama to be larger than life and if we find it smaller we can only adjust by feeling superior, by indulging the playwright, or if not him the characters. We may then weep for them, but not for ourselves, since *we know better*. We know that life ought to be more than it seems to be in Chekhov's plays, and we interpret the discrepancy as the mark of defeat on the brows of his people. And so *Uncle Vanya* is widely considered to be a central artifact of Chekhov's theater of melancholy and spiritual unsuccess as well as, in sociological terms, a specific document of middle- or upper-class anomie.

On the surface this reading seems to be accurate: the main characters fail in their ambitions, are disappointed in marriage or love, see the future as opaquely menacing and the present as the erosion of their human substance. They drink too much, live idly, secrete themselves behind designations: doctor, professor, wife. They make fools of themselves or, if not, their dignity is desperate, tenuous, held to as if to an almost-forgotten injunction.

Whether one thinks of Chekhov simply as the dispassionate observer of this beleaguered existence, as its active mourner, or as a social prophet indicting the present and sketching a desirable future based on a new kind of "will," the assumption is the same that almost all the lives *Uncle Vanya* exhibits are incomplete, unrealized, and to some degree morally culpable, and that Chekhov believes that they are. Yet such is not the case, and thinking that it is, more broadly thinking that Chekhov's great plays are tales of human ruin and defeat, has resulted in the long line of misunderstandings of his work that began with Stanislavsky's staging of the last plays, over Chekhov's own angry or rueful protests, as "heavy dramas," the Russian term for tragedy.

In fact, Chekhov called *The Seagull* and *The Cherry Orchard* "comedies," *The Three Sisters* simply a "drama," and *Uncle Vanya*, with even more deliberate neutrality, "Scenes from Country Life." This subtitle wasn't intended to suggest some sort of modest pastoral composition but, like the others, precisely to be a warning against interpreting the play as a tragedy or as what popular usage has made of that term: something over which one ought to weep. Above all, he wanted to deflect the impulse he knew the plays would arouse to rush in with political or social or, most destructively, moral judgments on its characters.

Chekhov once wrote to a friend that "to divide men into the successful and the unsuccessful is to look at human nature from a narrow, preconceived point of view. Are you a success or not? Am I? Was Napoleon? Is your servant, Vassilly? What is the criterion? One must be a god to be able to tell successes from failures without making a mistake." He knew that this penchant for playing God was nowhere more virulent than in the theater. Judgment—one or another sort of conclusion about human lives in combative terms; as crude as the matter

of who "wins" and who "loses" or as refined as that of who
becomes enlightened and who doesn't—was an inherent malady of the traditional drama he was engaged in finding a way
past.

The tradition rests on a perennial belief in the desirability
and possibility of a "good" or "right" life or at least an enlightened one, on the corollary proposition that lives can be
definitively bad, wrong, or in darkness, and on the assumption
that it is one task of culture to produce models of the alternatives. In short, it rests on the larger tradition of Western
moral consciousness, which because of its dualism, its inherent
principle of contention and conflict, is naturally "dramatic"
and so has been a mainstay of Western theater. At its most
vigorous and complex, in Shakespeare, say, moral triumphs
and defeats, rightness and wrongness, are never localized,
assigned to a single person, or embodied in wholly unambigu-
ous actions, but are dispersed throughout the drama's substance. Hamlet, for example, triumphs with extreme
ambiguousness, losing his life but "restoring" Denmark; Iago
is a villain, but his guilt is shared by Othello. Tragedy as a
dramatic mode produced models of the human universe seen
not as engaging in Manichaean warfare but in existential siege.

However, with the disappearance of tragic consciousness
(a subject beyond the scope of this book), "serious" drama
tended more and more toward the simplification of experience
and its conversion into a species of *false tragedy*, tragedy in an
outward form but with its moral complexity removed and its
sense of ontological fatality eliminated. Or else it turned into
what we might call anti-tragedy, a theater not of comedy in
the Dantean sense but of sententiousness, the world divided
into good and bad, right ways and wrong, heroes and villains,
with comforting denouements, in short into melodrama.
Where the tragic dramatists had seen disaster as the inherent
condition of existence and victory as the noble recognition and
courageous acceptance of such catastrophe, bourgeois drama

of the eighteenth and nineteenth centuries turned fate into a matter of the absence or presence of virtue, of luck, of social conditions, of personal strength or weakness; dramatic characters became the incarnations of "success" or "failure."

It was against this increasingly fixed convention that the great modern dramatists reacted, none with more subtle and daring invention than Chekhov. Beginning with *The Seagull*, he articulated a dramatic universe in which the questions of goodness and evil as ethical categories, heroism and villainy as combatants, no longer operate as decisive subjects, a universe in which there is no outcome or denouement of an absolute moral kind (or any other) and in which personal fate has been transmuted into a matter not of triumph or defeat as though in a paradigm of war, but of endurance, of lasting through one's experiences with open, accepting eyes or kicking blindly against the pricks.

What led to the reading of Chekhov as a miniaturist of social and psychic pathology is precisely the emptying out in his work of so much previous dramatic substance, and particularly the materials of moral choices and decisions. The famous "apathy" of his characters, their apparent inability to take hold of their lives and move them in "useful" directions, is a function of Chekhov's refusal to act as judge and, more radically, of his astonishing insight into the way in which time flattens out distinctions, renders human ambition futile, and forces us, or would if we would recognize the coercion as liberating, into a confrontation with the exact, and not the hoped for, quality of our lives.

Hidden, undramatic, scarcely qualifying for the word by our ordinary criteria, heroism in Chekhov is manifested by staying with one's life and resisting the temptation to exploit others; villainy, as subtle and untheatrical as its opposite, by being full of an idea of oneself and so, inevitably, using one's fellow humans for its implementation. There are of course degrees of this kind of heroism and villainy in the plays; in

Uncle Vanya Sonya is "better" than Astrov, who in turn has more "goodness" than Voynitsky, while Serebryakov is "worse" than his wife Elena. But these distinctions don't arise from an a priori moral scheme nor do they exemplify abstract ethical conditions. They exist as emphases, greater or lesser fullnesses along a continuum of possible experience, closer or more remote relationships to actuality. They are, to use the word once again, existential differences.

Her clear knowledge of her own situation is what makes for Sonya's heroism, in Chekhov's muted terms. She is not beautiful, Astrov doesn't love her, she isn't likely ever to be extricated from her lonely provincial life; and she persists. Persists, not succumbs. The notion that Chekhov's heroines (from Nina in *The Seagull* to Madame Ranevskaya and Anya in *The Cherry Orchard*, women are at the center of Chekhov's dramatic vision, for reasons we will take up later) are passive victims, unable to shape their own destinies, rises, as has been said, from a conviction that their condition of unhappiness or deprivation *can and ought to be changed* and that they are morally or psychically deficient for not at least making the attempt. Or else—the socio-political reading—their powerlessness has objective causes which a regenerated society will annul.

Against this critique based on an adamant optimism, Chekhov sets a quality of perception and morale that is not pessimistic but realistic in the most exact and rigorous sense. He has stripped his art of all purposes of consolation and exhortation, denied it a function of utility. We will not learn from his plays what is wrong with society or how to change it. In his notebook he once wrote that "Everybody goes to the theater to see my [plays] to learn something instantly . . . to make some sort of profit, and I tell you: I have not the time to bother about that canaille." An epithet as strong as that from this gentle man is indication enough of how strongly he felt about the independence of his art from *usefulness* in political or ethical realms.

The point is surely not that Chekhov was indifferent to the depressed conditions of life in Russia or disposed to offer fables of mournful quietism in the face of social malady. He was simply not interested in society—institutional reality—as the ground and referent of the experiences his characters undergo. Whatever his social and political interests might be outside the plays, and we know from works like *Journey to Sakhalin,* the account of his trip in 1891 to the Russian Far East, that they were "progressive" and responsible, the dramas don't reflect any social views, or rather they reflect so many that each is neutralized, refused effectiveness. He is advocating and deploring nothing; his characters don't change their lives because, dramatically, they are engaged in experiencing their lives as they are, not as they might be.

This doesn't at all mean that the future has no status for them; Chekhov's plays are notoriously full of talk about worlds and societies to come, about personal aspiration and hope. His characters are indeed full of the future, but as an idea, in the strictest sense of the word an illusion, since the time to come by definition does not yet exist. And it is just this tension between the future as what has not happened and the present as what has that constitutes the principal agency of Chekhov's drama, a drama which repudiates progress and solutions as it repudiates active "plot," the literary procedure that most centrally embodies the movement from present to future.

Time goes forward, but it doesn't carry the characters into accessions, earned rewards, or windfalls or, on the other hand, explicit defeats; there are no true "careers," whether of a physical, societal kind or an internal one. No one gains in wisdom or power or reaches a condition of ripeness, all of which means that the past has not been looked upon as preparation. The relationship of this to the question of physical plot is extremely intricate, establishing as it once again does how artistic vision discovers the necessary form for its articulation and is, in the end, the form itself. For the dramaturgical choices Chekhov made in converting *The Wood Demon* into *Uncle Vanya* are all designed to prevent plot—the concatenation of physical events by which, ideally, "meaning" is conveyed—from working toward fulfillments and solutions which would lower the intensity of or disperse the steady gaze Chekhov wishes to keep on what actually, *hope-lessly* (in a literal, neutral sense), is. His next play will carry this artistic action to its supreme realization.

In September 1900, with the tuberculosis from which he would die less than four years later growing more acute, Chekhov wrote in a letter that his new play was "very difficult to write, more difficult than my other plays." And when it was finished his first comment was that "the play turned out dull, verbose and awkward." He was to change his mind about *The Three Sisters* more than once, perhaps finally settling into the opinion most widely held now: that it is his greatest play. What he could not have thought is that *The Three Sisters* is one of the greatest of all plays, a drama as inexhaustible in its way as *Oedipus Rex* and *Hamlet* and *Lear* are in theirs.

Henry James once wrote that the criterion for any piece of fiction was "the amount of felt life" it contained. By *felt* life he did not simply mean raw experience but that which had been shaped into consciousness, with the further implication of such consciousness being a matter of the bestowing of aesthetic form. The standard is surely applicable to drama too, and by it *The Three Sisters* assumes its place as Chekhov's richest, most impregnable work. Coming after *Uncle Vanya* and before *The Cherry Orchard*, it throws its light backward and ahead to bring the other plays into the composition of a trilogy whose continuity is not a matter of narrative or subject but of vision, thought, and style.

"That the end of [*The Three Sisters*] reminds people of *Uncle Vanya* doesn't matter very much," Chekhov once wrote to Stanislavsky. "After all, *Uncle Vanya* is my play and not someone else's." In a manner for which there is scarcely any parallel among the important modern dramatists, Chekhov's plays, particularly the last three—and there are only five major ones altogether—do seem to merge with one another to form a long unbroken work. Its parts reflect one or another emphasis, one degree of felt life or another, but there are no major changes of style or setting or construction. In this respect he probably resembles Beckett most, Strindberg and Brecht least.

In *The Three Sisters* Chekhov's dramatic art reaches its culmination, so that the questions raised by that art make their most insistent demands on us. If drama, by definition, is "action," what sort of drama can a work be in which almost nothing physical happens? How do Chekhov's famous indirections find directions out? How does speech, dialogue, become wholly dramatic in itself, not merely the means of *expressing* dramatic actualities? Most centrally, almost all of us are extraordinarily moved by *The Three Sisters*, but why is this so, when it seems that it takes us nowhere, to no climax or revelation, no assured ending, and when there seems to be no central figure with whom we can "identify," as we are accustomed to doing as the essence of theatrical spectatorship?

To take up these questions is to see at once that they are intimately related, and to become aware once again how great and original plays change the very definition of drama, as imaginatively adventurous novels and poems change that of fiction or poetry. *The Three Sisters* has no protagonist, or, if you will, it has three, but they are scarcely heroines in any traditional sense and they provide us with very little incentive to do more than sympathize with their predicament in a detached way. Only if we come to see (or intuit, as many unlearned lovers of the play have of course done) that the predicament is without bounds or alleviation, that it constitutes the very subject and substance of the play, but in terms pitched far beyond social situation or idiosyncratic fate, can we understand the otherwise baffling depth of feeling *The Three Sisters* touches in us.

James had described Ibsen's plays as "that seemingly

undramatic thing, the portrait not of an action but of a condition." The perception applies with still greater exactness to Chekhov, most especially to *The Three Sisters*, and is the chief clue to the secrets of his astonishingly delicate and oblique yet indestructible art. The "condition" in this case is the situation of the sisters and, grouped around them at varying distances from their full conscious center, the rest of the characters as well, and this situation is, to put it as bluntly as possible at first, that of time.

Time as a dramatic situation? We could go further and say that time is the very subject of *The Three Sisters*, time in the sense Beckett intended when in his book on Proust he called it "that double-headed monster of salvation and damnation." I spoke before of Chekhov's affinities with Beckett and particularly of *The Three Sisters* with *Waiting for Godot*. In both plays, across their half-century separation so immediately alike in their "inaction" and their being filled with talk, something sought for is not attained, yet something unrecognized is preserved; in both, human existence unfolds, is extended, expressed, we could almost say *invented* on the spot, and left without decision or crystallizing outcome. For both Chekhov and Beckett the way to overcome the monster, time, is by refusing it its prerogatives, by not allowing it, *in their plays*, to save or damn.

As Jacques Guicharnaud has said in regard to Beckett's play, it is about waiting, not Godot, and more specifically about what the two tramps do while they wait for whoever or whatever it is that will justify and save them but does not come. In rather the same way, *The Three Sisters* is about what the women do while waiting or hoping to get to Moscow. For Moscow has a Godot-like sway over them, functioning in their imaginations and expectations as the site of their potential salvation or at least of their validation, their accession into dignity and true being. They were born there and they want to go home. Both the second and third acts of the play end with a cry for this place of deliverance from their unfulfillment: "To Moscow! To Moscow!" and "Let's go, oh please let's go!"

That they do not go, with its implication that they are fated to a "lesser" life, is generally considered their tragedy, but in fact their tragedy, if it really is one, lies elsewhere. It ought to be seen that nothing physically (or morally, for that matter) prevents them from leaving, nothing in the objective situation requires them to remain mired in the provinces. At the same time, they aren't weak or ineffectual, they don't lack will in the ordinary sense. Why then do they stay?

Everything suggests that they stay because to remain is the meaning of their lives, the condition of their existence, as to stay and wait for Godot is that of Beckett's tramps; staying is synonymous with their being alive, and everything exists beyond categories such as tragedy or its opposite and beyond alternatives like despair or hope. They stay, finally, because in this play, which is not a re-creation of actual lives but a creation exhibiting what it is like to be alive *whatever the circumstances*, Chekhov wishes to reveal how time, as we experience it, is always and only the present, how the future is always illusion, the past always absence or loss. The painfulness of the play is the suffering, at its deepest levels ontological and not simply social or psychic, of all of us, creatures whom time erodes while it is simultaneously promising us fullness.

The eroding action of time is most subtly manifested in *The Three Sisters* by forgetting. Andrey forgets his ambitions, the doctor his medical knowledge, Vershinin people's faces, Masha the title and author of the song she is humming, Irina, in a splendid instance of Chekhov's genius for the shattering commonplace detail, the Italian word for window. But there are more material or substantial losses. Love is lost to Masha and Vershinin, dignity to Andrey, her unloved but respected future husband to Irina, and, by implication, their house itself to the Prozorovs.

As they are consumed by the present, the characters yearn toward the future, all, that is, but the old servants, in whom desire is simple and meek, and the doctor, who is aging too but, more than that, emptied of pride. But the future, as we have said, is illusory, a matter for speculation, for talk which however passionate and "sincere" will not bring it about in its desired shape. The speeches in *The Three Sisters* about the new age to come, especially those of Vershinin and Tuzenbach about a future of honorable work and usefulness for all, are even more grandiloquent and extensive than those in *Uncle Vanya*, but they have the same function. And this is to deny themselves, to exist as evidence that the present is all we can know of life, all we can be truthful about.

It's worth noticing that the sisters' talk about the future is much less abstract, less socio-political than the men's. For them the future beckons in personal ways and promises love, or at least some element of palpable beauty. Chekhov is never obvious about it, but in all his major plays he gives to female characters a kind of stewardship of immediate bodily life, sometimes moving into the erotic and always having as its governing idea the principle of persistence that runs through *The Seagull* and *Uncle Vanya*. Whether or not he is objectively accurate, for the purposes of his art Chekhov thinks of women as being freer than men of the capacity for self-delusion through theorizing and literary constructions, and so more physically accepting.

At the same time, however (and as a proof, if one were needed, of his freedom from sentimentality), a woman, Natasha in *The Three Sisters*, is unquestionably Chekhov's most villainous character. Working mostly on the fringes of the play, she devours the family's possessions like an "animal," as they come to regard her. But she is really much more complex than that. Like the play's other evil or negative character, Solyony, she is an incarnation of aggression and acquisitiveness deriving from an incomplete sense of self. Solyony eats up all the chocolates, tries to possess Irina, and kills her fiancé; Natasha steadily appropriates the sisters' house and consumes their goodness. Both do these things out of feelings of powerlessness that can only be appeased by possessions, bulwarks against the void, and both think only of themselves, craving their "due."

That the other characters, especially the sisters, seem to bow to Natasha's depredations like helpless victims has led to a reading of the play as, on at least one level, a social and ethical drama in which a rising, aggressively insensitive but historically inevitable bourgeoisie pushes out a morally noble but enervated aristocracy. But this is once again to read Chekhov within the tradition of a theater of opposites, dramatic clashes; it is to read the play as a melancholy tale of materialism overcoming the spirit or of goodness bowing before brute strength.

But the play is one in which no such decisive encounters are allowed to take place, so that the reason the sisters don't oppose Natasha is that Chekhov, for the most stringent of artistic purposes, doesn't want them to. It is a condition of human life as the play exhibits it that rapaciousness of Natasha's kind be present in the world, but it is not the purpose of *The Three Sisters* to seek any large truth about human fate in that presence. Natasha is there, she is one of the conditions of the sisters' lives, they must survive her as they survive all other inroads and losses. And in the end, when the three women embrace one another in that last painful, loving communion and Olga's words about someday knowing "why we live, why we suffer" echo in our consciousness, we are aware of their victory, the only one Chekhov in his marvelous refusal of the world's hierarchies of success and failure, tragedy and triumph, will permit.

Yet such is his artistic quietness that even this fragile victory is hemmed in and denied full resonance. In that final scene the doctor, sitting apart from the sisters, reads a newspaper, murmurs the most frivolous song, and mutters, "What's the difference, anyway," as a counterstatement to Olga's closing expression of hope in the future. The play ends on a note of absolute non-resolution; the ambiguity and uncertainty remain. (It's significant that in the Moscow Art Theater production of *The Three Sisters* seen in New York in 1965 the doctor's final words have been deleted. The inference is inescapable that for the Soviets the play's ambiguity is unwelcome, that they wish to see it as an unequivocal declaration of faith in a future which they themselves were to bring about.)

This closing scene is a splendid demonstration of Chekhov's dramaturgy of indirection and what we might call lateral construction. There is no encounter or confrontation between Chebutykin and the women; they simply occupy the stage together, saying *what each has to say*, without the coercion by plot, the necessities of storytelling that in most naturalistic drama results in dialogue being linearly progressive, a question eliciting an answer, a comment a related one, a piece of information another.

One can even say that there is very little true dialogue in *The Three Sisters* but a series of utterances designed to fill out a world, to create it, the way much earlier (and of course unknown to Chekhov) Büchner had filled out the world of *Woyzeck* with speech that was not summoned into being by a narrative line but by the urgencies of consciousness. At times Chekhov's characters do speak directly to one another, to be sure, but much more often and even in many apparently straightforward conversations their words are as though momentarily suspended—for the time it takes to hear them—in an atmosphere which all breathe but where there is no obligation to "communicate."

The communication, that is to say, resides much more in the relations of the various speeches to each other and to the non-verbal elements of the play, in the texture of what is being composed, than in their substantive "meanings." When the doctor, sitting apart once again, mutters something he has just read in the newspaper—"Balzac was married in Berdichev"—the utterance exists with no discernible connection to what the others have been saying; it works in the play precisely to exhibit how such a fact, so useless a bit of information, has as much or as little significance as any other statement, as the grand descriptions of the future, for example. And when Tuzenbach ends one of those speeches with "We must get ready for it, we must work," Vershinin, to whom he has been addressing himself, replies, "Yes," then gets up and says to nobody in particular, "But what a lot of flowers you have!" The point is that the remarks about the future have their place, but so does the one about the flowers: they go to fill out a world.

This world goes forward in time, as that of any drama must: *The Three Sisters* covers a period of about four years and, in the dimension of "real" time, takes perhaps an hour to read and two and a half to perform. Within these physical restrictions it was Chekhov's whole effort, as it was to be Beckett's even more extremely, to try to overcome the sense of progression which is an ineradicable aspect of drama. This is both a thematic and a technical matter. For if, as has been argued, Chekhov's very subject is the "timelessness" of time, the necessity of living in the present together with the unreality of the future, then it became incumbent on him so to construct his play as to make each scene or unit of action live independently, as free as possible from causal relationships with what precedes and follows it. And in fact nearly every scene in *The Three Sisters* does exist in this way, moving through time but appearing, or being absorbed in our consciousness, like paintings, which is not to say they are static pictures, *tableaux vivants*, but that at any moment we can grasp the chief elements of the work.

The first act, which is one long scene, a gathering of the

characters into the Prozorovs' house and ambience, contains everything it is essential to know; what will happen afterward isn't so much development as the making of fullness. All desires are articulated, all personal relationships set forth. And the atmosphere reverberates with the presence of time. "Just a year ago, a year ago on this very day, Father died—on your birthday, Irina, on the fifth of May." These are Olga's opening words. The clock strikes twelve, "and the clock struck just the same way then," Olga says. And shortly afterward Irina raises the first cry of "To Moscow," Tuzenbach speaks of the storm cloud of the future sweeping society clean, Masha and Vershinin meet and almost immediately make their love obliquely known, Andrey exhibits his collapsing will, Chebutykin his sentimentality and self-hatred, Solyony his cruelty, Natasha her vulgarity.

It is all done with astonishing economy, an economy that isn't simply a matter of restraint but an active structural principle. "When a man spends the least possible number of movements over some definite action, that is grace," Chekhov had once written. This is one of the secrets of his method of indirection and helps to explain the elisions, the gaps between speeches and within them, the questions not replied to and the points not taken up, which many people have mistaken for a theme of "non-communication." Chekhov's characters communicate as much as any in dramatic literature—it is almost all they do—but only what he wants them to, only what the consciousness reigning in this imagined world requires.

An especially illuminating example of this is the scene in which the doctor drops and breaks a clock which had belonged to the sisters' mother, mutters in confusion and guilt a bitter pseudo-philosophical apologia—"Maybe I didn't break it but it only looks like I broke it. Maybe it only looks like we exist, and really we don't"—then abruptly, as a way of being "real" and in connection, says to the others, "Natasha is having an affair with Protopopov, and you don't see that. You sit there and see nothing and Natasha's having an affair with Proto-popov." He goes out, upon which Vershinin says, "Yes . . . (*He laughs.*) How strange all this is . . . When the fire started I rushed home . . ." and the matter-of-fact conversation picks up and goes on.

It isn't that they haven't heard Chebutykin or haven't noticed the affair before this, nor is it that they are repressing an unpleasant truth. Their failure to respond, Vershinin's changing the subject, is due to their *decision* not to allow Natasha's affair to concern them directly. It is there, a factor in their lives, part of their weather, but there is nothing to be done about it, they will not intrude into it with judgments, moral interference. And Chekhov will not allow the affair, potentially so rich in melodramatic energy, to move from the edges of the play, where its shadowy presence will be real but where it cannot draw attention to itself at the expense of subtler things.

One can discover at almost every moment of *The Three Sisters* Chekhov's marvelous capacity for making his dramas yield exactly the consciousness he wants, which is a power to exclude whatever would be false or irrelevant, what would disturb the balance of his world. A scene near the end is an unequaled example of this. Tuzenbach is going off to the duel with Solyony which he (and the audience) intuits will be fatal. He says goodbye to Irina, who has accepted his proposal of marriage, without love but with deep affection and respect. He looks at the trees:

TUZENBACH: See that tree, it's dried up, but the wind moves it with the others just the same. So it seems that if I die, still, some way or another I'll have a share in life. Goodbye, my darling . . . (*He kisses her hands.*) The papers you gave me are on my table under the calendar.

IRINA: I'm going with you.

TUZENBACH (*uneasily*): No, no! (*He goes away quickly, then stops by the avenue of trees.*) Irina!

IRINA: What?

TUZENBACH (*not knowing what to say*): I didn't have any coffee this morning. Tell them to make me some.

"I didn't have any coffee this morning." It would be hard to find a line in all drama as heartbreaking as that, or a scene in which such painful emotion is so stringently rendered. And it would be hard to find a play to equal *The Three Sisters* in its noble austerity and brave acceptances. Loss after loss after loss . . . and survival at the end. Chekhov once wrote in his notebook this enigmatic line: "There is not a single criterion that can serve as a measure of the non-existent, the non-human." Yet in its "inhuman" way, its creation of what we cannot otherwise know about our existence, its movement beyond our finiteness, art provides such a criterion, and Chekhov's art as enduringly as any other.

PIRANDELLO

Among the late entries in the journal or notebook which Luigi Pirandello kept during most of his life as a writer one finds this remark: "There is somebody who is living my life and I know nothing about him." The assumption of an unknown self, an *other* who fills the same space as one's own and breathes the same air, is by no means unheard of among writers, but in Pirandello it becomes central, obsessive, and, seized as a painful inspiration, one of the very principles of imaginative procedure. Pirandello is one of the great dramatic technicians of alienation, one of the foremost theatrical poets of self-division and internal abyss. He is also, as a function of the foregoing, the great modern playwright of the theater, or the theatrical, as *subject*; in his work the full, radical questioning of the stage as a place of formal pretending begins. To have instigated this is to have brought what we loosely call "modern" drama into a phase whose end is not yet in sight.

Pirandello's drama may be said to move between the key words "mirror" and "mask," both of which, in addition to being nouns of doubleness, implying something—a face, a self?—standing outside or beneath, are eminently theatrical metaphors. His dramatic work has been spoken of as constituting *il teatro dello specchio*, the theater of the mirror, and the word or object occurs over and over again in his writing. Furthermore, he gave to every volume of his collected plays the same title, *Naked Masks*, the implication of which is vulnerability in deception, the impossibility of being truly disguised.

Pirandellian drama comes into being at a point when that revolution in Western thought and art which we call Modernism is in full tide, having passed from unsettling discovery and invention to acceptance or at least legitimacy. Influenced himself by Nietzsche, Bergson, and—doubtless at first unconsciously, by cultural osmosis—Freud, Pirandello quickly takes his place among the masters of the displacement of values and the reorganization of consciousness. There is a story that after a performance in Germany by Pirandello's theater group Albert Einstein went up to him and told him that "we are kindred souls." The incident may be apocryphal, but in that case its having been invented testifies to Pirandello's position and stature.

It testifies more particularly to the generally held belief that Pirandello's central and peculiarly contemporary quality as a writer is his "relativism," and that his major achievement lies in having infused the drama, that obdurately absolutist medium, with a principle of uncertainty and doubt. There is truth in this, but elevated into a full-scale interpretation it has resulted in a kind of debased Pirandellianism. Here the description is of a mildly Satanic figure—neat, pointy Vandyke, eyes narrowed in an ironic, worldly glance—who presides over a theater of mockery and deflation, an exhibition hall for the overturning of intellectual pieties and the destruction of conventional, optimistic wisdom.

There is a coarser but somewhat related portrait of Pirandello as the dramatist par excellence of "illusion and reality," as if their relationship had not been either the outright subject or unstated ground of great segments of drama before him. Pirandello indeed sometimes seems to encourage this view of his art: "Why is he always harping on this illusion and reality business?" a character in one of his own plays asks. But it is a strategic move on the playwright's part; he knows what is being said about him and, most to his purposes, that the talk issues from the very misunderstanding of the nature of human existence his drama is partly designed to expose. Things are not either illusion or reality, but both, and to make this truth present on the stage is one driving purpose of Pirandello's complex dramatic art.

The complexity is great enough to account for the persistent popular and academic attempt to reduce it, to bring it into that system of abstract valuation and narrow identification by which we make cultural history manageable. It is easier for us to think of Shaw as "wit," and Chekhov as "mood," Ibsen as "social problem," Strindberg as "sexual struggle," and so on, than to try to discover the ways in which their respective arts transcend what may seem to be their own leading thesis or coloration. In the case of Pirandello, the "harping" on illusion and reality, on masks, mirrors, doubleness, estrangement, etc., has resulted in a widespread conviction that for better or worse (although mostly worse) he is an "intellectual" playwright, cerebral, moved by ideas rather than emotions, a dramatist who has forsworn the traditional passions of the stage in order to employ it for the exhibition of a species of exacerbated thought.

Once again, the mistake is to think in mutually exclusive alternatives: the heart or the head, passion or intellect. It's a commonplace to say that the source of an error like this is in our general need for dichotomy, our Manichaean division of ourselves and the world into competing systems or powers. But there is a specifically aesthetic origin—or rather one rooted in the sociology and psychology of traditional response to theater—of the notion that Pirandello is cerebral at the expense of emotion. And this is our assumption that the very purpose of the stage is to be an arena for the display of passions in conflict, that because of its physicality, its *fleshiness* and principle of palpable encounter, the theater gives us our own selves represented as embodied emotions.

What the theater of course gives us, or ought to give us, is consciousness; consciousness *enacted*, so to speak. Moreover, in this enterprise, emotion, or passion, figures as an element placed or located in relation to other things. The theater of the Greeks or Elizabethans or of the seventeenth century is one in which such situating of emotion is paramount, and it is the very mark of the decline of the stage in the eighteenth and nineteenth centuries that this action is relinquished and the direct presentation of emotion for its own sake becomes dominant. What we really mean by melodrama is theater in which emotion is offered without consciousness—which might be described as the *understanding of emotion*. In this case, action, which in Aristotle's sense meant the physical unfolding of morally and spiritually fraught events, is, as Henry James observed, converted into mere "sensation."

The modern theater, beginning with the isolated and only much later to be discovered plays of Büchner in the 1830's, can be said to comprise an effort to return the stage to its original function of the enactment of consciousness. In this light, innovation can be seen to involve strategies of the formal conquest of "bad habits," the restoration of health and efficacy to a corrupted or denatured organism. This is what Ionesco meant when he remarked that the avant-garde always seeks to return to some earlier condition, that it is not antihistorical but simply opposed to its own immediately preceding history, the time of an art's deflection or impoverishment.

As one of the dramatic imaginations who rescued the stage from its own long illness, Pirandello's innovative energy naturally took its own special form. In the roughest of classifications we can say that Ibsen infused social experience with moral awareness, Strindberg released unconscious truths, Chekhov set forth the action of time in human existence. Piran-

dello's accomplishment was to overcome the gap which had
been present between intellect and passion, and he did this
not, as his detractors say, by elaborating a cerebral drama but
by breaking down the reigning distinction. He himself wrote
that "one of the novelties [a word that might better be translated from the Italian as "newnesses," "new things"] that I
have given to modern drama consists in converting the intellect into passion."

He might with almost as much justice have said that he
had also given to passion a forgotten intellectual dimension or
mode. The point is that in Pirandello's work consciousness
plays back and forth between feeling and idea and is the very
result of their relations, their reciprocity and tension. We
know what we feel and feel what we know, he is saying, or
rather, we can *think* our feelings and feel our thoughts. The
source of the criticism of Pirandello for being overintellectual
lies in a wish to keep the categories separate, to keep intellect
from introducing a principle of abstraction into the pulsing
body of direct and hard-breathing representation of feelings
we consider serious theater to be.

This desire to keep uncontaminated the theater conceived
of as a place for feeling and not thought is persistent and
perhaps ineradicable. In 1970 the young Austrian playwright
Peter Handke, whose highly "intellectual" drama has discon-
certed audiences and critics alike, was asked by an interviewer
whether his work wasn't too cerebral at the expense of emotion. "I can't separate the rational and emotional effects," he
replied, and they are indeed inseparable in his work. "Doesn't
a stunning new thought, a new insight, a new view that is
based on reason, often make you feel wholly emotional
effects?" he went on. As different as Pirandello's theater is
from Handke's, they are both within the century-long line of
questioning of received wisdom about the place of thought on
the stage.

During the 1880's August Strindberg gave up writing

plays for a period of three or four years because he considered the stage to be "reprehensible." It was, he said, "mere pose, superficiality and calculation"; compared to fiction or poetry, it had no place for technical originality and, most crucially, for thought. Before this suspension of his dramatic work Strindberg had written a number of lengthy plays, mostly on historical themes and almost all of an unexceptionably traditional kind. When he returned to the theater he had found a principle out of which to elaborate a new dramatic consciousness, first expressed in the savage beauties and revelatory dissonances of *The Father* and *Miss Julie.*

Pirandello was never as explicit about his misgivings concerning the theater as a place for new consciousness as Strindberg had been (or Chekhov, who "swore fearfully" at the "conventions of the stage"). But the evidence is that for a long time after he had begun his career as an imaginative writer Pirandello thought of the theater as a very much lesser form than fiction and only turned seriously to it when, like Strindberg, he had succeeded in fashioning for himself a radically new approach to the nature of dramatic art and had gained the morale—the confidence, even arrogance—necessary to defy prevailing expectations and definitions.

Luigi Pirandello comes out of a Sicilian rather than an Italian literary tradition and, as shadowy as such regional distinctions may be, out of a Sicilian rather than an Italian psychic and imaginative ground. One biographical fact that may be significant is that he came from an upper-class and presumably sophisticated family, unlike his great Sicilian literary predecessor and influence, Giovanni Verga. His father, a wealthy owner of sulphur mines, could afford to send him to study abroad, and Luigi, who had indicated literary talent by writing poetry at an early age, went at eighteen in 1885 to the University of Rome and later to Bonn, where he was greatly influenced by that institution's notable school of philology.

Another pertinent biographical fact, though one of which perhaps too much has been made in an attempt to explain his "gloom" and dark humor, was his deeply oppressive marriage. This was an arranged affair; the bride was the daughter of a business associate of his father and Pirandello had scarcely seen her before the wedding day. A few years later she began to show signs of mental disturbance, which rapidly developed into full-scale psychosis. Her chief symptom was a paranoid suspicion that Pirandello was betraying her, even with their own daughter, and to appease her he refrained from going out at night for many years. Urged to have her committed, he declared it his duty to stay by her, and it was not until 1918, with the illness growing more severe, that he at last placed her in a mental institution, where she soon after died. Later Pirandello was to say that "a madwoman had led his hand for fifteen long years."

Before fame as a playwright came to him in the 1920's Pirandello had achieved a solid if not spectacular reputation for his short stories and novels and for a handful of influential essays on literary-philosophical themes. His earliest stories, written during the 1890's, were thoroughly Sicilian in milieu and tone, full of local color and, although largely "naturalistic" in style, characterized by a rather non-naturalistic interest in extreme and even bizarre passions and by an almost mythical sense of fatality. Later he transferred his fictional scene to Italy; his stories became more "modern," urban, psychological, and, as we would now describe them, existential.

He was to continue to write stories even after the stage had become his major activity (he once said that he wanted to write one for every day in the year, and ended about a hundred short) and, against the popular wisdom which holds that the two enterprises ought to remain wholly separate and distinct, maintained an unusually close relationship between his fiction and his theater work. The majority of his thirteen one-act plays and several of his full-length ones were directly derived from his short stories, and the seeds of a number of others are to be found in the fiction. This in fact has contributed to the criticism that his plays were mostly "dramatized" fiction, that he was not a "true" playwright because he thought narratively or novelistically and not in histrionic ways.

This judgment stems from the kind of rigidity in thinking about drama that was described earlier. To the academic or categorical mind, drama and fiction—like all the arts—ought to obey entirely different principles, so that the muddying of such distinctions, which is in fact one of the consciously engendered marks of modern sensibility, has been a source of disgust and even scandal. As we have seen, Pirandello himself felt a conflict between the two modes of expression, becoming able to reconcile them only after he had freed himself from his own submission to conventional notions of what drama ought to be and do.

In any case, it is possible to see in Pirandello's earlier fiction a number of ideas, themes, and imaginative dispositions that would naturally gravitate toward theatrical expression (not "dramatization") once techniques for their histrionic incarnation had been achieved. His first novel, *The Late Mattia Pascal* (1904), is a case in point. This startlingly "advanced" tale of a man who, when an accident victim is mistaken for him and buried under his name, is given the chance to create a new identity, is suffused in that atmosphere of agitated metaphysical concern and painful consciousness of the self's ambiguities which will characterize the great plays. In the same way, a later novel, *Shoot* (1916), the story of a movie cameraman who desperately wishes to get at the truth, the "real" lives of the performers whose fictive existences he records, is deeply involved with what will be one of Pirandello's central dramatic ideas.

For a long time Pirandello's writing for the theater was occasional and subordinate; his first play, *The Vise*, was written in 1898, but not produced until 1910, and there is no record of his having written another dramatic work in the interval. From then on, until his sudden emergence as a leading playwright toward the end of World War I, he wrote a handful of one-act plays and two or three full-length ones, whose generally minor status in his own mind is indicated by their having mostly been written in Sicilian dialect, something he had long since given up in his fiction. Later some of these plays were to be translated into Italian by Pirandello himself and others. But almost nothing in this early dramatic work indicates more than a conventional talent, although one might consider that its idiosyncratic violence and increasing psychological emphasis might be portents of something larger to come.

He had not yet found a way to make the stage serve the ideas which agitated and tormented him, ideas—perspectives on human dilemmas, really—that had already found their way into his fiction. These perspectives are to be found in their clearest and most direct form in an essay he wrote in 1908 called "On Humor." A humorist, which was what he considered himself to be, was, he argued, a person who worked, consciously or not, in the space between the convictions mankind has about itself and the world and the truth, which, whatever it might be, is not to be discovered in those convictions. "One of the greatest humorists, without knowing it," Pirandello wrote, "was Copernicus, who took apart not the machine of the universe, but the proud image which we had made of it."

The essay contains statements of what are to become the leading intellectual motifs of his great plays and reveals his large debt to Bergson, among others. "What we know about ourselves is but a part, perhaps a very small part of what we are," he wrote, and again: "To man is given at birth the sad privilege of feeling himself alive, with the illusions which come from it—namely to assume a reality outside himself and that interior feeling of life, changeable and various." Perhaps most Bergsonian of all is the following sentence: "The forms in which we try to stop and fix the continuous flow are the concepts, the ideals within which we want to keep coherent all the fictions we create, the condition and status in which we try to establish ourselves."

As a humorist his task was to try to deal with the discrepancy between the forms of the mind and the flow of life, between fiction and reality. Some years later he was to compose in the introduction to *Six Characters in Search of an Author* a coolly appraising intellectual self-portrait which went even further than had the essay on humor toward defining his particular literary character and temperament:

> To me it was never enough to present a man or a woman and what is special and characteristic about them simply for the pleasure of presenting them; to narrate a particular affair, lively or sad, simply for the pleasure of narrating it; to describe a landscape simply for the pleasure of describing it. There are some writers (and not a few) who do feel this pleasure and, satisfied, ask no more. They are, to speak more precisely, historical writers. But there are others who, beyond such pleasure, feel a more profound spiritual need on whose account they admit only figures, affairs, landscapes which have been soaked, so to speak, in a particular sense of life and acquire from it a universal value. These are, more precisely, philosophical writers. I have the misfortune to belong to these last.

The "misfortune" he speaks of has of course to do with the additional burden of consciousness such philosophical writers (and they include all the makers of modern drama) have had to bear; instead of being the re-creation of the world and of experience through a language and an imaginative mode ready at hand, the task of a writer like Pirandello is to find the language, the literary means, for a new creation. The position of the innovator is therefore that of one who has to invent, bring into being, what his temperament and sense of life find absent from the inherited artistic means at his disposal, and this has to be accomplished in the face of the innate conservatism, the entropic tendency, of already accomplished consciousness.

As distinct from his literary and philosophical influences, Pirandello's dramaturgical ones are, in the beginning at least, thin and inconclusive. At the time he wrote his first play the Italian theater was thoroughly conventional, imitative (in large part of French melodrama and domestic farce), and, in fact, lacking in any substantial recent history of achievement. More than that, with the minor exceptions of Goldoni and Gozzi in the eighteenth century the Italian stage had never had a master, a maker of models or paradigms for successors to draw upon or fruitfully reject. Pirandello would have had to go back to the high era of the *commedia dell'arte*, with its tradition of dark humor and its improvisatory emphasis, for anything that might be useful to his purposes.

But in the years preceding the writing of his major plays there were several developments in Italian theater which to one degree or another proved helpful to him. One came from the Futurist movement, which in so far as it addressed itself to theater elaborated a theory and a practice subversive of certain bourgeois values—fully fashioned characters, well-wrought plots, theatrical illusion, etc. The other, and more important, was the style or mode known as the *Teatro del Grottesco*, the Theater of the Grotesque.

Not a formal movement like Futurism, it was a loose grouping of playwrights who shared an affinity for extreme and sometimes Gothic situations and for psychological abnormalities, penchants that arose out of a revulsion from the proprieties and domestic pieties of the middle-class stage. Insubstantial and willed rather than truly imagined as were plays like Luigi Chiarelli's *The Mask and the Face* or Luigi Antonelli's *The Man Who Met Himself,* their very titles have a Pirandellian ring and it was their agitated, vaguely metaphysical quality that seems to have been an immediate propulsion toward his immeasurably greater accomplishment.

The first play of his that can be said to reveal any of the central meanings we attach to the adjective Pirandellian is *Così È, Se Vi Pare,* which has been variously translated as *Right You Are (If You Think You Are)* and *It Is So (If You Think So).* Eric Bentley has made out an intelligent case for *Liola,* written around the same period (1916–17). But although this drama of passions and amorous intrigue in a Sicilian village (which Pirandello seems to have written after a flying visit to his native soil) does possess certain elements of his mature imaginative perspective ("Pretending is virtue, and if you can't pretend you can't be king," a character says), its rural ambience, "sunniness," and basic naturalism place it considerably outside the true Pirandellian canon.

Right You Are (as for convenience it shall be referred to from now on) is derived from a short story called "Signora Frola and Her Son-in-law, Signor Ponza," which Pirandello had written about a year before. For much of its course the play seems to be participating in a familiar genre of domestic melodrama. The atmosphere is one of gossip and intrigue; the plot centers on certain mysteries having to do with the identities of some of the central characters and the play's structure seems conventionally organized to make these mysteries suspenseful.

A Signor Ponza has arrived in a provincial city to work in the local administration. It is learned that he has rented two apartments, one for himself and his wife, whom nobody ever sees, the other for his mother-in-law. Rumor quickly spreads that the arrangement is designed to keep the women apart, and this is confirmed when some inquisitive townspeople confront the mother-in-law under the guise of a sympathetic inquiry. She tells them that Ponza's passionate demands upon his young wife had driven her into a mental institution, that he had thought her dead, and that upon her cure and return he had himself slipped into madness, its form being the belief that the woman was his second wife. His mother-in-law keeps up the pious fiction out of regard for him, she says.

But the snoopers are swiftly thrown into confusion when they hear from Ponza that it is the mother-in-law who is mad. Her daughter has died four years earlier and her madness consists in refusing to believe it. In order to protect his new wife from the caresses and ministrations of the madwoman, whom he pities and loves, he keeps them apart. From then on, thoroughly at sea, the townspeople work furiously to try to find the truth. As Laudisi, a *raissoneur*-like character who clearly stands in for Pirandello, says to them, "You are in the extraordinary fix of having before you, on the one hand, a world of fancy, and on the other a world of reality, and you, for the life of you, are not able to distinguish one from the other."

According to the conventions of domestic melodrama, the ultimate "action" of the play would be the clearing up of the mystery, the revelation of the truth lying beneath the surface, and the audience's pleasure, beyond any incidental *frissons*, would lie in the satisfaction of its desire precisely that there be such a revelation, that there *is* truth to be found. As Laudisi says, "They all want the truth—*a* truth, that is: something specific, something concrete! They don't care what it is. All they want is something categorical, something that speaks plainly!" But such an expectation is wholly frustrated; in the play's culminating scene the woman whose identity is so passionately being investigated appears and with "dark solemnity" tells the townspeople that *both* stories are true, that she is the person her husband and her mother each, in total contradiction, say she is.

What is being said is that while "facts" about human

beings may be obtainable, exact truth is not, and that our desire to fix the reality of others is a mark of some profound deficiency in ourselves. "I find all you people here at your wits' ends," Laudisi says at one point, "trying to find out who and what other people are; just as though other people had to be this, or that, and nothing else." Against this cruel but also obtuse impulse, one stemming, Pirandello implies, from our disconsolate wish that human realities be in their places, like things (and also perhaps from a sort of atavistic nominalism: power through categorization), is placed the skepticism of Laudisi and the human acceptances of Signora Frola. "There is a misfortune here, as you see," she tells the assemblage, "which must stay hidden: otherwise the remedy which our compassion has found cannot avail." The "misfortune" is the very structure of human reality; the remedy lies in accepting the limits of what we can know, living in mystery and respecting that of others.

In these ways *Right You Are* converts the merely factual, vulgar suspensefulness of the particular story into the much more resonant and unlocalized enigma of the nature of human truth. In a dramaturgical action that almost perfectly illustrates what was said before about melodrama and consciousness, Pirandello forces the theatrical form of intrigue and emotional tension to yield up understanding of a moral and philosophical kind. It is a creative act extraordinarily analogous to that of Ibsen, who took the *pièce à bien faite* and compelled it to serve intellectual and aesthetic ends. In both cases the playwright, in making an increment to existing moral imagination, is simultaneously making a *correction* in the body of the art he practices; and this is an opening to new imaginative accessions, both for himself and for others.

What is radical about the Pirandello of *Right You Are* is, however, circumscribed, confined mostly to an idea about the purpose of drama and especially about what it ought not provide: the consolation of an assured ending establishing a specific truth or solving a mystery, a confirmation of the human world's logic and orderliness. For the most part the play remains structurally and in its texture within a familiar mode, so that what is new in it is, so to speak, detachable, capable of being told like an anecdote. It is a new event, a new outcome from an accepted form, not a new species of theatrical utterance.

Again the parallel with Ibsen is striking. The great Norwegian's "social" plays introduced moral and psychic meanings into melodrama; when with *The Master Builder* he moved on to his so-called "symbolic" last plays, the old structure of the well-made drama fell away and a new, infinitely more open, poetically ambiguous and aesthetically complete structure rose in its place. The movement by which Pirandello accomplished a similar revolution occurs in his imagination in the several years following *Right You Are* and the result appears to us, seemingly miraculously full-blown, in *Six Characters in Search of an Author*.

In 1953 a minor French playwright wrote the following lines to commemorate an anniversary: "Just thirty years ago today an elevator came down on the stage of the Théâtre des Champs-Élysées and deposited on it six unexpected characters whom Pirandello had conjured up. And, together with them, dozens, hundreds of characters loomed up before us, but we could not yet see them . . . It will be impossible to understand anything about today's theater if one forgets that little flying box out of which it stepped one April morning in 1923." The same year this was written a more illustrious dramatist, Jean Anouilh, could think of no better way to stress the importance of the opening night in Paris of Samuel Beckett's *Waiting for Godot* than to liken it to the Pirandello opening thirty years before.

Six Characters in Search of an Author is unquestionably Pirandello's best-known play and the one that has had the

widest and deepest influence on the course of the contemporary theater. Its reception in France, two years after it had
appeared in Italy, was, as the above quotations indicate,
ecstatic and profound, and for years afterward it held its position as an unrivaled source of ideas and possibilities for the
French theater. But the influence was felt everywhere. George
Bernard Shaw called it "the most original play ever written,"
and in America it quickly became a standard work in the
repertoire of "experimental" theater groups and, in time, the
very emblem, for numbers of cultured persons, of theatrical
avant-gardism, the way Picasso's green-faced, three-nosed
women had become exemplary of "modern" painting.

Pirandello was perhaps as widely misunderstood as
Picasso. Several years after *Six Characters* had entered public
consciousness, Pirandello wrote a preface to the published text
in which he attempted to deal with the distortions and mis-
readings it had encountered. After setting forth his position as
a "philosophic" writer rather than a "historical" one, he went
on to deny that the play was symbolic or allegorical, a vehicle
for "the presentation of some moral truth," and to make a
distinction between what he called his spirit's "inherent torment" and its "activity," that which had succeeded in "forming a drama out of the six characters in search of an author."
The distinction is one between autobiography, however disguised, and creation, and it is of course a warning against the
temptation, more extreme in his case than in that of any other
modern playwright except Strindberg, to find his work *settled*,
rendered unmysterious, by what we might know or surmise
about his life.

Beyond these matters the introduction, which is as important a document of modern drama as Strindberg's preface to
Miss Julie, articulates a great many of Pirandello's reigning
preoccupations in regard to experience and to art and, most
centrally, to their relationship. He speaks of the "passion and
torment" he has felt in the face of what he has undergone and

seen: "the deceit of mutual understanding irremediably founded on the empty abstraction of words, the multiple personality of everyone corresponding to the possibilities of being to be found in each of us, and . . . the inherent tragic conflict between life (which is always moving and changing) and form (which fixes it, immutable)."

This conflict between life and form, or physical reality and art, is a ruling obsession, the one which more than any other instigates his mature theater, becoming in fact one of its principal subjects. "All that lives," he writes, "by the fact of living has a form, and by the same token must die—except the work of art which lives forever in so far as it *is* form." In a marvelously arresting image he speaks of how when one opens *The Divine Comedy* to the story of Paolo and Francesca one will find the woman saying her "sweet, sad" words to Dante, and how if one opens the book to that page a hundred thousand times, a hundred thousand times Francesca will tell Dante her story, in those words.

He has pondered these subjects, letting his imagination move through the possibilities of a drama that will incorporate them, retaining all inherent tensions and contradictions, not seeking a "solution" or setting forth any sort of moral or social truth. "The result," he writes, is "what it had to be: a mixture of tragic and comic, fantastic and realistic, in a humorous [by his special definition] situation that was quite new and infinitely complex, a drama which is conveyed by means of its characters, who carry it within them and suffer it, a drama, breathing, speaking, self-propelled, which seeks at all costs to find the means of its own presentation."

In these headlong words one can detect the excitement with which Pirandello must have realized what he was on to, what was revolutionary in this play, which was discovering *its own means* of being presented. Elsewhere in the preface he tells us that its origin lay in a practice he used to engage in of granting weekly "auditions" to his prospective fictional characters. The practice is actually the subject of a short story of 1911, "The Tragedy of a Character," in which an author is visited by would-be characters, one of whom, an old doctor, pleads with special vehemence to be made the hero of a story and tells the writer, in words that will appear almost verbatim in the play, that "we are living beings—more alive than those who breathe and wear clothes. Less real, perhaps, but more alive."

In 1908 the Spanish writer Miguel de Unamuno had published a novel called *Niebla* (*Mist*) toward the end of which a character visits the author to inform him of his intention to commit suicide and is told that he has no right to take his life since he is a creation of the author from whom his life derives. It is almost certain that Pirandello had not read *Niebla* when he wrote his own story, but even if he had it would not diminish the originality of his accomplishment in *Six Characters*. For while in the Unamuno novel the confrontation was a discrete incident, throwing a valuable but limited perspective on imaginative processes, in Pirandello's play the relationship between author and characters, or between fictional beings and "real" ones, becomes the very substance of the work, its subject and principle of unfolding.

Six Characters in Search of an Author is popularly thought of as containing a "play within a play," rather like *Hamlet*, although the inserted drama is much more extensive and significant than in Shakespeare. In fact, this is not the structure of *Six Characters*, which is really a play *about* a play or, rather, about playing, about the stage, the human impulse to construct replicas of ourselves and, most centrally, the choices we make or avoid between imagination and reality. What Pirandello's drama does contain is a *story* within a play and two sets of "characters" between whom the destiny of this story moves back and forth in an unresolved tension which corresponds to the one we feel in our own lives between "truth" and fiction.

The play begins with the curtain open to expose a bare stage where a group of actors (a conventional stock company, we quickly learn) is rehearsing an unnamed comedy by Pirandello. The audience sees everything that would be visible at a "real" rehearsal—the stage's back wall, ropes hanging from the flies, fire extinguishers, the actors' personal possessions strewn about, etc.—and in fact the implication is that the rehearsal is going on in the very theater to which the audience has come in order to see *Six Characters*. In this way Pirandello puts his first visual emphasis on theatricality, artifice; in a far-reaching break with recent stage history, he shatters the pretense that the stage is *something else* or somewhere else, an image of reality outside the theater which we accept as actual through the operation of dramatic illusion, the suspension of disbelief.

The stage is nothing but the stage, a formal space, Pirandello is saying, and the "drama" of his play will consist partly in a debate over its uses and a struggle over its control. As Francis Fergusson has written: "The action of the play is to 'take the stage' . . . the real actors and the director want to take it for the realistic purposes—vain or (with the box office in mind) venal—of their rehearsal. Each of the characters wants to take it for the rationalized myth which is, or would be, his very being." In the light of this, in whatever way the characters arrive, or are discovered (they may come down in an elevator, as in Paris, or be revealed at the back or side of the stage through lighting, etc.), they must appear to be as "lifelike" as the rehearsing actors. They "must not appear as phantoms," Pirandello wrote, "but as created realities, immutable creatures of fantasy."

The first reaction of the theatrical company to the intrusion of the six characters is one of annoyance, which naturally turns into incredulity when the Father, the family's chief spokesman, reveals their mission. They have been brought into being by a dramatist who for some reason abandoned their story before finishing it (or perhaps before ever actually putting it on paper), and they are now seeking another author who will bring their tale to a close, "complete" them as fictional beings. "We bring you a drama, sir," the Father tells the Manager. "We want to live. The drama is in us and we are the drama . . . Isn't that your mission, to give life to fantastic characters on the stage, beings less real but truer?"

The Manager agrees to hear their story and to decide if a play can be made from it. The Father tells the following narrative. He is a businessman married to a woman (called the Mother in the stage directions, where the six are listed as the characters of a "comedy in the making") who has borne him one child, the Son, who is now twenty-two or -three. When he learned that his wife and one of his clerks were in love, he forced her to live with the man, keeping the Son himself. The wife and her lover had three illegitimate children: the Stepdaughter, who is now about twenty, the Boy, about fourteen, and the Child, three or four.

After some years the Father began to pay suspiciously ardent attentions to the Stepdaughter, now an attractive schoolgirl, upon which the horrified Mother moved the family to another city. On the death of her paramour they moved back and fell into deep poverty. The girl went to work in Madame Pace's millinery shop, a front for a high-class brothel which the Father had long patronized. One day Madame Pace set up an assignation for him with one of her girls. As the Father was about to take the girl, whom he did not recognize as the Stepdaughter, off to bed, the Mother burst into the shop and made the situation known.

The horrified Father agreed to take back his wife and try to build a home for all four children. But the tensions and submerged passions were too great, so that the house soon turned into a place of barely concealed resentments and hostilities. The situation climaxed one day in a terrible scene: while playing in the garden the Child fell into a pond, and her fourteen-year-old brother, who had seen her drowning and

allowed it to happen, then shot himself, presumably in remorse. At this point the creator of the story abandoned it.

Extrapolated from the play in this way, the narrative
constitutes a melodrama whose main themes are incest and
domestic strife but whose denouement is not yet known. The
mistake so often made by audiences and readers is to confuse
this melodrama with the play itself, to take it as the *play's
story*. But the story of the play is the outcome of all the
imaginative elements that compose it, and the melodrama of
the family is only one constituent. If anything, Pirandello
deliberately chose a flamboyant and unsubtle plot for the
internal story, for a more "artistic" and profound one would
have undermined his purpose. For what will be seen to matter
is not the fate of the six characters, considered as lying within
a discrete fictional form, but the destiny (to remain within our
schema of literary expectations) of their story within the form
of the play.

Pirandello's true subject begins to become apparent during the Father's recital. It quickly becomes clear that he and
the Stepdaughter are the only members of the family who
want the story told and completed by the actors. The Child is
too young to understand, the Boy seems dazed and apathetic
(an incomplete "character"), the Son is surly and withdrawn,
and the Mother full of shame. It is between the Father and
the Stepdaughter, the two most "conscious" and articulate of
the six characters, that a debate first rages, and it is a debate
over the "truth" of their experience, over its facts.

At one point, exasperated by the derisive challenges of the
Stepdaughter and the obtuseness of the Manager, the Father
exclaims, "Don't you see that the whole trouble lies here. In
words, words . . . how can we ever come to an understanding
if I put in the words I utter the sense and value of things as I
see them; while you who listen to me must inevitably translate
them according to the conception of things each one of you
has within himself." But the question is larger and more com-

plicated than that of "non-communication." The Father is furiously intent on clearing himself, anguished by the author's having left him without an opportunity for self-defense; having arisen in the mind of a writer, like Francesca in Dante's, he is doomed like her to repeat eternally the "truths" the author has decided upon.

The Stepdaughter, on the other hand, is scornful of his rationalizations and pleas, and wishes, much more sensuously, more fundamentally, *to live*. At this point the debate—the dramatic conflict—is between meanings and experience; abstractions, or values, and palpabilities. But it grows much more subtle. When the Father, who is given to disquisitions on illusion and reality and particularly on the greater "truth" of the six, is chided by the Manager, he asserts, "I'm not philosophizing; I'm crying out the reasons of my suffering." Indeed he is, and in doing so he is implicitly assailing the traditions of the popular stage—and of popular fictional forms in general—in which sufferings (or any emotional events) are presented without consciousness or intellectual structure . . . as melodrama, in other words.

This is made explicit near the end of the play when the Stepdaughter, who has revealed that she tried sexually to tempt the writer into continuing their story, says that "in my opinion he abandoned us in a fit of depression, of disgust for the ordinary theater as the public knows it and likes it." But the very action of *Six Characters* confirms the diagnosis. For when the actors and Manager attempt to fashion a play from the family's story they are absurdly inadequate, even to the large outlines of the melodrama; they "play" out of obedience to conventions, to ideas of how certain stock roles ought to be done, and, worse, try to cut out every bit of the "philosophy" with which the Father has moved the family out of the inner melodrama and into the wider milieu of Pirandello's artistic intention. "Drama is action, sir, action and not confounded philosophy!" the Manager impatiently shouts.

In one of the most astonishing scenes of the entire modern theater, Pirandello securely establishes the propositions that drama may in fact be a species of philosophy and that thought is a form of action. The acting company has reached the final stages of its lame attempt to "dramatize" the story of the six characters. As they are preparing the final scene, in which the Child is supposed to drown and the Boy to kill himself, a shot rings out. A great uproar follows. In desperate confusion, the company and the Manager carry off the Boy, who has been discovered lying with a pistol in his hand. "Is he really wounded?" the Manager asks. "He's dead," an actor screams, to which another replies, "No, no, it's only make-believe, it's only pretense!" Upon hearing this, the Father ("with a terrible cry") fixes the ambiguity forever: "Pretense? Reality, sir, reality!"

To anyone not deadened by the kind of scholarship that converts artistic phenomena into cultural data, to hear this shot during a performance of *Six Characters*—no matter how bad the production or how often one has seen or read the play—is to have one's ideas about drama changed in an instant or an earlier change reconfirmed.

What is dramatic "reality" and dramatic "illusion"? What does it mean to "act" on a stage? What is the relationship between the uses of the verb "act" to denote straightforward movements within the order of nature and sham movements, pretenses, within the order of artifice? Finally, what are the relationships between reality and truth, human characters and the characters of a fiction, imagination and actuality? These are the questions with which *Six Characters in Search of an Author* deals, and their having been raised is the basis for the play's impact on the theater and the wider culture.

This "philosophy" of *Six Characters* is much more complex than has often been seen, and it perpetually evades being made formulary. To begin with, it has to do with the Father's (and to a lesser extent the Stepdaughter's and even the other characters') *thinking* about the situation, forcing the banal "facts" of the story to yield up perceptions in a metaphysical realm. On another level, it deals with the question of how truth differs from reality. Fictional characters, Pirandello is saying, are "truer" than we are, though less real. For one thing, as the Father says, "a character has really a life of his own, marked with his special characteristics. But a man . . . may be nobody." Beyond that, characters are fixed in changelessness, whereas we are never who we were. One relationship between life and art is that we discover (or refuse to acknowledge) our own slippery truths through confrontations with our inventions of selves in art.

Yet the relationship between life and art is not simply fixed in this structure of aloof, artificial objects on the one hand and formal contemplation of them on the other. A remark of John Cage's throws light on one of Pirandello's implications in this play. "Theater exists everywhere around us," Cage said, "and it is the purpose of the formal theater to remind us that this is so." In establishing a perpetual tension between the characters, who incarnate the aesthetic or imaginative, and the acting company, who represent life or reality, Pirandello succeeds in forcing our consciousness to an acceptance of the lack of firm distinctions between "natural" and artificial behavior and between "reality" and pretense.

Moreover, he succeeds in making us aware of our longing to make fixed structures of our lives, which exists alongside our recognition that this is a doomed enterprise. Art is permanent, but we remain mutable in the face of our immortal creations. We oscillate perpetually between acting and "acting," playing, which is an attempt to escape mutability by fleeing into forms. But we are thrown back into a reverse impulse. The attempt of the six characters to break into "life" stems from their passionate desire to exchange truth, the fixed form of their existence, for reality, with its elusiveness but also its possibility of amendment, surprise, reparation. But once more the pendulum moves in Pirandello's imagination. In his next great play a man will be seen rejecting life in order to become a character, in order to substitute a form for a being.

Henry IV is considered by some critics to be Pirandello's masterpiece, a more important or more durable play than *Six Characters in Search of an Author* because it is fuller, less "schematic," and less exemplary of a sensibility consciously innovating. This may be true, although *Six Characters* seems certain to retain its place as Pirandello's most influential work in terms of its direct effect on the theater. More than that, it seems wholly unlikely that *Henry IV* could have come into being without *Six Characters'* prior inquiry into the philosophy of the stage and without Pirandello's having achieved in it the means for mounting a dialectic between the stage and the world outside it.

In any case, *Henry IV* stands fully on its own, a splendid work, although one with which admirers of conventionally tight and efficient dramatic construction can scarcely be satisfied. On the other side, there are those who criticize its abruptly "melodramatic" ending, as though this betrays the solidity and seriousness of what has gone before. But this is to make much the same mistake as that of confusing the story of the six characters with the play that contains it. As we shall see, the flamboyant and "extreme" ending of *Henry IV* is a conscious artistic decision on Pirandello's part and its strategic position in the play is an aspect of his wider strategy of dramatic revolution. For Pirandello is still innovating, even though what is new here is more hidden and implicit than what he had done before.

As in *Six Characters*, much of the "story" of *Henry IV* has taken place before the curtain rises and will be employed as a ground or set of references for the play's real action. The distinctions involved are essential to the question of what makes drama "modern." A central characteristic of much drama since Ibsen is the separation of narrative—causally linked events—from poetic or artistic action, the "soul," in Aristotle's term, of the work. Such action, one might say, is the *raison d'être* of the narrative and its principle of liberation from the fixed, clichéd implications of its own details.

In melodrama or the well-made play in general, as well as in naturalism in the broadest sense, narrative is more or less equivalent to action; there is no space for that movement of the imagination by which histrionic events are *placed* in relation to meanings outside the physical, the movement by which imagination becomes "philosophical." A murder is committed, an adulterous affair unfolds, etc., and the play's activity rests on the accepted meanings or values (or more likely sensations) of these events; drama functions here as a confirmation or exacerbation of previous experience.

But with Ibsen's later plays narrative increasingly becomes a pretext or occasion for meanings that cannot be confined to already accomplished experience; since the imaginative purpose is to release the previously unknown, to make visible (Ibsen's word) our hidden attitudes toward experience—or, more subtly, possible attitudes—the play ought not so much tell a story about its characters as place their story within a larger dramatic field of energy so as to generate new and uncontingent truth. Pirandello had certain temperamental difficulties with Ibsen, but he called him "the greatest playwright since Shakespeare," and his admiration doubtless rose from his predecessor's having extended the philosophical possibilities of drama in the ways just sketched.

As Ibsen had shown, to begin a play long after certain crucial events in the lives of its characters is to prevent those events from dominating the attention of the audience in the form of mere spectacle or sensation, as they would in melodrama. By this means the dramatic interest becomes attached to significances wider and less exhaustible—*less acceptable*—

than the events themselves, to disturbingly "thinkable things," as Henry James described Ibsen's themes. The thinkable thing in *Henry IV* is the destiny in consciousness and will of an occurrence that took place some twenty years before the opening scene; the play is the drama of the choices and decisions, shaping up to a mortally serious attitude toward existence, set into being by the event having occurred.

The play's protagonist is a Roman gentleman whose name we are not told. When he was in his late twenties he had participated in a historical pageant gotten up by some friends. He had dressed to represent Henry IV, the eleventh-century emperor best known to history as the ruler who knelt in the snow at Canossa before his archenemy Pope Gregory VII. During the procession he had ridden next to a woman named Matilda Spina with whom he was desperately in love and who had chosen to impersonate Matilda of Tuscany, the enemy of the historical emperor. When his horse suddenly reared up, he was thrown to the ground headfirst, the result of the fall being the swift onset of a madness whose only symptom was that he now believed himself to be the "real" Henry.

Instead of having him committed, his wealthy friends and relatives decided to humor him in his delusion. His villa was turned into as exact a replica as possible of Henry's castle; he was outfitted with historically accurate clothes and accoutrements and provided with young men as "private counselors." In this fashion he lived for more than twenty years. Now, as the play opens, a group of people—his nephew; the Marchioness Spina, the woman he had loved; her paramour, a Baron Belcredi; her daughter; and a psychiatrist—have come to the villa with a plan for rescuing Henry at last from the prison of his mania.

The details of this plan are too complex to be recounted here, but it centers on an attempt to shock Henry out of his madness by confronting him with his past in the person of the Marchioness's daughter, who at nineteen is the image of her mother at that age. "We may hope to set him going again," the doctor says, "like a watch that has stopped at a certain hour." For its first meeting with Henry, the group has dressed to impersonate people the historical emperor had known. The meeting is to be a preliminary to the plan's master stroke, but it is charged with tension and there is one especially disturbing note. "I could have sworn he knew me," the Marchioness tells the others afterward.

Indeed he did. In a wonderful *coup de théâtre* that is at the same time a demonstration of his having passed far beyond such theatrical norms as the phrase suggests, Pirandello has Henry reveal first to his servants, and later to the others, that he is not mad at all, that he is feigning his delusion and has been for years. The madness was real enough at first, but eight years ago he woke one day to find it gone. The remainder of the play consists of his relating—in the impetuous and violent speech, the fusion of passion and intellect that is the mark of every Pirandellian protagonist—the reasons for his decision to pretend, and the fateful consequences that decision finally brings about.

The possibilities for melodramatic maneuvering are obvious in the entire situation and it is the pure mark of Pirandello's genius to have gone so far beyond them. Even a "serious" playwright of conventional attributes would have made Henry's recovery the focal point of the play, would have perhaps drawn contrasts between what the world looks like to a madman and one newly "sane," would, in short, have used madness and sanity as the poles of his dramatic scheme. But Pirandello is interested in much more subtle and original matters: the *choice* of madness, the relation between time and the self, the relation of art—invention and pretense—to actuality.

These questions are thematically inseparable. When he had fallen from the horse Henry had been still a young man. But when he awoke from his dementia a dozen years later and looked in the mirror, he saw a man approaching middle age, his hair growing gray, his face filling with lines. (He would try with clumsy desperation to disguise himself, would tint his hair blond in patches, rouge his cheeks to simulate youthful color.) "I was terrified," he tells the others, "because I understood at once that not only had my hair gone gray, but that I was all gray inside, that everything had fallen to pieces, that everything was finished; and I was going to arrive, hungry as a wolf, at a banquet which had already been cleared away."

He had been the victim of time in a much more violent and unassuageable way than our own slow erosions. But he had been afflicted by more than the physical process of aging. Upon his return to sanity he had remembered that Baron Belcredi, his rival for the Marchioness, had deliberately pricked his horse and so caused his fall. He had thus suffered from both the remorselessness of time and the treachery of men, and so possessed a double motive for his flight into artifice. For that is what his impersonation of the historical Henry is. In a movement exactly opposite to that of the six characters, he has sought to become unreal but "truer," because a mask, a "character," and therefore fixed forever in form.

"To live in a world where nothing is stable and man grows old is lunacy itself," Robert Brustein has written, "while Henry's 'conscious madness' is the highest form of wisdom." Whether or not the latter part of this observation is true, Pirandello's intention is clearly to set against our conventional notions of sanity and madness a "higher" or more demanding perspective, one that assimilates the dimension of cunning, the strategic "lying" or madness of the artist. It is just his recognitions of mortality that impel the artist to cast his spirit or active principle into forms that are held in immutability. Both artist and creation, dramatist and character, Henry has entered a realm of fictive, hence unchanging, existence.

But of course this movement is itself a "fiction"; Henry,

after all, is still *acting;* he remains an aging Roman gentleman playing at being the historical emperor. Most damaging for his enterprise of demonstrating through his choice of madness "the misery which is not only his but everybody's," he continues to strike the others as merely the perpetrator of an elaborate, if ghastly, joke. He has to prove his *seriousness,* the lengths to which he will go in pursuit of his metaphysical intention, which can, however, only be convincing, or even explicable, to the others in physical terms.

At a moment of intense feeling and desire for the Marchioness, so utterly lost to him now, he stabs Belcredi, committing thereby an act of criminality which seals him off irrevocably, like Raskolnikov, from the "others," from mankind. As the dying Belcredi is carried out, he protests to the group that Henry is not mad, which is to say not mad in the sense they think. Belcredi has grasped the implications of the act, intuiting the nature of Henry's terrible passion for a way out of time. And Henry himself, "terrified by the life of his own masquerade which has driven him to crime," but grotesquely triumphant nevertheless, calls his valets to him and crystallizes his new, serious, and now irreversible condition: "Here we are . . . together . . . for ever!"

To think this ending melodramatic, in a negative sense, is to fail fully to grasp the strategies of Pirandello's innovative dramaturgy. Traditionally, the melodramatic, regarded critically, is something designed to function sensationally and not on the level of dramatic or artistic "seriousness." We speak of a work or part of a work, a play of violence or passion or a violent or passionate character, as melodramatic if it lacks complexity, is arbitrary, overblown, dependent on categorical and unexamined types of human behavior, if in short it fails to issue from and in turn enhance consciousness.

Now an apparently arbitrarily violent act such as Henry's may indeed be considered melodramatic, but this is harmful to the play only if we regard him as a traditionally "lifelike" stage character, if we think Pirandello's intention was to create a psychologically or morally or sociologically representative figure, one who is to be judged by the criteria we ordinarily use to determine the seriousness of dramas and their characters; if we think, finally, that he is someone we already know.

Yet Henry is someone we could not have imagined without this play; and the consciousness that it creates and exhibits is as much of theater and its relation to life as it is of existence in its historical, or non-aesthetic, modes. Henry is not meant to be judged as a "real" person, but as a locus of possible attitudes toward existence, one of these being the histrionic, the mode of pretending to be someone else which we employ because our finiteness and narrow identity become unbearable. He is not a simulacrum of a real person, such as stage characters traditionally have been, but a "character" playing at being a character, a creature designed to exhibit, in his exacerbated intellectual passion, an inconsolable state of consciousness about human change and the consequent thirst for a way out toward the infinitely seductive but impossible permanence of art.

He is on the stage, not to be an exemplary destiny offering us consciousness about human life from within experience accepted as given and merely in need of illumination or enhancement, but as a figure of the rejection of experience itself: he shows what it is like and what it entails to want to slay the self trapped in time and so escape into the eternal immutability of a form. In this he is the polar complement of the six characters, for whom form is precisely their prison. And just as the six characters' story is banal and conventional but the play which contains it is original and revelatory—for they are not portraits from life but metaphysical conceptions—so Henry's crime can only be considered injuriously melodramatic if plucked from the work which surrounds it and makes it meaningful.

Henry's whole movement has been toward the theatrical

(as the six characters' has been toward the real), and in the end this sweeps up and assimilates the melodramatic as an element of theater. What Pirandello saw, the principle of his originality, was that the theater and life are, or ought to be, in a dialectic relationship, rather than the theater being a discrete place for the formal display or illumination of life. The hardening of theatrical traditions, the turning of dramatic art into culture—something to use as a storehouse of "higher" feelings and recognitions—have always operated, however, to reinforce the stage (indeed all art) as something *to go to*, as to a museum or library, instead of an energy, an alternative, if unreal, means of existing.

Pirandello's dramas, especially his so-called "plays of the theater," of which *Six Characters* and *Henry* are the central works, attempted to reinstate a dialectic process. It was his intense if somewhat narrow, genius to perceive that we move between life and theater or art (imaginary life) in an unceasing tension, because we are existentially trapped between the claims of truth and reality, the desire for permanence, such as only forms possess, and for physical actuality, with its instability and ineluctable mortality.

By bringing "characters" and "real" persons onto the same plane and so dramatizing the conflict between ourselves and our creations—who are after all our selves, too—Pirandello helped free the stage from its dependence on a principle of illusion, a principle which is really a pretense that there is no pretense, that what is taking place on the stage is actual life. By drawing attention to the theatrical, the artificial nature of the stage, he further helped free dramatic imagination from the culturally induced idea that we live with illusion on the one hand and reality on the other.

Illusion—artifice, formal pretense—is an aspect of reality, a means of expressing reality's insufficiency; it is Picasso's "lie that leads to truth." In a deep irony, then, illusion has always to be seen through, known in its status as an arm or instrumentality of the real. Otherwise it becomes an escape in the fullest pejorative sense of the word, a way of losing sight of the tension, a diversion from the self instead of a means of knowing the self's unappeasable hungers and dilemmas, as well as of the strange pleasure that consciousness of these things affords us in art.

Out of his extraordinarily acute sense of the significance of the fact that we "act" in life and live on the stage, Pirandello fashioned a drama that fused illusion and reality, making them reciprocal sources of consciousness, and so released other playwrights from the tyranny of a theater which could only pretend to be real. If he was an "intellectual" playwright, it was because the theater needed thinking about, but more: it was because he understood that to think *in* the theater is to make passion articulate and so bestow upon the body its self-recognition.

BRECHT

When as a young man Eugen Bertold Brecht dropped his first name and changed the "d" at the end of his middle one to a "t," he was engaging in a form of poetic license that has been practiced in a more extreme way by other writers: Stendhal, Anatole France, Saki, George Orwell. The action is an extension of the principles of craft to life. But in most cases the new name represents a wholly new identity, a mask behind which to speak without the obligations of one's biography. For Brecht, though, it was simply a tactic designed to augment his potential effectiveness, both in society and as its critic.

He must have thought Eugen an anomalous or prissy name. The "d" of Bertold was too soft; "t" gave a sharper sound to the word, a bite, and armed with that tougher name he apparently felt more confident of his ability to cut a way into the world. Later he would shorten it still more to Bert Brecht: staccato, informal, with a common touch. He knew what he needed to be called.

He also knew what parts of his biography needed to be invented, and how to devise a persona, sincere enough but calculated too, that would draw glances. The black leather jacket, the bangs, the guitar, the big cigar in his twenty-year-old mouth; and boxers, six-day bike riders, exotic women, café celebrities in his company. Later there would be the owlish horn-rims and the workingman's clothes, emblematic of his innate polarities.

One of his best-known poems, "Of Poor B.B.," announces that "I, Bertolt Brecht, come from the black forests . . . and the coldness of the woods . . . shall remain in me until my dying day." Yet he had in fact been born and raised in the small industrial city of Augsburg near Munich in Bavaria, the child of thoroughly urbanized parents, a factory manager and the daughter of a civil servant. To ascribe his origins to the forest was to claim, without any wish to deceive, not a literal fact but an imaginative one: dark and even inhuman nature, the blackness of the forest as metaphor of the unknown and irrational, was what he understood his internal background to be.

A generation after Brecht's death we are still unsure what to make of these and other more far-reaching "deceptions," although we are pretty much agreed on his importance and his influence, for good or not, on the theater and even beyond. The only other modern writer whose life and personality seem to matter so much to us, whom we feel we have to *get straight* before being able properly to take hold of the work, is D. H. Lawrence, and he of course for quite different reasons. Lawrence was a mystery because of his psychic drama and doomed flame, Brecht because of his intelligence and endurance. And so, as with Lawrence, the literature on Brecht grows: reminiscences, studies, exegeses, polemical tracts, hagiographies, revisions and revaluations, claims and counterclaims.

He is variously the embodiment of human stamina or a wily time server; an acrobatic ego persistently holding center stage or a man who, as Hannah Arendt has said, was "scarcely interested in himself" and whose seeming egoism was a function of his absolute identification with epochal ideas and issues; a dedicated if unconventional Marxist or a man whose beliefs were shifting and wholly pragmatic. Brecht's Marxism has indeed been the source of the greatest controversy that surrounds him and of the wildest misconstructions of his work and intentions. It is used to denigrate his final achievement, interpreted as a rational overlay keeping in check his otherwise passionately anarchic nature, celebrated as unprecedentedly sophisticated and liberating, or dismissed as "doctrinaire," "ludicrous," and "not of serious concern," as Miss Arendt, otherwise quite perceptive about him, so strangely writes.

When we turn from the person to the work, the same multiplicity of view is present. Brecht is seen as a playwright who remained essentially a poet or as a poet who only found his true voice in the theater, a lyrical energy corrupted by ideology, or an *enfant terrible* who managed to mature into disciplined and responsible creativity. In the same way his dramaturgical theories and prescriptions are thought to exist as abstractions unvalidated by his specific works or are defended as being wholly inseparable from the plays and an equally persuasive aspect of his originality.

A critic (Herbert Lüthy) attacks him on the ground that "never has [he] been able to indicate by even the simplest poetic image or symbol what the world for which he is agitating should really look like," and another (Ronald Gray) thinks him a "brilliant innovator" but "still a dramatist more capable of momentary effects than integrated wholes." Most critics are full of baffled respect for his position as perhaps the indispensable modern figure in the theater; very few are able to restrain themselves from trying to shake that position—to make it appear that he hadn't *earned* it—or to bolster it by ingenious theories of their own.

There is a rather seductive critical notion that throughout his life Brecht was engaged in an interior war between his instinctual, anarchic private being and his reason and social sense, a conflict which entered a long stasis upon his adoption of Marxism as a sort of placating and restraining force but was not ended by it. The primary evidence for this idea is found mainly in the early plays such as *Baal* and *In the Jungle of Cities*, which are also considered his most directly "expressionist" theater works, and in the poetry of various periods. The argument is based on the undeniable "cooling" of his dramatic writing after his turn toward Marxism and on the presence until the very end in all his work of invocations to the body, erotic innuendoes, physical affirmations of many kinds, an expressiveness held severely in check by the rational necessities of his commitment to a practical and unremittingly "exterior" set of beliefs.

Yet to think of Brecht as the agonized protagonist of a personal drama such as this is ultimately to practice a melodramatic or romantic form of criticism, as well as to display the need, so deeply ingrained in our creation of intellectual history of all kinds, for order, succession, a sense of crisis, the presence of turning points, a final satisfying shapeliness in one's subject—all the attributes, that is to say, of a *properly written* history itself. (Intellectual history is seldom allowed by its practitioners to retain the waywardness and inconsistencies, or, conversely, the undramatic simplicity, of intellectual creation as it actually unfolds.) Beyond this, the theory naturally serves those who cannot credit Brecht's Marxism as an intellectual choice and therefore have to see it as a psychological necessity.

The truth seems to be that from the beginning Brecht laid out the themes and stresses that were in one form or another to be present in all his writings, that his works did not succeed one another as a progression toward anything final or definitive, that he several times quite consciously and deliberately changed his style and architectonics, for aesthetic and intellectual reasons and not out of psychic coercion, and that the three roughly determinable "major" periods of his work ought to be considered as making up a continuous field, a filled-in space approachable from every side, and not a flight of steps leading up or down as critical estimation would have it, or a congeries of discrete "positions." Brecht was a controlled if far from serene artist, almost perfectly in command of himself, and his artistic choices were never wholly out of reach of his conscious will.

Brecht's lifetime, from 1898 to 1956, began early enough and stretched far enough for it to have incorporated the twentieth century's central events, nearly all of them disasters of course; more than any other contemporary playwright, or poet for that matter, he made them his true, if only infrequently literal, subject. He was just old enough to take part in World War I, had reached his full manhood by the time of the Nazi surge and takeover, was at the height of his intellectual and artistic powers during his nearly twenty years of exile, and returned to his homeland, or the part of it which had become East Germany, in that state of canny, dispassionate superiority to fate and circumstances that characterizes the morale of certain turbulent artists when they reach high middle age and know precisely what they want.

His artistic lifetime opened in the era in which German art and literature were experiencing their first real upheaval and deep change for nearly a century. With what was loosely called expressionism, German imaginative culture was undergoing its modernization, so to speak, catching up with currents elsewhere. Brecht was to first come to prominence in the atmosphere of expressionism and be regarded as one of its important figures, to be touched as his art developed by the brief winds of Dada and surrealism, to pass through the nearly worldwide proletarian period of literature with his own species of agitprop or "democratic" theater, and to emerge with his last great plays as an unclassifiable imagination, outside movements and schools, one of the handful of originators.

André Breton once remarked that the painter he considered the greatest of the surrealists, di Chirico, was not a surrealist, because (although Breton did not think it politic to say so) his work had surpassed the boundaries the movement had been able to articulate. In much the same way, Brecht, by common agreement the greatest of the German expressionist writers, was not one. Sharing in its ambience, particularly its violent repudiation of what it considered bourgeois spirit and mentality, and participating in some of its procedures, its architectural looseness and general movement away from naturalism, he was nevertheless temperamentally and in his artistic aims at an opposite pole from most of expressionism's practitioners. The movement was once described by a leading exponent as a "new eruption of the soul," and it took its vitality from a fervent affirmation of the self and the self's inner, transcendent life in the face of mechanical and coldly organized social reality. A principle of anarchic self-will ran through its compositions and a new, if undeclared, romanticism inflamed its aspirations.

Brecht was never interested in the "soul," even as a concept, or in the self apart from its situation among others. Or, more accurately, his earliest plays lying somewhat aside, his interest in the self centered on its apprehensible, one could almost say "reportable," qualities, not its mysteries, and particularly on its behavior in social and objective contexts. Above all, he cared about the self's capacity to endure (and the cost of such endurance) and to be "happy," which, as we shall see, he considered its natural condition, thwarted by the political and economic structures of the world. Thus, as Walter Sokel has observed, Brecht "does not begin with the individual but with the problem." His dramatic characters operate in an arena designed for the exhibition and struggle of public issues, transformed by his art into metaphors for the difficulties of personal, though never idiosyncratic, existence itself.

His earliest writings, poems, and dramatic sketches, which beginning in his fifteenth year he contributed to school publications and later to Augsburg newspapers, are closer to his mature creation than is usually the case with precocious genius. This was not always seen. Until research turned up a number of previously unknown documents, it was thought that his early works exhibited Brecht's wholly immature sentiments and rhetoric, their worst aspect being a highly jingoistic appreciation of German grandeur and mission, and that by some mysterious alchemy he was suddenly metamorphosed into the immensely gifted and wholly skeptical author of anti-war (and anti-Prussian) poems such as *The Legend of the Dead Soldier* and of his supremely original first play, *Baal*. But as Reinhold Grimm has recently shown, Brecht's early works follow no clear-cut line of growth and show no sudden leap but alternate thematically between a belligerent Teutonism and a mistrust of all things assertively German and, more subtly, contain in their textures the nearly complete elements of everything that was to follow in his writings.

The Legend of the Dead Soldier was a direct product of Brecht's wartime experiences, which were in turn a profound basis for all his later sensibility and thought. He had been studying medicine in Munich, was drafted as a medical orderly, and served in a military hospital during the waning months of the war. Later he described to a friend how "I dressed wounds, applied iodine, gave enemas, performed blood transfusions. If the doctor ordered me: 'Amputate a leg, Brecht,' I would answer, 'Yes, your excellency,' and cut off the leg. If I was told: 'Make a trepanning,' I opened the man's skull and tinkered with his brains. I saw how they patched people up in order to ship them back to the front as soon as possible." *The Legend of the Dead Soldier* is a bitterly satiric poem on such a theme, relating how a soldier killed in battle is dug up from his grave, reoutfitted, and marched in triumph through his hometown on his way to the front again.

But whatever the subtlety and vigor of Brecht's early poetry, *Baal* still seems to have risen almost without background or preparation from his imagination. Completed in

1918 before he was twenty-one (although it was not produced until 1923, after his second play, *Drums in the Night*, had been staged, and underwent revisions as late as 1926), *Baal* is surpassed only by Büchner's *Danton's Death* as perhaps the most impressive first play ever written. There are remarkable parallels between Büchner and Brecht. In addition to their having shared such early-ripening genius, both studied medicine before turning to the theater, a training which was to give their work unprecedented "objectivity" and concreteness, and both were instrumental in bringing about revolutions in dramaturgy and in the philosophy of dramatic imagination. Brecht's whole artistic enterprise may in fact be thought of as the extension and reconstruction—after an interval of three quarters of a century—of Büchner's. The earlier playwright had remained unknown for almost fifty years after his death, until he was rediscovered by Gerhart Hauptmann and the naturalists in the 1880's and passed on by them to the Austrian innovator Frank Wedekind, through whose published enthusiasm for *Danton's Death* and *Woyzeck* Brecht seems to have come upon their liberating existence.

Technically, *Baal* was deeply influenced by Büchner, as we shall see. But as an imaginative act it seems to have been instigated by Brecht's impulse, notable throughout his career, to use existing works as jumping-off places and, especially at this earliest stage, to make his mark by writing against an established mode and work. (He was never reticent about his belief that a writer had actively to win attention; together with his penchant for "borrowing" from other writers, it has cost him the approbation of cultural purists.)

He spoke later of his antipathy for a currently popular play by a well-known dramatist named Hanns Johst, who was later to become a highly placed official Nazi writer. *Der Einsame (The Lonely One)* had appeared in 1917 and was a celebration, in the extravagant tones and lyric flights that made up one strand of expressionism, of the life of the poet or artist—in this case, thinly disguised, that of the gifted and half-mad contemporary of Büchner, Christian Dietrich Grabbe—as tragic outsider, whose painful triumph lay in his scornful superiority to the materiality and gross ambitions of bourgeois society.

There is a story that Brecht made a bet with a friend that he could write a better play and proceeded to turn out *Baal* in four days. Whatever the truth of this, *Baal* was initially undertaken as a parody and shocking exposure of both the romantic myth of the heaven-storming artist—"I am the cosmos!" Johst's hero declaims—and the expressionistic cult of the sensitive individual. Brecht's protagonist is also a poet (in one draft he was an iconoclastic drama critic, as Brecht himself was to be for a year or two after writing the play), hugely scornful of bourgeois considerations and driven by a ruthless sense of destiny, and as in Johst there is a homosexual affair between the central character and a man named Ekart. But the similarities between Brecht's Baal and Johst's hero quickly end, and the new play moves steadily past parody, greatly transforming its original subject and entering a new dimension of poetic vision. Like many other works of literature which begin in a mode of opposition to something extant, *Baal* far outstrips its origins in artistic polemics.

Along with *In the Jungle of Cities*, the play is Brecht's darkest, most mysterious, and most "unconscious" work. Struggling with its opacities and enigmas, critics have misread it at least as widely as they have any other of his dramas and in a familiar kind of irony have often interpreted it precisely counter to Brecht's intentions. *Baal* may be full of particular mysteries, but its general movement and purport are clear. The play is a theatrical poem, darkly lyrical, moving between praise and lamentation, in tones that are vulgar and literary, low and majestic by turns, which describes an arc of existence pitched beyond social or political or moral boundaries. Baal, in Eric Bentley's words, is "man stripped of character . . . asocial man."

Although Brecht, looking back, was thirty years later to describe its subject as "the love of pleasure, the search for happiness," a theme reminiscent of books like Alain-Fournier's *The Wanderer* or Boris Vian's *Mood Indigo*, the play is anything but the straightforward celebration of erotic or physical life it has been described as being ("a passionate acceptance of the world in all its sordid grandeur"—Martin Esslin) nor, from another perspective, is it a cautionary portrait of an immoralist. Its protagonist incarnates experience instead of representing it, and this experience is of the irreducible duality of the world, of boundless appetite meeting implacable limits, and of an inconsolable nostalgia for earth, sky, water, bodies, repletion.

In the "Chorale of the Great Baal," which is a prologue to the play proper and contains poetic statements of all its themes, Brecht's protagonist is described as lying first in his mother's womb and finally "rotting" in "the dark womb of the earth" under the same "young, naked and immensely marvelous" sky. Between the two poles of conception and death stretches Baal's destiny as "criminal" and animal being, which is to say his existence outside human laws and definitions of acceptable human behavior, beneath a primitive, uncorrupted sky. If he is stripped of character, he is also beyond rationality, or rather beyond *reasons*; unappeasably voracious, he takes what he wants—food, drink, lovers of both sexes—out of primal, uncontrollable appetite, like that of an infant or small child.

And in fact Baal may be said to incarnate the infancy of the race, not in any historical or even allegorical sense but in a dimension of sensuous imagination: he is *what it would be like* if society had not constructed us all; if time, empowered by human misgivings to inflict its metaphysical coercions, did not hold us to responsibilities and thoughts of consequences; and if our desire for a "natural" existence free of the inhibiting pressures of rationality and communal life were not thwarted by conscience. Yet Brecht is far from imagining a noble savage. Baal is no figure of splendid, lusty innocence. Immensely seductive, irresistible to others because of his lack of constraint and apparent possession of sovereign bodily wisdom, he is nevertheless, in the literal sense, a monster. "Your teeth are the teeth of an animal: grayish yellow, massive, uncanny," someone tells him, and another character says, "You are ugly, so ugly a girl is frightened." In a passage which throws the clearest light on the play's anti-romanticism and complex perspective, his homosexual lover, whom he is later to murder, asks him, "Are you drowned in brandy or poetry?" and calls him a "degenerate beast."

The epithet issues from a moral realm, in which all the subsidiary, "unreleased" characters necessarily exist, but Baal is never confined to a moral dimension. "Your world seems a very poor one, my man," a parson tells him, to which he replies, "My sky is full of trees and bodies." It was Brecht's genius to place him at the exact intersection of values and physical actualities or, in Freudian terms, between the pleasure principle and the reality principle. Baal's quest for immortal pleasure is unbounded, but boundaries are inescapably there: the limits of the flesh, the remorselessness of physical time. A line of the "Chorale" has Baal "trot[ting] toward the cure of the disease"; the disease is life itself, life which in its plenitude and inexhaustible fecundity mocks our finiteness, and the cure is of course death. Baal dies, that is the crucial thing to know about his sacred-unholy quest.

Most revealing of the anti-romantic counterstrain to expressionism in Brecht's imagination is that he dies meanly, in squalor, after having become increasingly swollen, gross, and solipsistic. He had begun his Nietzschean lope through experience with an attitude of ferocious insubordination:

> I'll fight every inch of the way. I want to go on living even after I lose my skin. I'll withdraw into my toes. I'll fall on the grass where it's softest, fall like a bull. I'll swallow death and pretend not to notice.

But death notices him. He is the played-out demiurge, the fertility god who will not be resurrected.

The chief thematic beauty of *Baal* lies in its almost-miraculous poise between extremes of passionate impulse and recognitions of mortality and in its refusal to tip over—against the temptations inherent in such a subject—into pure Promethean outcry on the one hand or despairing exhaustion on the other. Throughout the career of his impossible divinity, Baal never lapses into repentance and he is preserved from a rigid missionary seriousness by Brecht's dark and visceral humor. Baal knows the fatality of his appetites, the dark side of the sensual universe. "I see the world in a mellow light; it is the Lord God's excrement," he tells Ekart, who replies in a passage reminiscent of Swift, "The Lord God, who sufficiently declared his true nature once and for all by combining the sexual organ with the urinary tract."

Baal accepts this too. One major constituent of the play and of Brecht's imaginative intention at this period is a deep thrust into carnality as a corrective to intellectuality in life and intellectualization in what Brecht considered the "upper-brow" theater. "Don't overrate the head," Baal says at one point. "You need a backside, too, and all that goes with it." Baal indeed exists for the other characters as the embodiment of instinctual being, and his utterance is often a poetic imagery of fiercely lyrical physicality:

My soul is . . . the groaning of the cornfields when they roll in the wind and the glitter of two insects that want to gobble each other up.

Love's like letting your naked arm drift in pond water with weeds between your fingers. Like torment at which a drunken tree, when the wild wind rides it, starts singing with a groan.

But images of decay and decomposition accompany the celebratory speech throughout. Drowned bodies turn to "carrion" in the river; well-fed vultures circle overhead. "The worms inflate themselves," Baal says. "Putrefaction crawls toward us. The worms sing each other's praises." And beneath this recognition of the body's inevitable destruction is an even more profound disillusionment, a nihilistic repudiation that incorporates the entire world of experience, which does not endure and which mocks even the poet's attempt to immortalize it. "The most beautiful thing is: nothing," a character says, standing in for Baal at the moment.

But even this has its counterweight. In a superbly understated formulation of one of the play's deepest significances, Baal remarks to the churchman who has lectured him on his immoral ways: "I love people who have miscalculated." The kind of mistake he means is of an ontological order; in his violent Dionysianism, he himself has "miscalculated." We are left in no doubt that, for Brecht also, such an error is lovable, since it testifies to risk and immortal vitality. He will draw back from the extreme of such a sortie against the world's body as this first play, but his work will never fail to exhibit a love, crafty, sober, theoretic, or impassioned as the case may be, for the human struggle to find a way through errors into a fullness of life.

Unsurprisingly, *Baal* reveals many debts to previous writers, but it is very far from being derivative. D. H. Lawrence once wrote that an artist gets from an earlier one he admires not so much detailed technique as the spirit of technique, a morale, so to speak, of style. The young Brecht seems to have fallen under Büchner's sway not long before the composition of *Baal*, and it is from Büchner, especially from *Woyzeck*, that he draws, without flagrantly expropriating them, his largest dramaturgical ideas—his sense of what a dramatic universe ought to be like—and his chief structural principles. Like the earlier play, *Baal* is composed of a number (twenty-one) of short and narratively discontinuous scenes, and its flow of action is broken up by somewhat the same alteration of lyrical and declarative modes and, though more markedly in Brecht, by songs and soliloquies which appear without preliminary and contain their own justifications out-side the strict canons of plot.

In fact, the abandonment of causal, linear plot—the unfolding of a "story" through the concatenation of incidents that build logically to a climax—which it had been Büchner's revolutionary stroke to initiate, is carried still further by Brecht. Baal's history is laid out as a succession of images, verbal encounters, and poetic events whose significance is to be apprehended sensuously more than as an act of literary "information-giving," musically rather than as exposition. Hugo von Hofmannsthal wrote that *Baal* marked the "disinte-gration of the European idea of personality"; at least as important for the theater, it marked the furthest point yet reached in that process of the destruction of plot-as-paraphras-able-story which was to culminate in Ionesco and Beckett. The motive, one might say, is the protection of mystery and the integrity of the stage as revelation. In *Baal* a character remarks that "tales that can be understood are just badly told"; it was not willful mystification that lay behind the enigmatic surfaces of the play but Brecht's intuition that in art what is immedi-ately understood makes nothing happen in the imagination.

In the sense that he provided a liberating precedent, Büchner also stands behind Brecht's use of both a vulgar and an educated speech, the colloquial and the literary. The dia-logue in *Baal* is alternately tough, racy, elevated, and epigram-matic, and this alone sets it apart from the earnest magnilo-quence of the majority of expressionistic plays. Brecht's language, and to a certain extent his entire aesthetic percep-tion, are also influenced by Rimbaud, especially the extreme imagery and dislocations of *Le Bateau Ivre*, and the Ophelia poems, by Paul Verlaine, and, more remotely, by François Villon. The *Lulu* plays of Wedekind, with their bawdry and impulses of perversity, and the *Moritat* or street ballad of Bavarian popular culture are his most immediate sources of ideas and procedures. But *Baal* easily absorbs its influences and comes forth as unassailably original, the outcome of an imagination still forming but powerfully itself.

Brecht's second play gained him immediate attention and even a measure of fame. At first glance *Drums in the Night* seems to be a wholly different sort of drama from *Baal*. For one thing, the new play is much less oblique and mysterious, more within a recognizable tradition of dramatic narrative. More important, it is rooted, as *Baal* is not, in a concrete if slightly mythicized social actuality. Its protagonist is a soldier who has been presumed dead at the front but who returns after the war to find his homeland in chaos and violent conflict; the reality, never literally identified, is the Spartakus rebellion, which flared abortively during the terrible German winter of 1918–19. Pressed to declare himself for the revolution, Kragler, the resurrected soldier who has witnessed too much death and suffering, refuses to participate, and the play becomes a vision of anti-politics, governed by a plague-on-both-your-houses attitude which years later, after he has committed himself unreservedly to political concerns, Brecht will find somewhat embarrassing, like a youthful indiscretion one would like to keep secret.

Yet *Drums in the Night* was true to Brecht's thinking and perception at this point and is closer to *Baal* than their surfaces might indicate. Like its predecessor, it derives much of its energy from a nostalgia for life outside social organization and is informed by rather the same sort of anarchic individualism. Along with *Edward II*, a reworking of the Marlowe play which he wrote a year or two later, *Drums in the Night* is in fact Brecht's most direct expression of what would continue covertly to be present in his work to the end: a disgust, mounting at times to nausea, over political reality at the level of its existence before programs and policies, before, that is to say, its immediately palpable oppressions have been converted into data and intellectual matériel.

In this connection, the notion that Brecht arbitrarily and mechanically stifled this instinctive revulsion through his adoption of Marxism is simplistic and naïve. What he did was to suppress and transcend it in order for his dramatic work to be able to grapple with newly conceived tasks issuing from, and in turn shaping, a changed aesthetic in which what is repugnant about the politically organized world is precisely what the dramatist has to illuminate, so that regeneration might be possible. The embarrassment over his early nihilism undoubtedly issued from his sense of position, his natural desire to seem to be and to stand for what he always had.

While more discursive and "conversational" than *Baal*, *Drums in the Night* shared to a degree the earlier play's verbal richness, its startling new fusion of sensuality and epigrammatic wit, reason and outcry. The influential Berlin critic Herbert Ihering, who was to remain a steadfast admirer and champion of Brecht to the end, summed up what had happened to German drama with the play's appearance in 1922. "With Bertolt Brecht," he wrote, "a new note, a new melody, a new vision have entered our time. Brecht is impregnated with the horror of this age—his language is brutally sensuous and melancholically tender. It contains malice and bottomless sadness, grim wit and plaintive lyricism."

Toward the end of Brecht's third play, *In the Jungle of Cities*, one of the two central characters asserts that "if you cram a ship's hold full of human bodies, so it almost bursts—there will be such loneliness in that ship that they'll all freeze to death." The passage reminds one of Danton's remark to his wife in Büchner's play that we are all so separate and unknown to each other that "we would have to crack open one another's skulls and drag the thoughts out by the tail" in order to have any mutual understanding or connection. *In the Jungle of Cities* is Brecht's drama of human isolation, a strangely violent sortie into depths of personal alienation and a bizarre quest for relationship, whose intensity and painfulness his work was never again quite to display.

The play is set in Chicago, the first of Brecht's mythical or geographically exotic locales, and concerns a duel for psychic and even bodily possession of each other by two men, Garga, a bookseller, and Shlink, ostensibly a grain dealer but also a species of white-slave trader. Much interpretive comment on *Jungle of Cities* has fastened on the play's homosexual and sado-masochistic elements, and they are surely present. But they are not decisive, so that to make them into the play's theme or subject is to miss its central reality, its mysteriously carnal and yet at the same time curiously abstract investigation of human relationships at an even more basic level than that of sex, on an irreducible plane of existential encounter.

Along the same lines, it has been pointed out that the play can be thought to be "about" the commercialization of relationships, the buying and selling of persons, particularly of their minds and thought, as though they were products. But this reading also misses the point; what Brecht is interested in at this stage of his career is still human loneliness and the vulnerability arising from it, not their social background or causation. The city is still to him a "jungle," in a sense broader and less socio-political than it was for Upton Sinclair, whose famous novel would indeed greatly influence Brecht when seven or eight years later, steeped now in political theory and with an altered dramatic intention, he would sit down to write another "Chicago" play, *Saint Joan of the Stockyards*.

In a prefatory note to *In the Jungle of Cities*, Brecht offers the play's prospective audiences a principle for viewing and regarding it. "You are observing," he writes, "the inexplicable boxing match between two men, and you are witnessing the downfall of a family which had come out of the savannah into the great city. Do not wrack your brains about the motives of this match but concentrate on the human stakes involved, objectively judge the style of the antagonists, and fix your whole interest on the finish." The note is an important revelation of Brecht's technical interests at this period, of his attitude toward what drama conventionally was and what he thought it ought to be like.

By the time he wrote *In the Jungle of Cities*, Brecht's theatrical experience had been varied and extensive. Besides his own plays, he had written drama criticism of an extraordinarily acerbic and rebellious kind (rather like that of a predecessor he quite admired, Bernard Shaw) and for a time had served as a dramaturge for a theater in Munich. His indictment of the contemporary stage thus arose from the most intimate acquaintance. What he most objected to in it at this time was its pretentiousness, its artificiality—in the sense of being remote from true contemporary feelings or concerns—and its lack of principle or theoretic basis. When he was a dramaturge, he had had posters put up in the lobby of the theater which read: "Stop goggling like a bunch of romantics," and later he set down his impressions of a typical audience at a "serious" play:

> Looking around one discovers more or less motionless bodies in a curious state—they seem to be contracting their muscles in a strong physical effort, or else to have relaxed them after violent strain. They have their eyes open, but they do not look. They stare—they stare at the stage as if spellbound, which is an expression from the Middle Ages, an age of witches and obscurantism.

Like many contemporary writers, Brecht was fascinated by athletes, seeing them as a type of modern secular hero whose skills pressed against limits and whose style defined a clear-cut occupation of the physical world. But he also saw in sports, particularly in boxing, with its simplicity and elemental structure of combat, a model for the theater. To begin with, a boxing match or other athletic event is familiar, unmystifying, conducted in an atmosphere of easygoing, masculine cama-raderie (later Brecht was to propose an "epic smoking theater" as a means of deflating the stage's pretentiousness) unlike the presentation of a drama which, especially on the most *elevated occasions*, makes for false earnestness, heavy sobriety, and drummed-up emotion. Beyond that, a sports contest has its well-formulated and precise rules; one witnesses it in order to share in the pleasure of seeing those rules obeyed, tested, and cleverly bent, and to marvel—if the thing is well done—at the grace and economy of the body rising to a specific challenge.

"The decadence of our theater public," Brecht wrote in this connection, "derives from the fact that neither theater nor public has any idea of what ought to go on here. In the sports palaces, when people buy their tickets they know exactly what will happen; and that is exactly what does happen when they are in their seat: namely, that trained people with the finest feeling of responsibility, and yet in a manner which makes one believe that they are doing it principally for their own fun, exhibit their particular powers in the most agreeable fashion."

Brecht's description of the combat between Garga and Shlink as a boxing match ought not of course to be taken too literally; he was up to rather more complicated matters in the play. But the comparison is important because of the stress it puts on drama as something precise, bounded, and *viewable:* the theater, he is saying, should be as clear—not, it goes with-out saying, in its meanings but in its physical unfolding—as an event in sports. Moreover, the theater ought to afford the same pleasure in technical prowess as sports and, going still further, ought like the athletic enterprise and that of art itself to be something *unserious*, which is to say an area of activity invented for the precise purpose of affording relief from, and so a perspective on, the "real," the tyrannical presence of everything having to do with sheer physical survival. "The

theater," Brecht was later to write, "must in fact remain something entirely superfluous, though this indeed means that it is
the superfluous for which we live. Nothing needs less justification than pleasure."

As we shall see, Brecht's ideas on what constituted theatrical pleasure and especially on its relationship to instruction
were to undergo some radical changes, but through all his
periods, even the most avowedly didactic, he never lost sight
of the fact that art is a form of play in the root sense of the
word. Concomitantly, he also understood it as a species of
thinking, a mode of knowledge unobtainable by ordinary
cognitive processes; this is a familiar recognition on the part of
creative minds, but in Brecht it had a particular importance.
Nothing could be more indicative of this and of his lack of
interest in the psychopathological inquiry which so many
critics have made out of *In the Jungle of Cities* than his
remark about the play that "this is a world and a kind of
drama where the philosopher can find his way about better
than the psychologist." More broadly, he flatly asserted around
this time that "the theater's future is philosophical."

He was no doubt using the word in a very loose sense.
Still, it was a word he meant to use; it illuminated his intentions and helped describe his quarrel with the existing stage,
which he considered mindless, bereft of the pleasure that
comes from making intellectual connections and of that which
comes from constructing the relationship between feeling and
significance. That, after all, is what we mean by "consciousness."

Even in *Jungle of Cities*, a play which still draws heavily
from unconscious and dream-like sources, he wished to pro-
voke thought, if as yet simply on the level of calling attention
to patterns and away from raw emotions. About this time he
coined his famous phrase "culinary theater" to describe the
prevailing stage, where people went to be fed, to be satiated
instead of aroused. From then on his work would proceed

with deliberation and increasing technical mastery to try to wake consciousness and not, as the theater almost universally did, to placate it.

In the spring of 1926 a newspaper interviewer asked Brecht, whose reputation in Germany was by now wholly secure, what he was working on. "A comedy called A *Man's a Man*," Brecht told him. "It's about a man being taken to pieces and rebuilt as someone else for a particular purpose." "And who does the rebuilding?" the interviewer asked. "Three engineers of the feelings." "Is the experiment a success?" "Yes, and they are all of them much relieved." "Does it produce the perfect human being?" "Not especially."

The play's title in German is *Mann ist Mann*, which translates most literally as *Man Is Man*. But the title under which it is usually offered in English is A *Man's a Man*, and this, with its ironic echoes of Robert Burns, seems more in keeping with Brecht's intentions. For the play is a document, pivotal in Brecht's own development, of what we might call twentieth-century counterhumanism, that tradition of mockery and derision in which the older literary tradition of human dignity and individual worth is exposed as sterile and bitterly unreal. Modern technologized mass society has rendered mythological the uniqueness of the human person and brought an unprecedented kind of suffering into the world, the painfulness of seemingly interchangeable identities.

Brecht's play is a fable of human interchangeability based on modern functionalism and of the "processing" of the individual by a social order organized for effectiveness instead of personal well-being. Set in a fantastic India whose physical details and iconography derive mainly from Rudyard Kipling's *Barrack-Room Ballads* and the tales of the East, A *Man's a Man* tells the story of Galy Gay, a humble water carrier or porter who is transformed into a British soldier and, even more extreme a change, into a perfect "fighting machine."

A machine-gun unit of four men loses one of its members in a grotesque incident (he is taken prisoner in a Buddhist temple and exhibited as a god to admission-paying tourists, a "metamorphosis" which paves the way dramatically for Galy Gay's) and seizes on the porter to fill its ranks. "This is a man who can't say no," one of the soldiers remarks. But Galy Gay's docility is in no sense idiosyncratic or pathological; Brecht makes it clear that he is representative of contemporary help- lessness in the face of the quantification of the person. "Why all this fuss about people?" one of Galy Gay's manipulators asks. "One's as good as none at all. It's impossible to speak of less than two hundred at a time."

The porter's transformation is by no means mechanical or perfunctory; he suffers through its stages, although with wry fatalism rather than explicit pain. Under the threat of being shot on a trumped-up charge, he "forgets" who he is, so that the intended victim must be someone else. And he slips acquiescently into his new name and role: "Jeriah Jip is no harder to say than 'good evening'—and you're just the man people want you to be—easy." At the end, trained solely to fight, a mere element of an army and, by implication, of a functioning imperialism, he poignantly expresses the new hier- archy of values into which he has been inserted and which he must make his own: "A cannon is something for a man to live up to."

But the play is much less schematic and tendentious than this summary might suggest. To begin with, Brecht's whole imaginative manner stands in fertile opposition to the straightforward instruction and general tradition of the *pièce à thèse*. The play takes much of its spirit and a good number of its techniques from English music-hall and German political cabaret models; the dramatic scenes are interspersed with songs, skits, and projections, and the prevailing atmosphere is one of bawdy mockery and sardonic, hard-bitten wit. In the midst of the ideas he is beginning to turn into subjects,

Brecht's inventive vivacity continues to reign; the locale itself —that land of Kilkoa, Cooch Behar, and the Pagoda of the Yellow Monks—out-Kiplings Kipling, and has the effect of forestalling earnestness, as well as of turning literature itself, with its pretensions to humanizing influence, into one of the play's ironic targets.

In the matter of his locales, Brecht chose to set the great majority of his plays in remote and generally exotic places— India, China, the Caucasus, America—or at distant historical periods—the Thirty Years' War, seventeenth-century Italy. This served to remove the works from political or social literalness, with its danger of turning them into topical dramas, and, further, to give them that "strangeness" which was the quality he thought was needed for the spectators' eyes to be opened, as we shall come to. It's significant that with almost no exception Brecht's least effective, most strained and unrealized dramas are those with immediate and familiar settings, his anti-Nazi plays, for example.

Just as his "historical" settings make no pretense at accuracy of detail, so his geographically exotic ones are in no sense made up of physical observations. They could not have been, for he was never in any of the places he wrote about, except America, and then only *after* the composition of his three Chicago plays. For those works, as for the others, he drew upon his reading, in large part that of childhood; America, he once said, had been his "familiar, unmistakable boyhood friend," and in his plays, its details colored by Wild West and crime stories, it is as bizarrely imagined and as mythically inspired as the Amerika of Kafka's novel.

Beyond this, Brecht deepens his theme by placing in counterpoint to the man who loses his identity the figure of one who retains his—but at an even greater cost. Sergeant Charles Fairchild is nicknamed Bloody Five for having once killed five natives in a single encounter, and he is fanatically proud of the terror his name evokes. But he is troubled by violent erotic impulses which threaten his self-control and thus the maintenance of his legend, so that to preserve it, to continue to *deserve his name*, he shoots off his sexual organs. He has traded carnal vitality for a literally nominal power; "on account of his name," Galy Gay remarks, "this gentleman did something very bloody to himself."

There is an anticipation here of Genet's ideas about the "nomenclature," the categories through which true power is exercised in the world and from which men take their identities, and also of Georges Bataille's theories about eroticism as being in perpetual conflict with the social demand for self-mastery in the interests of economic efficacy. For Brecht's sensibility is too subtle to allow him simply to decry contemporary mechanization or argue romantically for some abstract freedom. In A *Man's a Man* what we see is the world with its choices given, its possibilities *as they are now;* the implication is that Galy Gay acts as he has to, coerced by the structure of present existence. No "solution" is offered, or any theories about the origins of social malaise. Brecht's vision is as yet largely unpolitical, although in this play he is on the edge of making it almost wholly so.

A few months after having finished A *Man's a Man* (which he seems to have rewritten at least ten times), Brecht wrote to a friend that "I am eight feet deep in *Das Kapital.*" He had been moving very slowly and fitfully toward the acquisition of formal political knowledge and theory, and now the process has evidently been speeded by the inferences he has drawn from his own play. The imagination that had located itself outside political structures, when it wasn't actively and indiscriminately condemning them, is now perturbed by its recognition of the inescapability of politics; Galy Gay's fate would seem to impose an obligation to seek its causes and possible amendment.

Brecht's Marxism will from this point affect everything he

writes, but its particular uses will be varied and, after a time, extremely subtle. Its presence is most direct and methodical in the didactic plays of the late 1920's and early 1930's. Later it appears as a factor of morale, a tacit element of his opposition to Nazi tyranny and fascism in general, in plays as diverse as *Arturo Ui*, *The Private Life of the Master Race*, and *Señora Carrar's Rifles*. Finally it becomes absorbed into the larger, more open and "epic" structures of Brecht's last great plays; it entirely loses its argumentative edge, gains in subtle wisdom, and comes to operate as a principle of *wakefulness*, of sobriety about the dilemmas of existence, instead of either a source of philosophic assurance or a ground of political adherence.

Yet except for the avowedly didactic plays, Brecht's Marxism is mostly original and undoctrinaire, and even in these works it is never a matter of egregious ideology-mongering or party-line politics. What made Brecht suspect to the end in the eyes of official Communism was precisely his subordination of dogma to perspective, his imaginative use of Marxism as a method of inquiry rather than a storehouse of conviction. In a sense he was far truer to Marx's spirit than were the commissars, since, unlike them, he never used dialectical materialism as a means of confirming assumptions about the world or for the validation of power.

For Brecht, Marxian dialectics was at one and the same time a double mode of perception and a way of seeing the doubleness of the world. It was his means, wielded more explicitly at first and then assimilated into the very fabric of his imaginative method, of becoming able to deal with the perennial gap between men and their social organizations, between values and power, between, in its most profound formulation, human desire and ontological fact. In *The Threepenny Opera* (written in 1929 and the work that gained him his first international reputation) the character Peachum expresses what is to be Brecht's dominant theme or dramatic concern from then on: "Who would not be a good and kindly person, but circumstance won't have it so."

The observation reminds one of Henry James's description of Ibsen's plays as dealing with "the individual caught in the fact." Human beings plan moral universes or systems of ideal behavior which are brought to ruin by the inimical structure of the actual world; we are not allowed to be what we might be. For Ibsen this is more purely a matter of self, the self which cannot find a way out of the abyss between the ideal and the actual except through interior knowledge. But this knowledge remains in the aesthetic realm, impotent to physically change things, so that such triumph as there is lies in what we call tragic awareness.

Brecht's consciousness, however, has moved beyond tragedy, or eliminated it entirely as a mode of dramatic vision. Suffused now in politics and economic theory, his notion of aesthetic reality having become increasingly functional, he wishes now not simply to understand the world or even, in Ibsen's manner, to perceive it without illusion, but, like Marx, to alter it.

He is still the "philosopher" he had called himself at the time of *Jungle of Cities*. But now, as he later recalled, "I wanted to apply to the theater the saying that one should not only interpret the world but change it." For the dramatist to play his part in the alteration of social existence meant that the theater—his instrument and arena of consciousness—had to be altered along with existence outside it, in a reciprocity that would, theoretically, continue without end. Brecht's early works had indeed helped overthrow conventional wisdom about the stage, but they had done this nearly instinctively and by an almost-visceral reaction against the bourgeois theater. From now on, Brecht was to elaborate a flexible, continually changing body of theory to accompany his theater works which, in a significant step, he began in 1928 to call *Versuche*, or essays, experiments.

Because of his pragmatic approach to theory as well as practice, there is no single work in which Brecht's ideas about the theater can be definitively studied and no period in which they can be said to have become fixed into doctrine. *The Little Organon for the Theater,* a work of twenty-seven concise and lucid but unsystematically arranged paragraphs which he put together in 1948 (and published five years later), is the nearest thing we have to a compendium of his thinking, but even some of the principles enunciated here underwent revision in the few remaining years of his life, largely under the pressure of what he had learned from the experience of having for the first time a theater of his own.

Still, the broad elements of Brecht's theatrical ideas persist without radical change throughout his writings, so that it is a sort of intellectual mug's game to try, as a number of commentators continue to do, to catch him in contradictions or make him appear, through chronological investigations that focus on details, to have been eclectic, inconsistent, or capricious. The fundamentally unchanging constituents of his thought, the basis of his unparalleled influence on the contemporary theater, are these: that the stage ought to instigate consciousness and not lull or confirm it; that drama ought not to be a surrogate for experience but an experience in itself; that acting ought to be the physical or "gestural" expression of consciousness and not a species of emotional enticement.

Out of these convictions—or, really, these intuitions fortified into convictions—Brecht elaborated the particularities of his theatrical theory and practice. They were implacable yet supple too. They remained always subject to the test of experience, and Brecht remained ready to learn from his own temporary dogmas. The central Brechtian terms—"epic theater," "alienation effect," "gestus," etc.—entered his vocabulary, for example, as "attempts" (his own word for them) and not as completed pieces of wisdom, and he was ready to change or scrap them as the need showed itself. What he never abandoned was his vision of the theater as a scene of active consciousness, a needle against slumber.

None of his governing notions was wholly original with Brecht, nor did he ever pretend that they were. For instance, his work with Erwin Piscator, who in the twenties had mounted experimental productions in Berlin that employed film strips, direct addresses to the audience, and other devices aimed at reducing traditional dramatic illusion, gave him the seeds of his idea of the epic. And his thinking about acting was influenced by Oriental examples and by such well-known treatises as Diderot's *Paradoxe sur le comédien*.

But in the same way that his plays drew on other writers, seized great chunks of plot or incident and thrust them into a transforming imaginative environment, his ideas fed on others in order to reconstitute them as parts of a new system of thought. This is perhaps the manner in which all innovation proceeds: originality is much more a matter of new relationships between known things than of pure invention. The charge of eclecticism is in part ironically based on Brecht's modesty, his understanding of there being nothing new under the sun but of there surely being things seen newly in relation to one another, under the same sun.

In 1930, as a set of notes to his "opera" or musical play, *Rise and Fall of the City of Mahagonny*, Brecht outlined what he called the "changes of emphasis" between the traditional "dramatic" theater and the epic one he was in the process of trying to establish. The list would be modified, developed, undergo relinquishments and additions, but remain the basis of his theatrical thinking from then on:

DRAMATIC THEATER	EPIC THEATER
Plot	Narrative
Implicates the spectator in a stage situation	Turns the spectator into an observer but:
Wears down his capacity for action	Arouses his capacity for action

DRAMATIC THEATER (*cont.*)	EPIC THEATER (*cont.*)
Provides him with sensations	Forces him to make decisions
Experience	Picture of the world
The spectator is involved with something	He is made to face something
Suggestion	Argument
Instinctive feelings are preserved	Brought to the point of recognition
The spectator is in the thick of it, shares the experience	The spectator stands outside, studies
The human being is taken for granted	The human being is the object of the inquiry
He is unalterable	He is alterable and able to alter
Eyes on the finish	Eyes on the course
One scene makes another	Each scene for itself
Growth	Montage
Linear development	In curves
Evolutionary determinism	Jumps
Man as a fixed point	Man as a process
Thought determines being	Social being determines thought
Feeling	Reason

Governing everything was Brecht's wish to move the theatrical spectator away from empathy or identification with the play's characters, for this put him in the presence of what he already knew and left consciousness unchanged. He sketched this confirming action of conventional drama and his own developing theater's counteraction in this way:

The dramatic theater's spectator says: "Yes, I have felt like that, too—just like me—it's only natural—it'll never change—the sufferings of this man appall me because they are inescapable— that's great art; it all seems the most obvious thing in the world —I weep when they weep, I laugh when they laugh."

The epic theater's spectator says: "I'd never have thought of it—that's not the way—that's extraordinary, hardly believable —it's got to stop—the sufferings of this man appall me because they are unnecessary—that's great art: nothing obvious about it. I laugh when they weep, I weep when they laugh."

It followed from this that acting had to undergo a transformation as far-reaching as that affecting dramatic writing, and indeed from the late twenties most of Brecht's plays were written with new styles of performance in view. But his thinking about acting applied with equal point to the interpretation of classic plays. The phrase "alienation effect" seems not to have appeared in his essays until 1936, but long before that he had indicated his belief that the function of acting was that of creating a new reality by estranging the spectator from what was familiar, whether in his actual experience or in the realm of inherited artifice, of formal culture.

In the thirties he had written: "Oughtn't the actor try to make the man he is representing understandable? Not so much the man as what takes place. What I mean is: if I choose to see *Richard III* I don't want to feel myself to be Richard III but to glimpse this phenomenon in all its strangeness and incomprehensibility."

Later, in *The Little Organon*, he wrote: "In order to produce Alienation-effects the actor has to discard whatever means he has learned of getting the audience to identify with the characters which he plays. The verdict: 'he didn't act Lear, he was Lear' would be a devastating blow to him."

As has been said, Brecht's prescriptions for acting and for drama in general functioned in the manner of ambitions, were elements of an effort to bring into being a new potency for the stage. Like any creator of imaginative works, however, he fashioned *what he could,* as the times, the state of his technical prowess, and his interior dispositions determined. At certain periods, therefore, theory exerted more pressure than at others or was more easily assimilated; in certain frames of mind he felt the need for greater immediacy or narrower scope, at others he could relax into the perspectives of relative distance and expand into a spaciousness rising from greater confidence in the coherence of policies and practice.

This is why his work can't be charted like the progress of an expedition up Mount Everest or the colonization of a discovered and staked-out territory. He went where he had to go and then went elsewhere. In the first flush of his enthusiasm for his own Marxist-oriented and utilitarian turn of thinking, for example, he wrote his so-called "didactic" plays, during the several years following *A Man's a Man*. That these were the years of the rise and imminent triumph of Nazism in Germany has the most intimate connection with their origin in his imagination. For Brecht, this playwright who had come to wish to do something about the world, the sense of crisis was now extraordinarily acute.

Yet the didactic plays are not directly anti-Nazi; that would come later. Emerging from Brecht's new historical sense, they are proposals for a changed society, models of an approach to reorganization of communal existence along the lines of a "scientific" morality and grounded on the subordination of individual ego to social necessity. In these *Lehrstücke*, or "learning pieces," the function of drama becomes that of presenting a problem or dilemma, in order to compel recognition that dilemmas do exist and to urge the spectator toward solutions which are always on the side of the good of society and its protection from both institutional injustice and personal rapacity.

Schematic, dialectically conceived, and often ritually laid out, works like *The Baden Play of Learning: On Consent* or *The Flight of the Lindberghs* are exemplary of Brecht as half-pedagogue, half-prophet. Is individual heroism sufficient or even possible in the new scientific era? Can personal morality survive in the face of dehumanizing institutions? The plays pose questions like these and offer answers that point to a new age in which the dilemmas will no longer exist, once consciousness has become effective in implementing the good in human beings that history has so far prevented from being more than an impotent, abstract value.

Described this way, the didactic plays might seem to be extraordinarily cold and unsatisfying as theatrical occasions. And in fact the worst of them, or the best ones at their worst, do present the mind with the almost insufferable appearance of a lecture (no matter how the topic is dispersed among a dramatis personae) or with the tightly controlled stages of an argument whose outcome is foreordained. Yet there are saving qualities. Like Pirandello, Brecht had the power to make thought take on an attribute of passion, to give us a sense of the consequences for total existence of the clash between precepts and cognitions. The plays sought to teach, to rouse their audiences to political commitment, but what survives in them, their true "drama," is their struggle—indecisive, never explicitly acknowledged, at times wholly suppressed—to escape from the emotional seductions of conventional theater without losing its human subject.

At times during the thirties and early forties, the world was too much with Brecht to allow this ambition to be realized. The human subject pressed forward, demanding attention to its present plight, not wanting to be mediated by the formal strategies of an innovative art; in this atmosphere of crisis and despair, dramatic theory must have often seemed a luxury to Brecht. In exile and wandering flight from Nazi Germany after 1933, he looked back at his homeland—over his shoulder, so to speak—and composed a number of plays whose purpose was to warn, indict, or lament. If they increased consciousness, they did so directly, in the old manner, as a matter of statement and not of dialectic.

These plays were straightforward portraits of life under the Nazis (*Fear and Misery of the Third Reich*, 1935–8), allegories of aggression (*The Horatians and the Curatians*,

1934), or of Nazi racial theories (*The Roundheads and the Peakheads*, 1932–4), or of the growth of Hitlerism (*The Resistible Rise of Arturo Ui*, 1941), or dramas of anti-Fascist action (*Señora Carrar's Rifles*, 1937, which is set in Spain during the Civil War). They represent Brecht in his most urgent political moods, his most immediate commitments, and yet they all figure among the least interesting, least memorable of his works.

As different from one another as they are, they all exhibit a wholly inadequate understanding of the history and nature of Nazism. Brecht seems to have suffered a loss of imaginative energy and to have relied on theory, even ideology, for his perspectives. The general level of interpretation of the Nazi phenomenon was grossly unsophisticated in the thirties, and Brecht failed to rise above it, sharing, for example, the popular notion that Hitler was a creature of powerful German industrialists and the fatal underestimation of him as being merely "anti-Semitic." Most peculiar of all was his failure to see the profound irrationality at Nazism's core; it was as though he had temporarily suppressed the impulse toward the irrational in himself in an effort to have things make sense.

Whatever took place within Brecht toward the end of the thirties and of this series of insubstantial plays will remain mysterious. He did not suddenly wake up to himself or "snap out of it"; *Arturo Ui*, one of the most egregiously bad works of the group, was in fact written in 1941. But surrounding it, the result of a creative burst that began with the first version of *Galileo* in 1938 and ended with *The Caucasian Chalk Circle* in 1945, are some of the greatest of all his plays: the two just mentioned, together with *Mother Courage*, *The Good Person of Setzuan*, and, on a somewhat lesser level, *Puntila*. They make up what is widely considered Brecht's "major" accomplishment, the heroic epoch of his art.

The time is one of exile; Brecht is in Sweden, then Denmark and Finland, finally the United States. With the exception of *Puntila*, whose locale is a barely identifiable Finland, the plays are set in remote places and/or times: *Mother Courage* in the central Europe of the seventeenth century, *Galileo* in Italy of the same period, *The Good Person of Setzuan* in twentieth-century China, *The Caucasian Chalk Circle* in Russian Georgia at the end of World War II and in the region's distant past. In each case a liberation is thereby gained from political immediacy and "direct" relevance, but parables like *The Roundheads and the Peakheads* had had the possibility of that freedom too. What is different now is Brecht's spirit; he has somehow regained his detachment, become subtle and imaginatively canny again.

The full title of the play that is most widely considered to be Brecht's finest achievement is *Mother Courage and Her Children*, the subtitle being "A Chronicle of the Thirty Years' War." That the shortened form of the title—*Mother Courage*—is used in nearly every published text and production and in nearly every critical or scholarly reference is often simply a matter of convenience, but to the unwary it has acted as a source—or confirmation—of the wide misunderstanding to which the play has been subject.

Our habit of identifying almost exclusively with the play's protagonist, to the detriment of the work as a whole, is strengthened when the title is, or includes, a name. The obvious examples are the Greek tragedies, and Shakespeare almost irresistibly. What happens is that the plays then become a kind of invented biography, the *personal story* of Oedipus, the *life of* Hamlet or Lear, instead of the drama of Oedipus at the juncture of human and divine design, Hamlet caught between feeling and fact, Lear in an arena where appetites strike down values. We convert the protagonist into a surrogate self whom we embrace or expel, but who *exists as we might*, and the play into our own possible history, but one narrowed into a single meaning or quality: Hamlet is the indecisive man, Oedipus the reckless one, Macbeth the ambitious, Lear the blind. Tragedy then becomes not the great imaginative map of the world as extremity, disaster, and ennobling awareness but a species of cautionary tale.

This process of reduction to the personal, drama being made into an extended moral or spiritual anecdote, is at work in more recent genres. If instead of being regarded as a cautionary figure, Mother Courage is thought of as an exemplary one, a being who *doesn't die*, the same inability is present to see her in a set of environing circumstances which constitute the true tale, to see her as a locus of meanings and significances having to do with the structure of the world and not with a merely personal fate. By calling his play *Mother Courage and Her Children*, Brecht wished to guard against what we might call the protagonistic fallacy, the notion that a drama (or a novel) is equivalent to its hero's or heroine's fate, which fate ought to be able to be distilled, so to speak, into one or another kind of "value."

Walter Sokel's remark that Brecht doesn't begin with the individual but with the problem applies to all the late major plays but to none with more force than to *Mother Courage* (as, *for convenience*, I shall call it hereafter). In narrative or physical terms, the "problem" is for Mother Courage to get through a long war with her children; in sociological or historical ones, it is the organization of society into structures which promote rapacity and violence; in moral or philosophical ones, it is the internal costs of survival and the relationship of spirit to implacable physical necessity.

To summarize the play's main line of action: Anna Fierling, called Mother Courage (Brecht took her nickname and occupation and the drama's setting, but almost nothing else, from Grimmelshausen's seventeenth-century satirical chronicle), is a sutler who follows the shifting campaigns and battle lines of the Thirty Years' War, selling supplies to one or another of the armies. She is tough, salty, "indomitable," and her steadfast purpose is to preserve her life, for its own sake but that in turn for the sake of her three children, in the midst of unending devastation and death. One by one, however, the children die and the mother is left alone, hitched to her wagon, a survivor in only the narrowest bodily sense.

From the very beginning the ironic perspective is present that will issue in this survival at the cost of everything that has seemed to matter. Mother Courage's own nickname has a grossly ironic origin; as she tells the story, she received it after driving madly through the bombardment of Riga "with fifty loaves of bread in my cart. They were going moldy . . . I was afraid I'd be ruined." Is her virtue therefore founded on a sham? The point Brecht is making is that it is founded on an overwhelming practicality, a business sense that dominates everything she does and that is seen throughout to be in mortal, insoluble conflict with all other "values," including, in the deepest irony of all, that of life itself.

The deaths of her children all take place as more or less direct results of her making the living that is designed to sustain them. She loses one son to the blandishment of a recruiting officer when she lets him out of her sight in order to make a sale (he will later be killed in the war) and the other when she tries to bargain over the ransom demanded of her after he has been captured by enemy soldiers. (Her only means of raising the money is to sell her wagon, which would mean that she could not provide for her other child.) And her mute, defenseless daughter is killed when she is off on business.

In each case there is a further thematic significance, a deepening of the play's vision of personal destiny controlled by ineluctable social forces that have constructed our existences along lines of physical power and that thus force us to betray our most "positive" qualities. In one more irony, Swiss Cheese and Kattrin die in the war for the possession of an attribute that would have been honored in peace, he for his modesty,

she for her capacity to love, and Eilif is killed during peace-
time for virtues most negotiable in war, his impetuosity and
élan.

These particular deaths are the immediate source of the
widespread reading of *Mother Courage* as an anti-war play.
Less directly, the interpretation rests simply on the play's
permeation by images of and references to violence and destruction. Yet it's difficult to see how any sensitive reader or
spectator can fail to perceive that if *Mother Courage* arraigns
war, it does the same to peace, that, in fact, one of its governing ideas is that war is simply an intensified form of peace,
which is a condition possessing its own warlike character.
This theme finds expression most directly in Brecht's use of a
humor of reversals: "Peace has broken out," a character says,
and another speaks of the war as unlikely ever to stop because
whenever it "gets in the hole" it has friends to pull it out, so
that it can look forward to a "prosperous future."

It may seem reductive or merely witty to say, as Eric
Bentley does, that *Mother Courage* is actually a "business
play," but the description has much point and is a useful
corrective to the notion that it is anything so painless to conceive as an anti-war epic. Its movement and atmosphere
incorporate the narrowly conventional meaning of business as
"the supplying of commodities" but go beyond this to suggest
a world of *quid pro quo*, of ruthlessness (ruth: compassion),
and of the triumph of the material. "The business of the
United States is business," a famous American once said, and
the remark touches on one aspect of Brecht's perception: the
human world as institutionalized profit and loss, which in turn
of course institutionalizes greed and aggression on the one
hand and, literally, "emptiness," deprivation, on the other.

In such a world, values are made material, virtues become
a matter of degrees of physical power, and moral being is
consequently rendered impotent. Mother Courage is neither a
heroine nor a villain (the exquisite balance between the condi-

tions is most splendidly indicated in the scene in which, when she realizes that her captured son is going to die, she murmurs, "I believe—I've haggled too long") since there is no moral dimension in which she can act. She can only try to make a "living"; she cannot choose among values and particularly not an abstract or spiritual value over a material one. Yet she retains the impulse or memory of love, the most spiritual value of all, doggedly attempting to implement it in the face of an institutionalized savagery to which love is not merely super-fluous but inimical, and in despite of her own hard-bitten rejection of "sentiment."

She is held in the bitter contradiction by which the attempt to maintain her children in life—to "love" them in the only way she can, materially, by providing sustenance—be-comes the very principle of their being lost to her. For to make a living is to participate in the world on its warlike terms of profit and loss, and so be mechanically stripped of human substance. She is therefore, in the deepest way of all, deprived of choice, the basis of moral life, and her "courage" becomes in the end, as Joachim Mennemeier has said, "nothing more than the form in which she hides from herself the conscious-ness of the fruitlessness of all virtues."

Though this is not all it is, the play is an image or dramatic legend of such fruitlessness, and not a tale of stamina in the face of adversity or an inspiring story of how "little" people can survive the depredations of the powerful. As Brecht wrote, his "merchant-mother" is a "great living contra-diction who is disfigured and deformed beyond recognition." In her, "antitheses in all their abruptness and incompatibility are united." She is not an image of "the indestructibility of a vital person afflicted by the inequities of war" but almost wholly the opposite: one of the destructibility of humanity within the prevailing system, no matter how tenacious, sinewy, and energetic a particular person might be.

Why then has *Mother Courage* been so widely regarded

as precisely the sort of indomitable heroine Brecht was at such pains not to create? Why do audiences identify with her, weep over her misfortunes, and leave the theater full of admiration for her capacity to endure? The usual answer is that she somehow managed to escape Brecht's control, that his own rich humanity won through, transforming what was intended to be a coldly analytic drama into a work of celebration. And this triumph-in-spite-of-himself is then used to cement the argument that Brecht's theories and practices are at variance and, more generally, that drama cannot exist without characters with whom audiences can identify and without having as its purpose an increase of passion or sentiment.

We know that Brecht rewrote several passages in an effort to make Mother Courage less sympathetic than he had discovered audiences found her. This would seem to be damning evidence in the case for the failure of his theories of estrangement and alienation. Yet must we ally ourselves on one or the other side of the controversy? Something subtle and immensely important for an understanding of the changed drama we call "modern" is at work here.

To begin with, that Mother Courage is in some respects an appealing figure is undeniable; she is lusty, sharp-tongued, durable. At least she is these things at the outset and even in spasmodic, nearly disembodied movements at the end—like memories of another condition. But to be seduced by these qualities into wishing to embrace Mother Courage as a heroine is to want to embrace air; it is to be blind to the drama itself, wherein she functions less as a biography than as an occasion, a demonstration of how even the wiliest strength will be ground down. If we would allow it, against the pull of our temptation to make dramatic characters into emblems, our consciousness would be aroused to her status as a victim, but more importantly to the fact of victimization in the world, as societies, including our own, have constructed it.

This is not to say that Mother Courage ought not to be

appealing; what critical perversity that would be! The point is that her attractive qualities are part of the data of erosion, the substance of what will be lost, as her love is, in the persons of her children. She is exemplary not in being a survivor but in being one at a terrible cost; her virtues thus function dramatically not as attributes to be admired but as annihilated possibilities to be mourned. That she has been seen otherwise is not so much the fault of Brecht as of a certain radical defect in a great many people's experience of drama, a defect that will show itself once more ten years later when Beckett's two tramps will exhibit their nearly historyless condition and critics and theatergoers alike will foolishly struggle to write a history for them.

There is something mean-spirited and obtuse in challenging Brecht to the proving of his theories, which in the first place were never absolutes or even firm doctrines but attempts, dispositions, or perspectives, and beyond that have been immensely valuable in the pointing of directions in which the theater ought to, and has, moved. With the partial exception of the formally didactic plays, Brecht never wished to write a wholly "analytic" drama, and it is a mistake to interpret the notions of alienation, estrangement, and the like as leading to responses of pure cognition, pure rationality.

What he considered indispensable to a modern theater, theater in the age of the authority of science and technology and the depletion of mythical acceptances and beliefs, was a power to cause thought; but thought fused to emotional realities and directed, as its ultimate intention, toward an understanding of how sensuous being is itself destroyed by our wrongly erected lives. Mother Courage's own vitality and implicit sensuality are powerless to declare themselves; and it is this very powerlessness, the silent anguish of her thwarted nature, that is the consciousness we ought to make our own. But we can only do this by being "estranged" from her as a *character*, in order to see her as a battlefield.

Traditionally, drama has been based on nothing so securely as the idea of choice, on the granting of opportunities for characters to elect their destinies, whether trivial or noble, triumphant or disastrous. The fact of consciousness is not essential: the various "blindnesses" of Oedipus, Lear, and Othello do not remove them from a realm in which choice and, therefore, responsibility operate as the central human capacities, the very capacities that most significantly distinguish men from beasts. Drama has largely been the *enactment of choices*, and one reason for the perennial status of *Hamlet* as perhaps the greatest (certainly the least exhaustible) of all plays is the way it moves at the deep center of the mystery of choosing, with its difficulties and pain.

The disappearance of tragedy (which we might describe as the representation of human decisions at their most consequential) as a dramatic mode is due, as much as to anything else, to the erosion of belief in the power of moral or spiritual or existential choice, with a corresponding acceptance of the *chosenness* of our destinies in a secular, technologized, and politically intrusive world. Yet such is our persistence in the habits of our classical and humanist tradition that we suppress such knowledge and are confined in our illusion of freedom by—among other cultural forces—the theater, which has continued to enact moral dramas as though they still had exemplary power, as though we ourselves still had the power of choice.

Perhaps it was Bertolt Brecht's greatest intellectual achievement, the fulfillment of his belief in the dramatist as a species of philosopher, to have placed the problem of choice—or, rather, the fact that we have difficulty being conscious of it—at the center of his late plays. In one way or another, each of these dramaturgically spacious works takes up again the dilemma announced by Mr. Peachum: "Who would not be a good and kindly person, but circumstance won't have it so."

Yet not only goodness or kindliness in a circumscribed ethical sense is at stake. *Galileo* takes up the question of the truth of self, integrity in the face of social coercion, *The Caucasian Chalk Circle* that of justice in a world ruled by power. Moreover, all the plays are informed by a recognition of how concepts like goodness or justice are the enemies of ordinary corporeal life as long as they remain not simply "ideal" but without basis in an organized physical reality.

The Good Person of Setzuan and *Puntila* are the most schematic of the group, although in neither case does the schematism result in a narrow or "theoretical" drama. In *Puntila*, the slighter of the two, a man is shown to be kind and affectionate while drunk, and hard, cruel, *businesslike* when sober. His drunken state may be thought of as one of unconsciousness, closer connection to instinctual life, while his sobriety is the acceptance of the ruthlessness demanded by social actuality. The idea is eminently Brechtian that we are "better" and not more savage in the unconscious, and is an echo of his original dream in *Baal* of a freer, because less socially corrupted, life.

The Good Person of Setzuan is usually translated as *The Good Woman*, etc., but the German word is *Mensch*, which means person, not man exclusively, and, moreover, signifies the qualities that make up a fully human being. In it a young woman finds that the only way she can reconcile the necessity of economic survival with claims on her natural goodness is to divide herself into two separate personae, her own, which is that of a good person, and that of her "cousin," whose pitiless economic realism keeps her alive. Since they are of course the same physical "character," the play can never present them at the same time, which is a brilliant visual way of demonstrating the split between the self and its external necessities and not the dramaturgical flaw it has sometimes been said to be.

In *The Good Person* Shen Te speaks of the future of her son, who will be, perhaps, an aviator, a useful man, when usefulness and not power has become the human criterion. *The Caucasian Chalk Circle* extends the vision into fully social terms: those who work the earth and tend it shall possess it. In the greatest of all the ironies that bristle about his name, Brecht has been accused of not offering a fuller description of this world of the future and, from a meaner perspective, of not tendering "solutions" to the present. The irony is of course that these criticisms come from those who already find him dogmatic and would evidently prefer him to be complacent and tendentious as well.

What gives all these plays their fullness as dramatic creations, preserving them from being programmatic or merely expository of a problem, is their abundant sensual and affective life. Through them run images and gestures out of a dominion of desire, expansiveness, embrace; in them we encounter a dream of children, home, order, and love, a buried or barely emergent human universe possible to see beyond the realities of our imprisoned condition. In *The Good Person* and even more *The Chalk Circle*, there are the fullest suggestions Brecht was ever to give of what the future might be like when it would again become possible, through attentiveness to our reality, to choose and so be made whole.

In a magnificent movement on the part of an imagination that saw ahead and yet remained anchored in the present, Brecht created the dialectic that was the true fruit of his Marxism, which in the end turned out to be not a dogma but a principle of possibility. In his essay "The Mirror and the Dynamo," the Yugoslavian critic Darko Suvin has written with fine perceptiveness of the relationship in Brecht between present and future—and therefore between fact and aspiraion, reality and dream, truth and hope—as both the constituents of his philosophy and the materials of his dramas:

The strategy of the look backward . . . presented the plays' situations simultaneously as "human, all too human" history for our sympathetic involvement and as inhuman, alienated pre-history for our critical understanding. It created tension between a future which the author's awareness inhabits and a present which his figures inhabit; this utopian tension between antici-pated and empirical human relations is at the root of the most significant values of Brecht's work.

Brecht was to write more plays, but his vision and powers had reached their fullness with *The Caucasian Chalk Circle*. He died in the atmosphere of controversy in which he had lived. We try to grasp him and his work, to *place* him accord-ing to our notions of monolithic truth and being, but he escapes our reductions. What might serve for his epitaph are the last lines of his *Saint Joan of the Stockyards*, lines which celebrate all the contradictions, the contrarieties held in ten-sion—actuality and possibility, reason and passion, instruction and pleasure—that made up his life and work:

> Humanity! Two souls abide within your breast!
> Do not put either one aside
> for life with both is best.
> Be two in one! Be here and there!
> Keep the lofty and the low one
> Keep the righteous and the raw one
> Keep the pair!

BECKETT

In a nondescript room in Paris during the fall of 1948 Samuel Beckett, who was forty-two years old at the time, began working on his second play, the first he would allow to be staged and published. A year or two earlier he had written a drama called *Eleutheria*, a rather sprawling, unremarkable piece with a large cast of characters which he seems to have worked on in a tentative, experimental fashion and which he has kept almost entirely to himself ever since. After that he had written the first two volumes—*Molloy* and *Malone Dies*—of the fictional trilogy he would complete, once the new play was out of the way, with *The Unnamable*. Asked afterward by a critic why he had decided at that late point in his career seriously to try his hand at drama, he replied that he had been working with some rather deadly materials in the fiction and thought that to do a play might serve as a relief.

There is no reason to suppose that Beckett wasn't speaking the truth, but every reason to think it was far from the whole story. Like other important dramatists, he had turned to the theater only after having spent years writing fiction, and though we tend to think of him as a writer apart, a very special case, he is not so special as to escape entirely the influences at work on one's choice of genre or medium. The stage seems to lie in wait for the novelist, its varied seductivenesses suddenly asserting themselves; one can get rich and famous very quickly in the theater (or be brutally slapped down: witness Henry James); one can feel more connected to physicality, to living beings, after the abstractness of fictional creation. And if, whatever the motive, you succeed on the stage, commercially or not, it can mean the end of writing fiction, as it did for Shaw, Ionesco, and Genet, or plays will take precedence over stories, as in the cases of Strindberg, Pirandello, and Beckett.

Since *En Attendant Godot* the bulk of Beckett's writing has been for the theater (or for radio or television), and he is surely better known to the public as a playwright than as a novelist. In the case of a writer as austere and ascetic as Beckett, there can't be any question of the potentially easier popularity or greater remunerativeness of working for the stage. Far from it; in one of the half dozen or so anecdotes which are all we possess about his actual life, we are told that when in 1949 he sent the script of *Godot* to the director Roger Blin and was asked why he had chosen him, he replied that it was because the production of Strindberg's *The Ghost Sonata* Blin was currently directing was faithful to the text and because the theater was nearly empty every evening.

There was nothing tactical in this latter remark, no strategic modesty, nor was there the slightest possibility of a pose. Beckett's whole work is about "unsuccess," so why shouldn't that be true for its physical fate in the world? In the dialogues on modern art he engaged in with Georges Duthuit in 1949 (his only public appearance of which we have record) he asserted, or rather let fall that "to be an artist is to fail, as no other dare fail. Failure is his world." The same dialogues contain of course his best-known description of the impossible function of art in the present: "The expression that there is nothing to express, nothing with which to express, nothing from which to express, no power to express, no desire to express, together with the obligation to express."

Beckett seems to have turned to the theater for reasons beyond that of "relief" from the exigencies of his unprecedentedly rigorous prose. Drama is another case of the obligation to express. Like Pirandello, whose plays rose out of the same intellectual atmosphere and metaphysical compulsion as his fiction and were in a number of instances directly based on his own stories, Beckett began to write for the stage as an alternative mode of expression from a unitary source. Neither his nor Pirandello's plays are theatricalized or histrionic versions of the themes of the fiction, but represent a natural and necessary movement of imagination, the extension of a single voice that had been speaking in the monologues of which at bottom all fiction is composed, into dialogue, embodied conversation.

The relationship of the plays to the fiction is therefore extremely close, without being at all parasitic. Beckett once told a critic, Colin Duckworth, "If you want to find the origin of *Waiting for Godot*, look at *Murphy*." In fact *Murphy*'s world of the "nothing new," where there are no high or low points, where everything tends toward stasis and the sun shines because it "can't do otherwise," is very much the world of Beckett's first play. Similarly, the action of *Waiting for Godot*, as of other of his plays, in both a physical sense and as an aesthetic process, is nowhere better described than in the following key passage from his second novel, *Watt*: "Nothing had happened, with all the clarity and solidity of something, a thing that was nothing had happened with the utmost formal distinction."

But the fiction everywhere offers clues, connections, pointers to the plays, is full of monologues that are going to be transformed into enactments, with the different order of recognition that will then be present: the last words of *The Unnamable*—"You must go on, I can't go on, I'll go on"; Molloy's cry—"To be literally incapable of motion at last, that must be something!"; the Unnamable's lament, whose burden

is that of Beckett's entire work, fiction and drama alike—
". . . time doesn't pass, don't pass from you, why it piles up
all about you, instant on instant, on all sides, deeper and
deeper, thicker and thicker, your time, others' time, the time
of the ancient dead and the dead yet unborn, why it buries
you grain by grain neither dead nor alive, with no memory of
anything, no hope of anything, no knowledge of anything, no
history and no prospects, buried under the seconds, saying any
old thing, your mouth full of sand . . ."

Like his fiction, Beckett's plays are built out of the most
unpromising themes and conditions for an enterprise of imagination: occluded movement or outright immobility; a refusal
of hierarchies in personal experience or in the organization of
the social world; a negation of the distinctive characteristics of
objects; a violent mistrust of language; most generally, as he
has himself told us in one of the rare interviews he has given,
"ignorance and impotence." In his words, he deals with "a
whole zone of being that has always been set aside by artists as
something unusable," and this is perhaps even truer of the
plays than of the fiction. Again, even more than the fiction,
the plays follow a descending path toward a destination close
to invisibility and silence. His last theater pieces have been
Come and Go, which he wrote in 1965 and calls a "dramati-
cule," and *Not I,* written in 1972. *Come and Go* is barely two
pages long and can take no more than three or four minutes in
performance, while *Not I* is all of ten minutes long.

By now there is a large body of criticism of Beckett's
theater, some of it of a very high order: Jacques Guicharnaud's,
Hugh Kenner's, Ruby Cohn's, among writings in English.
But like that of the fiction, this criticism often suffers from a
scanting of the works' aesthetic reality, their mysterious functioning as drama, in favor of their being seen as closed philosophical utterances, histrionic forms of the vision Beckett had
previously shaped into intense, arid tales, structures of intel-

lectual despair placed on stage. Or else, if they are accepted as proper dramas, they are made local, particularized into anecdotes or fables of circumscribed and idiosyncratic conditions.

Thus an observer as acute and wrongheaded as Norman Mailer could detect the motif of impotence in *Waiting for Godot* but interpret it as sexual, delivering the play over to his own anxious concerns and so brutally shrinking its dimensions. In the same way an astute critic like the Yugoslavian scholar Darko Suvin can call Beckett's entire theater "relevant" only in "random and closed situations of human existence: in war, camps, prisons, sickness, old age, grim helplessness . . ." Yet if these plays are not "relevant" to everything, coherent with human situations everywhere, then they are merely peripheral games of the imagination, grim and transient jests. But they are nothing of the kind.

When *En Attendant Godot* opened in Paris in the spring of 1953, it was received with widespread incomprehension and even revulsion on the part of the general public and the conventional press, and with great praise, amounting in places to a kind of ecstatic gratefulness, by a number of influential persons who were able to assure it a modest commercial success. Jean Anouilh, who thought the opening the most important in Paris since that of Pirandello's *Six Characters* thirty years before, described the play in one of the first reviews to appear as "the music-hall sketch of Pascal's *Pensées* as played by the Fratellini clowns," a characterization that has never been improved upon. And the playwright Armand Salacrou spoke of it in another early review as the fulfillment of a generation's hopes and expectancies: "We were waiting for this play of our time, with its new tone, its simple and modest language, and its closed, circular plot from which no exit is possible."

The play was presented in America several years later, in Beckett's own English translation. He had started writing in French in 1945 with a novel, *Mercier et Camier* (which has just been published), after naturally having written his first poems, fiction, and the essay *Proust* in his native language. Asked on several occasions why he had turned to French, in which he had in fact become wholly fluent during the seventeen years since he had come to Paris following his graduation from Dublin's Trinity College in 1927, he replied once that "I just felt like it. It was a different experience from writing in English," and another time, much more pointedly, that it was because "you couldn't help writing poetry in English." French, the more severe, emotionally limited language, suited his new intentions more closely.

Waiting for Godot was a commercial failure in the United States in 1956. Its critical reception was very much like that in France: bewilderment and distaste among the middle-brow reviewers, intense enthusiasm in avant-garde circles. Marya Mannes wrote a representative notice: "I doubt whether I have seen a worse play. I mention it only as typical of the self-delusion of which certain intellectuals are capable, embracing obscurity, pretense, ugliness and negation as protective coloring for their own confusions." Norman Mailer wrote two reviews for the newly founded *The Village Voice*. The first was a scornful attack, the second, a week later, a grudging admission that the play had something after all. He added, however, that he still believed that "most of the present admirers of *Godot* are . . . snobs, intellectual snobs of undue ambition and impotent imagination, the worst sort of literary type, invariably more interested in being part of some intellectual elite than in the creative act itself."

This peculiar emphasis on what was considered to be the effeteness and self-deception of both Beckett and his admirers was characteristic at the time, and was only gradually moved to the fringes of cultural history as a die-hard position of know-nothingism when the years passed and Beckett's genius and his enormous influence on younger writers became evident to nearly everyone. The phenomenon of course resembles the various stages of reaction to Joyce and more broadly to modern art and literature in all their successive movements. In this case an idea of dramatic procedure was being violated; the theater, which was supposed to be an emotional matter, to present images of action, was being employed for inaction, and its tradition of completions and endings was being flouted by an almost intolerable irresolution. These things more than the play's ostensible "content," its melancholy view of human power and possibility, were what so disturbed conventional minds (or minds which like Mailer's had large areas of conventionality).

If *Waiting for Godot* is now widely accepted as the greatest dramatic achievement of the last generation, some would say the greatest imaginative work of any kind during the period, it is obviously because its once radically new form has with time been assimilated into educated consciousness, becoming at last a kind of norm itself. Diderot once wrote that "if one kind of art exists, it is difficult to have another kind," and Alain Robbe-Grillet has described the difficulty more precisely: "A new form always seems to be more or less an absence of any form at all, since it is unconsciously judged by reference to consecrated forms."

The new forms or dramatic methods that Beckett and others introduced in the early fifties found their own consecration in the collective designation Theater of the Absurd; along with Eugène Ionesco, whose work his in fact scarcely resembles, Beckett continues to be identified as one of that artificially created "movement's" chief practitioners. Dissimilar as their plays are, Beckett and Ionesco did however share a common ground in the abandonment of sequential action (their ancestors, though not their conscious influences, being Büchner and the early Brecht), their exclusion of almost everything that could be thought of as plot, and their creation of a general atmosphere of illogic, of not "adding up." If anything, Ionesco's first plays satisfied more strictly than did Beckett's the dictionary definition of absurdity as being "that which is contrary to reason"; Beckett's dramas have always been closer to Camus's meaning in his description of the absurd as "that divorce between the mind that desires and the world that disappoints."

This separation between desire and reality is in the largest sense what *Waiting for Godot* is about; it is a play of absence, a drama whose binding element is what *does not take place*. The fierce paradox of this provoked the search for the identity of the Godot of the title, as a way of uncovering the play's meaning, that became a minor critical industry in France and elsewhere. Richard Coe and others have found the source of the name in a well-known French racing cyclist, Godeau; Eric Bentley has pointed out the existence of an obscure play of Balzac's in which someone named Godeaux is expected throughout the evening but never arrives; and Roger Blin has said that Beckett told him the name comes from the French slang word for boot—*godillot*—and was chosen simply because of the importance in the play of boots and shoes as physical properties.

It has become clear that whatever the origin of the name, Godot is not to be sought outside the boundaries of the play itself, just as he is not to be encountered within them. What the two tramps do encounter is his possibility; they are held to their places, their stripped, rudimentary existence on "a country road" with its single tree, at evening, by the possibility that he will come to them or summon them to him, and their task, we might call it their *raison d'être*, is just to wait. The play was originally called simply *Waiting*, and there is a significant clue in the final French title: *"en" attendant*, "while" waiting. The drama is about what Vladimir and Estragon do while waiting for Godot, who does not come, whose very nature is that he doesn't come. He is a sought-for transcendency, that which is desired beyond our physical lives, so that these may have meaning.

But the meaning, the validation the tramps seek for their

lives is never forthcoming; there is no transcendent being or realm from which human justification proceeds, or rather—and this is the crucial difference between *Waiting for Godot* and so many modern works of despair—we cannot be sure whether there is or not. In the space this doubt creates, Didi and Gogo exist, neither "saved" nor "damned," unable to leave, which is to say, unable not to exist, held there by an unbearable tension which it is their task—or rather the play's task; the play as formal human invention—to make bearable. Godot is not a figure for God or for immortality or, conversely, for the absence of these; he or it is a term within an imagined structure of life as we would feel or experience it if we were reduced, as Didi and Gogo are, to sheer, naked, non-contingent being, without theories, rationalizations, or abstract consolations of any kind.

For as Jacques Guicharnaud has said, the figure of the tramp represents "man as such, as detached from society," and so from the mental and behavioral constructions by which social organization hides from us our real condition. Society is by nature optimistic, progressive (in the sense that it moves forward, develops new forms, believes that it improves), and self-sufficient. Man beyond (or beneath) society is pitched past such categories as optimism and pessimism, is existentially static (except that he moves physically toward death), and is radically insufficient. *Waiting for Godot* is a drama of man in such a state. It thus resembles in its themes and attitudes a number of plays of the modern past: *Peer Gynt*, with its motif of the destruction of the self through a belief in its sufficiency; *The Three Sisters*, with its static extension of lives that do not find culminations; *Baal*, with its protagonist placed beyond society's laws and claims.

But since the state with which all these plays from one perspective or another deal is itself an abstraction from the *real world*, since man only exists physically in society or by reference to it—as in the case of a hermit or a shipwrecked person—the dramatic imagination has to create, as a gesture toward reality and to fulfill the requirements of drama itself, some kind of social ground. That is to say, there has to be exchange, community of some sort, dialogue; in a paradox that is at the heart of the theater's art, the state of non-contingent existence, of pure being, together with the feeling of what it is like to be alive whatever the circumstances, is rendered only through contingencies and circumstances. Without these a play would be a philosophical disquisition, just as without the presence of at least two characters it would be a solipsistic exercise. We shall see how in all Beckett's plays the necessity of there being more than one character is met, even if, as in *Krapp's Last Tape*, the "other" is simply the one's recorded past self.

Vladimir and Estragon are thus linked together by something much more mysterious and elemental than what we think of as friendship. The connection is of an imaginative and metaphysical order; they are under the obligation *to be two*, a pair, a social unit outside society. "Don't touch me! Don't question me! Don't speak to me! Stay with me!" Estragon abjures Vladimir at one point. And when one or the other, but especially Estragon, the somewhat more spontaneous and childlike of the two, expresses a desire to leave his companion, he is unable to, just as neither can break the invisible bond that ties them to the possibility of Godot's coming.

For to leave each other or to quit the place where they have been told to wait (by whom or what? by the intention of the playwright, communicated to them as his creations) would be a contradiction of the terms of their existence. This is a difficult notion for us, who have been nurtured on the value of free will, which is at its most sovereign in literature and drama. There characters must be seen to act freely, to bring about their own fates however disastrous, or else be thought of as pawns in a mechanical, unlifelike game. That

Didi and Gogo are as "lifelike" in their way as the characters of classical drama and far more so than those of a debased classicism, such as the modern conventional theater had been offering, is one basis of the play's stature, its new beauty.

Their lifelikeness on the stage derives from their very unfreedom, or rather from their attitude toward it. To begin with, they do not question it, since that would mean they could be something other than what they are—the men who must wait. And in the face of this unfathomable compulsion to remain where they are, they devise—it is the exact word—a provisional, tactical liberty, one of speech and small gestures. They are like prisoners free to amuse one another or to take advantage of the penitentiary's game room, the crucial difference being that for them the prison walls are as wide as the earth. No *idea* of existence itself being free afflicts or consoles them; and their wit and raillery, their wry or bitter utterance within this larger unfreedom, give them their dignity, for if they do not rebel, neither do they quietly submit.

Held there then, without a say in the matter, they must contrive to exist, not hopelessly, but in a strange sort of indeterminacy in which hope is not an emotion or state of mind but an absence of proof that one ought to despair. And they must fill out this existence, which stretches from a vague historical beginning—they speak of having been together perhaps fifty years, of having once been "respectable," and of having been "in the Macon country"—to an unknown end, through their own resources, unaided and unjustified by anything outside themselves.

In this regard they are almost wholly theatrical, for in its essence theater is that which shows us life being fabricated, so to speak, from scratch; when an actor steps onto a stage, he appears to have emerged as by spontaneous generation and he must live in this artificial environment by the inventions—the created words and gestures—of the playwright. What modern realism had done (and continues to do), however, was to disguise behind a multiplicity of detail, a surface of likeness to our ordinary lives, this radical nakedness and *ab ovo* quality of both theater and the life it is designed to illumine. One central strand of *Waiting for Godot*'s originality is its having recovered a lost principle of theater at the same time as it displays us to ourselves in our root condition.

It is the tramps' *presence* on the stage which, like ours on the earth, is at bottom unaccountable; as Robbe-Grillet has written, "They must explain themselves," defending their right to be there, although the plea is not offered to any judge or jury but to the void, which it helps to fill. Once again the connection between theater and life is intimate. The tramps are compelled to speak, are indeed, as Estragon says, "incapable of keeping silent," just as we are, since it is only through our words, those most abstract and insubstantial of our possessions, that we overcome—temporarily and with an illusory solace—our actor-like isolation and sense of arbitrary being.

And so a great deal of *Waiting for Godot* is conversation, between Didi and Gogo in large part, between them and the boy (or boys) who brings news of Godot, and between them and Pozzo (whose significance along with that of his servant Lucky will be taken up shortly). The conversation, like that proposed in *Murphy*, means to be "without precedent in fact or literature, each one speaking to the best of his ability the truth to the best of his knowledge." The ability the tramps possess is that of sheer verbal invention; it is as though they ad-lib for their very lives, talking endlessly for fear of the annihilation silence would bring, "keeping the ball rolling" between them in an action which gives them the necessary "illusion that they exist." And the truth they utter is not about anything external to themselves or even about their internal state; *Waiting for Godot* doesn't give information of the world or of the emotions or psyche but of what it is like to "be there," to have to be.

In doing this it offers no meanings in the traditional

sense, an absence which is the source of its being designated "absurd." Like Beckett's fiction, the play works tirelessly against just that desire for explicit meaning that has so often forced literature and the theater into a pedagogic function at odds with their aesthetic one. "I do not teach, I am a witness," Ionesco has said, a remark that applies with even more pertinence to Beckett and his tramps. For neither he nor they know why they are waiting or for whom ("If I had known who Godot is, I would have said," Beckett has told us); all they know is that they do not know and that the hole their ignorance makes, Pascal's void felt at one's fingertips, must be filled in by words, the way space is filled by a juggler's balls or an acrobat's parabola.

Such analogies to the world of the circus and the music hall have often been made in regard to Beckett's theater, Hugh Kenner having gone so far as to locate the antecedents of his plays not in previous drama but in "Emmett Kelly's solemn determination to sweep a circle of light into a dustpan." The perception is shrewd but is a bit beyond the mark. For while the plays do indeed rise from the atmosphere and morale of circus rings and vaudeville stages, as well as from those of American silent-film comedy, their historic action is to have used those sources for a regeneration of theatrical art, whose elemental shapes and procedures were always firmly in Beckett's grasp. It was the desperate nonsense, the splendidly adroit accomplishment of insignificant acts (in a literal sense: without meaning or use) of trapeze artists, one-man bands, and people who stand on their index fingers—or the equally grand failure on the part of clowns and stooges to attain the simplest physical results—that Beckett borrowed in order to compose dramas of immediate presence as opposed to narrative unfoldings and of gratuitous being instead of portentous humanistic conviction.

These influences are much more directly physical than verbal in *Waiting for Godot:* the bowlers and baggy pants, the ill-fitting shoes and difficulties with laces, the carrots and turnips—fundamental, inane foods eaten like haute cuisine— the vaudeville routine of exchanging hats, the general impression of a succession of "turns" being done, unsequential, self-contained epiphanies of corporeal wisdom and folly. But the speech also emerges shaped and ordered like a program on an announcement board: now we say this, now we say that, we fill up the time. In actuality the circus is a place of pure physicality, as is of course the silent screen, and what Beckett has done, the essence of his innovating or renovating method, is to have thrown language, the chief bearer of our weighty significances, into a physical world of farcical gesture and knockabout comedy whose effect is to undermine all intellectual pretensions. One cannot speak "meaningfully" with a turnip in one's mouth and wearing shoes two sizes too big or too small.

In the same way that the "meaning" of the circus and of physical comedy is in their relation to the sober significances we attach to everything else in life, that of *Waiting for Godot* is in its relation to the values of logic, purposefulness, psychic or moral revelation, etc., we have been trained to expect from drama. Like the clown and the tap dancer, Didi and Gogo instruct us, by their improvisatory presence, in unseriousness, in a revivifying frivolity whose desperate edge is the result of a recognition that it is covering over an abyss. Their talk is not so much anti-intellectual as counterintellectual; in the course of the play they mock or demolish all our myths of meaning, using language against itself so as to prevent it from disguising their radical vulnerability. After an absurdly grave exchange about radishes, Didi says, "This is becoming really insignificant," to which Gogo replies, "Not enough."

This process of what we might call a decantation of meaning is continuous in the play, which takes up themes of many kinds—religious, philosophical, psychological—without allowing any of them to become the drama's motif, and with a fierce comic opposition to their pretensions. "We have kept our appointment and that's an end to that," Didi orates at one point. "We are not saints, but we have kept our appointment. How many people can boast as much?" Gogo's wonderfully deflating reply is "Billions." In another exchange Didi asserts, "We are happy," words which Gogo mechanically repeats before asking, "What do we do now, now that we are happy?" Didi's answer is a pressure back to the naked ground of their existence, beneath emotions, psychic particularities, or humanist values: "Wait for Godot."

Beyond this, language and gesture are in a wholly ambiguous causal relationship. In another break with dramatic tradition, speech does not predict gesture or gesture speech. Instead of instigating physical actions or articulating their relevances, language now operates to ignore, question, or annul them. The most striking examples of this are the last lines of both acts—"Yes, let's go"—which are followed in the text by the words "They do not move" and on the stage by the tramps remaining immobile. There is no explanation of the failure to stir, only the presence of the gap. In this way the orderly universe of utterance followed by logically related movement, of volition succeeded by steps taken, which we inhabit as our very air, is disrupted, pulled asunder. And in the spaces this leaves we feel comically and harrowingly deprived of support, for here language, instead of controlling or shaping the world, has established its own wayward dominion.

Pozzo and Lucky. These two are emissaries from the realm of time and from the life of society, with its institutionalized relationships, its comforts and delusions, above all its thirst for hierarchies. Didi and Gogo live in an atmosphere in which time barely moves forward and in which all values are flattened out under the arc of Godot's possibility, the value whose absence empties all judgments. Here one thing is as important or as unimportant as any other—a carrot or a memory, a shoe or love—and here nothing has power over anything else. In Pozzo and Lucky, on the contrary, are embodied the very principles of human power and exploitation, delusory, ultimately disastrous, but maintained by them as the foundation of their lives.

They are thus a contrast to the tramps' perpetually self-invented, powerless beings, which hunger for a net under the void in whose air they dance, like cartoon characters arrested in mid-fall from a cliff. For Pozzo and Lucky are creatures of the society from which Didi and Gogo have been extricated in order that they may wait, without histories or plans, for validation. Agents of "reality," these intruders have been shaped by its exigencies and values, which divert us from our condition of helplessness, and by time, which blinds us to our fateful, deep lack of change. Unexpected signs of Beckett's genius, their presence in the play helps, along with the brogans and radishes, to preserve it from an overbuoyancy, a lightness arising from its deprivation of the ordinary materials and weights of "realistic" drama. They are reminders of the actuality the imagination has to leave behind.

In the way Godot's identity has been sought for and worried over, those of Pozzo and Lucky have been traced to numerous objective sources. Bertolt Brecht is said to have been planning at his death a socialist version of the play in which Pozzo would incarnate capitalist exploitation and Lucky proletarian subjection. More broadly, Lucky's relationship to Pozzo has been taken to be that of intellect enslaved by materialism, and the former's presence with a rope around his neck (the mind at the end of its tether) and his famous speech—a broken, mad onrush of scraps of theology, philosophy, and scientific information—do suggest some such structure. But there is a danger in this kind of interpretative pursuit. *Waiting for Godot* is no allegory but a marvelously concrete work to which we are asked to lend our senses, our unrationalized affective capacities as spectators; the social or political relevance may or may not follow.

The difficulty is of course that we are used to experiencing in drama emotions we have felt in life, enhanced and given formal structure on the stage, and that these emotions are always attached to narrative situations, however brief or self-contained. We live by telling ourselves tales out of the materials of our experience or reveries: stories of love, hatred, moral or physical triumph or disaster, anecdotes of happiness or regret, all with progressive movements and outcomes, endings. But there is no recognizable story in *Waiting for Godot* and hence no development, no suspensefulness (except that of whether or not Godot will come; but to respond to the play at all is to understand at once that he will not), and no denouement, the very principles of dramatic interest, as we have been taught.

Moreover, the emotions that are thus offered in suspension, as it were, are continually balked, stifled, canceled out. Whenever a character appears to be feeling some definite emotion or to have entered some decisive area of commitment, it is all undone, by an opposing remark, a corrosive scornfulness, a physical jape. This process of undoing is also one of the chief functions of Beckett's famous pauses and silences, intervals of emptiness which resemble those in Chekhov and which in both playwrights serve as agencies of negation or ironic undermining. In one sequence Gogo asks "if we're tied." "To Godot?" Didi replies. "Tied to Godot. What an idea! No question of it. (*Pause.*) For the moment." Into the pause rushes our own awareness that there is every question of it, and Didi's subsequent "For the moment" simply adds a further irony to the exchange.

The result of all this is that we find it difficult to "identify" with the tramps, and this will be true as long as we wish them to be traditional protagonists carrying forward an active narrative full of recognizable events to a point of resolution and summing up. We have to see them as figures provisionally outside time and cumulative circumstances, placed on stage in order to show us what being on earth, beneath social fate and personal distinctiveness, is like. As Büchner made Woyzeck into an embodiment of pure oppressed creatureliness, the victim as hero, Strindberg split his characters into faculties and impulses, and Chekhov kept his three sisters immobile so that their truthfulness as survivors might be seen—all blows at dramatic rules and rubrics—so Beckett, in the most far-reaching revolution of all, deprives his characters of a story and an ending in order to demonstrate how we wait for these things, how the waiting is our bitter, comic task.

Yet the demonstration is no abstract exercise but a form of invented life, and this life at the extremity moves us deeply in ways we could not have foreseen. We have not had these emotions, for we have not knowingly lived this existence; but we recognize it now. There are moments in the play of great poignancy—it is the wrong word, but this is Beckett, in which no word is ever quite "right"—when we fully intuit the mysterious, unexampled humanity of the entire work and are moved to tears through our laughter. Perhaps the deepest of these occasions are when the Boy appears at the end of each act with word that Godot will not come "today." "What am I to tell Mr. Godot, Sir?" he asks them once. Didi's reply contains the essence of the longing, the uncertainty, and the painfulness of this clown show, this juggling act in stricken space: "Tell him . . . (*He hesitates.*) . . . tell him you saw us."

If such categories as optimism and pessimism pertain at all to Beckett, then *Endgame* is much more pessimistic than *Waiting for Godot*. In its seedy room whose windows look out on empty ocean, the living world seems to have been narrowed down to four survivors: Hamm, who cannot see or stand; Clov, his servant, who cannot sit; and Nagg and Nell, his parents, who exist throughout in ash cans. Everything is winding down to a finish, as in that ultimate phase of a chess match which gives the play its title. Humanly, it is dissolution rather than explicit death that seems to be in the offing. There are no more coffins, we are told; death as a rite, and therefore as connection to human truth, has been abrogated.

In this burned-out world, which has been compared to that of Lear at the end of his drama but perhaps more closely resembles that of Woyzeck, despair is an axiom. When at one point Clov tells Hamm that his father is weeping down in his ash can, Hamm replies, "Then he's living." He then asks Clov, "Did you ever have an instant of happiness?" to which the response is "Not to my knowledge." "You're on earth," Hamm tells him, "there's no cure for that." Only Clov seems to have any desire or capacity for a change of circumstances; he grumbles or protests bitterly throughout at his subjection to Hamm, and in fact seems in the end to have made good his repeated threats to leave, as though from a doomed house.

It is tempting to see in all this a parable of man at the end of his rope, more specifically post-atomic man, and the play has indeed been staged along the lines of a vision of the world after nuclear holocaust, as well as, from a different but equally "contemporary" perspective, along Freudian and Marxist ones. But this is in a peculiar way to take the play too seriously, to give it a weight of commentary and social earnestness its imaginative structure continually subverts. We ought to know from Beckett's entire body of work that of all living writers he is the least interested in the present, in the changes time effects, and in what we might call local, temporally or spatially differentiated existence. His imagination functions almost entirely outside history: what is, has been, and what has been, will be, so that writing for him is the struggle to find new means to express this proposition of stasis. In this struggle is one source of the tension of his work.

Another related source is in the unending dialectic between what he is "expressing" on an immediate level in the words and gestures and his obsession with the literary and dramatic impulses in themselves, the human need to say and show. This is his truest subject: the illusion that our speech

and movements make a *difference*, the knowledge that this is
an illusion, and the tragicomic making of speech and gestures
in the face of the knowledge. The materials may vary, like
those of an orator on different occasions, but they remain
those of a voice engaging in utterance precisely for its own
sake, for the sake, that is, of meeting the obligation of making
human presence known.

Such materials do not add up to a reassembling of the
phenomenal world, such as we ordinarily expect from literature and drama, nor do they constitute a commentary on the
present state of personality or society. "He is not writing about
something, he is writing something," Beckett once said of
Joyce, and it is even truer of himself. What he is writing—
bringing into being—in *Endgame* is another version of his Ur-
text on the human self caught between actuality and desire,
the craving for justification and its objective absence; at the
same time it is a drama to show the impulse of playing—by
which we fill in the void—to show it up. If it is more desperate than its predecessor, this isn't because Beckett has seen the
world grow grimmer or has less hope than before (he had
never had any) but because he has pushed the undertaking of
artifice closer to the edge, cut down the number of possible
ways out. There is not even a Godot now to provide by his felt
absence a prospect of a future.

From the opening "tableau," as the stage directions call
it, with Hamm sitting covered with a sheet like a piece of
furniture in storage, Clov standing "motionless by the door,
his eyes fixed on him," and the ash cans adding their silly,
mysterious presence, the play proceeds to unfold as though it
were the partly self-mocking work of a weary company of
barnstormers who have set up their portable stage in some
provincial town and laid out their shabby scenery and props.
The text they speak has a "content" of desolation and end-of-
the-world malaise, but it is interpersed with literary ironies
and internal theatrical references and jokes, all of which go to

sustain the thesis, most brilliantly propounded by Hugh Kenner, that *Endgame* is a play about playing, a performance "about" performing.

"What is there to keep me here?" Clov asks at one point, to which Hamm (ham actor? the reading is now a commonplace) replies, "The dialogue." "What about having a good guffaw the two of us together?" Hamm says. Clov (*after reflection*): "I couldn't guffaw again today." Hamm (*after reflection*): "Nor I." "Let's stop playing!" Clov pleads near the end; Hamm calls one remark of his an "aside" and says that he's "warming up for my last soliloquy"; Clov says of his departure at the end that "this is what we call making an exit." It is all theatrical, rehearsed, in a deeply important sense *perfunctory*; the scene is not one of despair in a darkening world as much as a weary, self-conscious enactment of what such a scene is supposed to be like, of what it would be like *in literature*.

The importance of this is hard to overestimate, for it is what lifts the play wholly above the chic status of a "God-is-dead" document or an allegory of Life after the Bomb. *Endgame*'s thoroughgoing artificiality as tragedy, its self-derision—in his opening speech Hamm says, "Can there be misery—(*he yawns*)—loftier than mine?"—point directly to its imaginative purpose. As in all of Beckett's work, what is being placed on sorrowfully mocking exhibition is not the state of the world or of inner life as any philosopher or sociologist or psychiatrist could apprehend it (or as we ourselves could in our amateur practice of those roles) but the very myths of meaning, the legends of significance that go into the making of humanistic culture, providing us with a sense of purpose and validity separated by the thinnest wall from the terror of the void.

It is not that Beckett doesn't experience this emptiness—no living writer feels it more—but that he is more pertinently obsessed, as an artist, with the self-dramatizing means we take to fill it. The mockery that fills his first plays is a function of his awareness of this activity, not a repudiation of it: we can't do otherwise, *Waiting for Godot* and *Endgame* are saying; we fill the time with our comic or lugubrious or tragic dramas. Still, we have to know that they are inventions, made up in the midst of indifferent nature—stone, tree, river, muskrat, wasp—all that has no question to ask and no "role" to take on.

Thus the derision does not deny the horror or the stress on artifice annul the real. But palpable actuality isn't Beckett's subject, which is, as has been said, the relationship between actuality and our need to express it, to *express ourselves*. Such expression is always "artificial," always self-conscious (since it is consciousness of being conscious that we are impelled by), and never directly "true." "Matter has no inward," Coleridge had said, and it is this truth that we are trapped in, material beings who crave inwardness and have the capacity to imagine it. At its most formal level the expression of our inwardness becomes literature, drama, which, as Ibsen beautifully described it in *The Master Builder*, make up "castles in the air."

What *Endgame* demonstrates is how our self-dramatizing impulses, our need for building Ibsen's castles, is inseparable from the content of our experiences, how we do not in fact know our experience except in literary or histrionic terms. And this is independent of whether the experience is solemn or antic, exalted or base. We give it reality and dignity by expressing it, we validate it by finding, or rather hopelessly seeking, the "right" words and forms. This is what is going on in *Endgame* beneath the lugubriousness and anomie: "Something is taking its course," Clov says, not their lives—they are actors, they have no "lives"—but their filling in of the emptiness with their drama.

"By his stress on the actors as professional men and so on the play as an occasion in which they operate," as Kenner has written, Beckett turns the piece from a report, however fantastic, on the state of the world to an image of the world being dramatized. In this performance the actor is not an interpreter or incarnation of surrogate emotion for the audience but simply the professional embodiment of an activity we all engage in, at every moment, to build the wall against silence and non-being. "Outside of here it's death," Hamm says, and what he means is not that death is closing in but that *inside*, in this stage-as-room and room-as-stage, the play goes forward to enact the human answer to it, the absurd, futile, nobly unyielding artifice of our self-expression.

If the true action and subject of the play are therefore the enactment of despair rather than despair itself, then the relationships of the characters to one another have to be seen in an untraditional light. Like Pozzo and Lucky, Hamm and Clov have been thought of as impotent master and sullenly rebellious servant (capitalism and the working class? imperialism and emerging nations?) or, more subtly, as paradigmatic of every human relation of exploitation and tyranny. But once again this is to take their connection too literally, at its verbal surface. We ought to remember that Beckett is not interested in human relations as such but in human ontology, in the status of the stripped, isolate self beneath social elaboration. It is the requirement of the stage that there be at least duality, tension demanding otherness, that turns his play away from the nearly solipsistic interior monologues of his novels.

Yet something is carried over from the fiction to the drama, and it is a central clue to Beckett's new dramaturgy. If Hamm and Clov do not represent or incarnate any types discoverable in the social world, they are not even discrete personalities, except as they possess a sort of provisional and tactical individuation as a source of dialogue and therefore of dramatic propulsion. For many things about the play suggest that there is really only one consciousness or locus of being in the room, a consciousness akin to that of the "narrator" of the novels, so that it is more than plausible to take the room or stage as the chamber of the mind and the figures in it as the mind's inventions, the cast of characters of its theater. This is almost irresistibly indicated by a passage in one of Hamm's soliloquies: "Then babble, babble, words, like the solitary child who turns himself into children, two, three, so as to be together and whisper together, in the dark."

Clov would then be an extension of Hamm, the seated, reigning, perhaps dreaming figure. Hamm has invented a servant to be his eyes and agent of mobility, as we speak of our senses and legs serving us, and he has reinvented his parents, turning them into his own grotesque children. He is now complete, the play can be staged, the desperate drama in the dark. And Beckett's play *Endgame* takes on still another implication: that it is an illusion that there are fellow actors in our dramas, we have to invent them as they invent us; we are all children in the dark, solitary, babbling, inconsolable. But we play, in this case the *end game*, the last phase of an abstract life worked out in the mind.

The recognition that there is nothing beyond this last invention except silence—the scenery trundled off, the props put away, the stage lights down—is the true source of the feeling of extremity that rises from *Endgame*. There is no doom impending from outside, no tragic or deracinated situation to live through. There is only that silence on the other side of the wall . . . and we are running out of scripts.

Since *Endgame* Beckett's plays have become shorter and emptier of what we think of as dramatic action. But in direct relation to this they have become technically even more astonishing. Like the fiction, where the superficially diverse and active cast of characters of *More Pricks than Kicks* dwindles down to the solitary crawler in the mud of *How It Is*, the plays have followed a more or less steady course toward the elimination of everything extraneous. But how is that decided? What is essential? In both the novels and the plays it is as though Beckett has attempted with increasingly narrow fervor to make the obligation to express function with the absolute minimum of support from the traditional materials of fiction and drama. The result is that he would seem to have reached the taut, dry, naked spirits of literature and theater themselves.

In this, his later dramatic work is the textual equivalent of, as well as almost surely one inspiration for, the Polish director Jerzy Grotowski's "poor theater," a theater stripped of nearly every conventional physical means of seduction and allure. In both cases the motive (although much less conscious and deliberate on Beckett's part) is to purify the stage of its contamination by the obvious, by "lifelikeness," which leads to surrogate, reflected experience instead of the new and autonomous. It is to make the theater yield dry, linear gestures rather than expansive ones, to allow what we might call its metaphysical *raison d'être*—its purpose as the enactment of presence—to detach itself from the banality of the merely sensational.

These later plays of Beckett's pose and answer fundamental questions about the nature of dramatic action and interest. Even more than *Waiting for Godot* and *Endgame*, plays like *Krapp's Last Tape, Happy Days,* and *Play* assimilate the spectator to a static world of essences, experience abstracted from contingency and set forth with a sort of unchanging, rhythmic beat. What is being rehearsed are irreducible human responses to the actuality of being alive: to the grip of time, the illusion of freedom, the coercion by what has been. All the "action"—to a great extent verbal—of these stage pieces is extraordinarily formal, precise, ritualistic; in elaborating it, the characters (if we can still use that conventional term) seem as if dazed or spellbound, under mysterious orders to march in place, to repeat themselves, to surrender to being specimens, exemplary victims.

Krapp's Last Tape has a single character, divided between

his present physical existence as a "bearish old man" and his past voice, or self, fixed by means of tape recordings. His "den" is like a lair in which he hides out from the present. There is an unseen back room to which he ploddingly retires from time to time for alcoholic refreshment, as the stage directions indicate, while the other room contains nothing besides a table and chair, a tape recorder and microphone, some cardboard boxes with reels of completed tapes, and a ledger in which their contents are catalogued. The rest of the props include a banana Krapp eats and another he peels and an "enormous" dictionary in which he looks up a difficult word— "viduity"—from one of the tapes he plays.

With the exception of the trips to the back room and the bits of business with the banana and the dictionary, the play consists in Krapp's recording a few sentences and, for the greater part of the time, listening to several tapes and muttering an occasional comment on what he hears or what is set off in his mind by it. Bits of his history float to the surface: he has apparently written a book that was a disastrous failure, his father died before his mother, he has never married.

The key tape seems to have been made thirty years before and describes an incident in which he had taken a young woman boating on a river. They had been lovers and were now at the end of their affair, and the tape, as well as Krapp's present remarks about it, mostly moves from nostalgia to bitterness and a kind of surly impatience. But there is another strain. Near the end he is listening for the third time to a strangely lyrical section: "I lay down across her with my face in her breasts and my hand on her. We lay there without moving. But under us all moved, and moved us, gently, up and down, and from side to side."

The tape now runs silently. Krapp speaks in his present voice: "Perhaps my best years are gone. When there was a chance of happiness. But I wouldn't want them back. Not with the fire in me now. No, I wouldn't want them back."

"The fire in me now." The irony of this is of course extreme and is one source of a plausible reading of the play as a vignette of self-deception, the lies of old age. Yet on this level, or that of any natural sentiment such as regret or vain longing, *Krapp's Last Tape* is almost wholly unsatisfying, a bathetic anecdote. But it is not meant to satisfy in any such way, for it is clearly not a character study but a play about time, not so much the emotions time arouses but the terrifyingly contradictory situation in which it holds us. For Krapp the past is the only occupation of the present, all that fills it. And this is because time is what "doesn't pass" but "piles up all about you," so that you are simultaneously what you have been at different periods and there is no beginning or end.

Except for the body. It is in the violent contrast between Krapp's physical decrepitude and weary crotchets and the freshness, the immortality of his voice preserved out of time on tape, that creates the tension and so the interest of the play. In his conscious mind, out of what we might call his psychic and social individuation and hence his existence from habit, he repudiates the past, doing the "right" thing, the bearable thing. This is what we would identify with in him if we found his story moving; we would forgive the lies, having felt the tacit pain. But the identification is carried past this to his wider situation, to a victimization unheard of in our psychologies or analyses of emotion.

For metaphysically Krapp is the past's absolute prisoner, drawn to its purity, its fixity, mesmerized by its inviolability and imperviousness to physical change. More extremely, if much more narrowly than in the previous plays, *Krapp's Last Tape* exhibits human life as implicated in an unfathomably rigorous set of positions: we are both in and out of time; we change and do not; we are what we are and are not. The essence of Beckett's dramatic art might be said to be the making palpable, the granting of physical and verbal lineaments to these metaphysical actualities. If drama is characters-in-conflict, then *Krapp's Last Tape* clearly and astonishingly fulfills the requirement, for the characters here are a being in the present and one in the past, and the conflict, unresolved and unresolvable, is over which of them is "truer."

Happy Days is Beckett's most savagely ironic play, if one can speak of so detached a literary principle as irony operating at the level of intense vision he attains here. A tour de force for an actress, it is doubtless the most difficult of his theater works to do well, for no other of them combines such fierce precision of *mise en scène*, such exactly calibrated movement and speech, with so full a complement of what we think of as homely sentiment and even sentimentality. It is in just this relationship of the play's commonplace emotional substance to the counterweight of its grotesque physical schema and unrelenting procedures that, as in similar kinds of antinomies in Beckett, the play's fascination lies.

Winnie, the woman buried up to her waist in sand in the first act and to her neck in the second, is a victim of time in an even more explicit and so more theatrically visible way than Beckett's earlier characters. His obsession with the Greek story of Zeno and the heap of millet is well known, and from this he no doubt derived the central physical situation. Once again it is time piling up around you, not carrying you to a destination, but burying you where you are. This shift in metaphor from the traditional one of time as a current to that of an inert substance is crucial in all of Beckett, but nowhere has it been made more palpable. Winnie is *in* time, the phrase we use so lightly; imprisoned there, she lives with decreasing mobility, being able at first to move her head and arms and later only her head. The implication is that were the play to go on, the sands would finally cover her up, like an object in the desert.

More than this, she lives without past or future, since these imply continuity, extension. When Beckett directed the play in Germany in 1971, Ruby Cohn tells us, his *Regiebuch* (production book) contained a note that the script's broken speech and action should be related to the discontinuity of time, the fact that for Winnie time is experienced as "an incomprehensible transport from one inextricable present to the next." He also told the actress who played Winnie that the bag, from which she takes the objects—toothbrush, comb, lipstick, etc.—that are the basis for almost all of the physical action, was her "friend," while the bell which sounds at the beginning and end of each "day" was her "enemy."

Together with the "blazing light" which Beckett calls for in the stage directions, this bell may be taken as a materialization of the harsh compulsion to exist, the inescapability of time as brutally indifferent jailer. The bag would then be the source of relief from such unopposable duress, the container of those objects of daily use that help make up the thick web of habit by which Winnie protects herself from the knowledge of her true situation. (It also contains an object to be used if such knowledge breaks through: a pistol.) In his essay on Proust, Beckett wrote that "habit is a compromise effected between the individual and his environment, or between the individual and his own organic eccentricities, the guarantee of a dull inviolability, the lightning conductor of his existence." And he went on to quote Proust's remark that "habit is a second nature," keeping "us in ignorance of the first" and being "free of its cruelties and enchantments."

It is habit, then, that makes Winnie's existence in the sand acceptable to her, as it makes life bearable for us all, at the expense of cruelties and enchantments. This is the human truth of the play, the burden of its insight. Dramatically, the utter lack of awareness on Winnie's part that there is anything frightful or even untoward in her situation is exemplary of one of the most profoundly original aspects of Beckett's art. Neither Winnie nor any of his other characters ever gives an indication of being in anything but the most unremarkable set of circumstances; the effect is to give the fantastic a natural quality, to eliminate the usual distance between the grotesque and the normal, and so to reveal the quotidian and commonplace as the unknowing harborers of realities beyond the actual.

The play's deep irony, which is entirely without malice or authorial self-satisfaction, strikes us of course in the title (the French—*Oh! les Beaux Jours*—is more active, hence even more distressing) but is present at every moment. Winnie's gratefulness, her repeated references to the "great mercies" that are visited upon her, the way she finds so many things "wonderful"—all this contrasts violently with the horror of her situation and with the rigidly mechanical way she is compelled to act—"Smile on . . . smile off . . . head down," etc. It is not that she is blind to what we see but that she has accommodated so thoroughly to it, that she continues to behave *as though she were free*, fussing, commenting on things, fretting about her appearance, putting on her make-up, dreaming of love, comforting herself with sentimentalities. When at the play's end she sings the "Merry Widow Waltz" to Willie, the man who has been behind her mound throughout and has now crawled around to her, the effect is of heartbreaking banality, the recognition of a pathos to which irony itself must defer.

Willie's presence has led to various sociological interpretations of *Happy Days*, the most extreme and vigorously argued being that of Albert Bermel, who sees the play as a study of a dead marriage. There is a certain thin plausibility to this but it is quickly exhausted in the light of Beckett's whole body of work and that of the play's internal evidence. Willie and Winnie may indeed be husband and wife, but marriage is scarcely the play's subject. If it were, why should almost all the dramaturgical energy be expended on Winnie, and what are we to make of the mound of sand, the bell, the blazing light? Are they symbols of domestic routine and marital moribundity? Beckett is hardly the writer to provide us with such triteness.

Kenneth Tynan made the same kind of reductive error when he interpreted Ionesco's *The Bald Soprano* as a satire on English suburban life instead of seeing it as a play about the nature of language. In the case of *Happy Days*, Willie is there to be the *other*, to keep Winnie from solipsism, and so keep the play from becoming an anecdote of isolation or loneliness, and also to provide by his marginally greater mobility a perspective on her own immurement. Neither Tynan nor Bermel can imagine a play without an "objective" subject, a theme transcribable into social or psychic data. But Beckett has always functioned at a level much beyond that; his effort has been to reconstitute human life as dramatic or literary artifact, not to offer an account of it as though he were simply a gifted savant.

Since *Happy Days*, written in 1961, Beckett has produced very little for the theater, although he has done a few short pieces for radio and television and a film script for Buster Keaton called, simply, *Film*. The most impressive stage work during these years has been *Play*, which appeared in 1963. These generic titles are indications of how closely his attention had become fixed on the natures of the mediums, on the way the forms function beneath their ostensible contents. A piece that runs no more than seventeen or eighteen minutes—although the script calls for it to be repeated without a break—*Play* is a work in which dramatic action has been reduced to an absolute minimum, or rather one in which such action has undergone another change of definition.

The direction of his theater had been toward decreasing movement, with Winnie's incarceration the culminating point until *Play*. Here the "characters" are two nameless women and a man, whose heads protruding from urns are the only parts we see and whose speech, together with the movements of a spotlight that shifts in a strictly arranged choreography from one speaker to another, makes up the work's entire scheme of action. They presumably are dead, which is to say past all possibility of change; immured in time, now wholly arrested, they can only rehearse certain events and recognitions of their lives, the central experience being an adulterous affair which the man had had with one of the women (the other is his wife), repeating the frozen "drama" again and again.

"What a curse, mobility!" Winnie exclaims in *Happy Days* and the words are more than simply another of the play's ironies. For mobility is that which defines creaturely life, but it is also the agency of human illusions, for illusion rests on the capacity to imagine *something not present* and so implies movement, change. This is especially true in literature, our formalization of illusion, for there the freedom to move, from one abstract place or time to another and so from one condition to a new one, is absolute. All fiction and drama, no matter what its content may be, supplies us with the illusion, in Beckett's terms, of difference, change through movement.

And so his perhaps doomed effort has been to make literature and drama out of as little of such mobility as possible, in order to force the mind to attend to unchanging— unmoving—realities. From the passivity of Belacqua in his first stories to the incher through the slime of *How It Is*, his fiction has reduced the area in which his creatures can move, so that it might be seen what it means to be in the human condition, to know oneself at the metaphysical—beyond the corporeal—heart of things. The plays have proceeded in much the same way. An impossibility, this presenting of significances or perceptions detached from our recognizable days and hours, our progress through sensate life . . . but that is the paradox of his art.

The story the three voices tell in *Play* is of desire, jealousy, egoism, disgust, in some ways a conventional narrative of sexual entanglement. But it is not this tale that matters nearly so much as the manner of its telling, more precisely the terrifying inability of these "dead" souls to keep from speaking. The material is not a matter of indifference; if they were talking about a croquet game or a memorable meal they had shared, we would feel a discrepancy between such a subject and their present condition, an excessive quality to their fate. As it is, the moral and emotional substance has an almost classic gravity which is balanced by the despairing need to go on giving it expression.

And it is this need to express themselves, to account for their passion and torment, in short *to be actors*, that constitutes the damnation, if we want to call it that, of the three. In the stage directions Beckett refers to them as "victims" and to the spotlight darting from one to another as an "inquisitor." Once again he is placing the theatrical at the forefront of his theater: a spotlight, instrument of publicity, conjuror of presence, coercer of the expressible. It holds them in this rehearsal of what their lives came to, of what life comes to. Beyond morality or emotions, beyond memory even, is speech, words with their traces of our truth, whose body lies elsewhere. "Is it that I do not tell the truth," one of the women says, "is that it, that some day somehow I may tell the truth at last, and then no more light at last, for the truth?"

Voices, ghostly faces, in the light still. The theater in Beckett's hands has abandoned events, direct clashes, inquiries, representations. What remains is the theatrical impulse itself, this thrust toward the truth about our condition: that it consists in enactment, presence, the painful necessity to remain visible. "Tell him you saw us," Didi says to Godot's messenger. To be seen, heard, by a Godot, by each other, and, in the darkness, ourselves: this is an obligation, a fate, and, finally, a story.

HANDKE

> The results of philosophy are the uncovering of one or another piece of plain nonsense and of bumps that the understanding has got by running its head up against the limits of language. These bumps make us see the value of the discovery.
>
> WITTGENSTEIN, *Philosophical Investigations*

We are taught to consider philosophy and literature as being separate in both intention and procedure, but the lines don't seem so clearly drawn when we are able to give up categorizing. We have all had the experience of reading certain philosophers as imaginative writers, makers of self-sufficient worlds out of language charged with affective power and out of animate, revelatory ideas. Plato is of course the greatest of these philosopher-writers; then there are Pascal, Nietzsche, William James (who, it was said, wrote philosophy like a novelist, while his brother wrote novels like a philosopher), and Wittgenstein in our own time. Even where the philosophical style is entirely dry, systematic, and abstract, there may be a drama of the self on display more compelling than most outright fiction; think of Descartes's vertiginous journey through his own mind in search of its basis and relation to his breathing life.

In the same way, fiction or the theater can afford us what we rightly feel is a kind of philosophical knowledge, more sensuous usually than explicit philosophy, more fully bound to our physical situations, and of course less a matter of logical inquiry, but opening out to the same meaning of meaning (or description of description) that is philosophy's traditional field. For example, beyond dead-level naturalism, fiction or the stage can instruct us not so much in what we do as in questions such as these: how are we what we are? what forms do our existences take beneath appearances? what is our relationship to the structure of the world? Like the philosopher, the novelist or playwright begins in innocence of the answers; when Wittgenstein says that "a philosophical problem has the form: 'I don't know my way around,'" he is describing the writer's initial problem too. Camus acknowledged as much when he said that "if the world were clear, art would not exist."

Imaginative novelists have always taken the clarifying function of their supple, spacious art, its philosophy-like action of inquiry and illumination, more or less for granted. But playwright-artists are forced by the immediacy and physical directness of their enterprise—the placing of "characters" who will be impersonated by live persons in a narrow space where they are driven to "act" much more than to think or be thought about—to put in claims for wisdom and not merely emotional knowledge or home-truthfulness. In our century Pirandello, Brecht, Ionesco, and a theater prophet like Artaud have all insisted on drama being a species of philosophy, applying the word to their own work (the "philosopher in the theater," Brecht called himself) and basing their repudiations of the conventional stage on the very fact that it possesses no philosophical dimension.

Peter Handke hasn't felt called upon to make the same claim as these writers, but the justice of it applies with perhaps even greater force in his case. A native of Austria just past his twenties, Handke has written plays (as well as some fiction and poetry) that go an extraordinary distance toward implementing in artistic terms Wittgenstein's sketch of the philosopher's task and method:

> Philosophical problems . . . are solved . . . by looking into the workings of our language, and that in such a way as to make us recognize those workings: in despite of an urge to misunderstand them. The problems are solved not by giving new information, but by arranging what we have always known. Philosophy is a battle against the bewitchment of our intelligence by means of language.

Wittgenstein goes on to say that "the philosopher's treatment of a question is like the treatment of an illness." Compare Handke's remark in an interview in 1970 that "one should learn to be nauseated by language, as the hero of Sartre's *Nausea* is by things. At least that would be a beginning of consciousness." Again, Handke has referred to the "idiocy" of language and spoken of his own intention, at least in his earlier plays, of "point[ing] out the present forms of linguistic alienation" in order to make possible a less-fettered life for the mind. Nothing could be closer in spirit to Wittgenstein's philosophical adventure, his wish to "show the fly the way out of the fly-bottle."

This is not to say that Handke's work is a sort of theatrical equivalent or transliteration of Wittgenstein's speculations but, to begin with, that they rise from a common ground and atmosphere. As Stanley Kauffmann has pointed out in a review of Handke's latest play, *The Ride Across Lake Constance*, much postwar literature in German has been deeply influenced by Wittgenstein's inquiry into the relation between language and reality. This philosophical quest has its roots in the modern European experience of deracination and intellectual estrangement, and was one central response to it, as

Sartre's existentialism has been another. Although Handke has turned away all questions about Wittgenstein, there's no doubt that he has read and pondered his fellow Austrian, but even if he hadn't, the pressures, enticements, and directions were in the air to be succumbed to and followed.

We may think we have heard all we want to hear about European intellectual estrangement, deracination, and the like. In the era of McLuhan, Norman O. Brown, and R. D. Laing, the purported revolt against our overly verbal consciousness and the increasing urge to make the arts more "physical," the very words smack of a superseded phase of cultural history, just as the appellation "avant-garde" seems no longer applicable to any literature being written. Yet we are no less estranged than before, our dilemmas are still chiefly reflected and embedded in, if not heavily caused by, language, and there is still a function for literature which, whatever we may call it, breaks new ground or, in a better image for the effect of imagination, breaks up the old ground in order to release its stifled fecundity.

Wittgenstein's renewal of philosophy has had its continuing efficacy precisely because of its recognition of our perennial verbal confusion and consequent victimization by experiences wrongly analyzed and described and hence wrongly known. Instead of attempting a new and grander synthesis in the line of philosophy's overlords, he plunged directly into the facts of language. "We do not realize that we *calculate*, operate with words," he wrote, and spoke of his action as "bring[ing] words back from their metaphysical to their everyday use."

Peter Handke might say that what he has done is to have brought words back from their traditional "dramatic" or literary uses, their existence as elements of unfolding narratives which provide surrogate emotional or moral experiences, and placed them directly before us, in their own right, so to speak. His plays demonstrate how we operate with words and are operated upon by them; what they reject is language thought of as containing meanings requiring no further investigation, language employed to communicate pre-existing truths about the world and our natures.

The chief revelation in these plays is of the truths of language itself, and of our relation to our own speech and expression. Handke's dramaturgy comes directly out of his "nausea," the sickness induced by the sight of language escaped from our control, the feeling of helplessness in the face of its perverse and independent life. The cure is homeopathic; in Handke's theater, language, exposed, assaulted, wrestled with, driven to limits, and pursued still further, begins to take on, like the color returning to the cheeks of a nearly hanged man, the signs of a strange and unexpected resurrection.

With one exception, *My Foot, My Tutor*, a play with no speech at all—which serves as a relief from language but also to throw an eerie perspective on its absence—Handke's stage works are in large part dramas about the nature of language, even where they contain "characters," which is to say figures whom actors embody. As he has said, he has "abstracted from modes of speech the basic grammatical elements" and dramatized these, in order to release into consciousness the ways in which language really works, how we build up the world through inherited verbal forms, and how these forms propel us on courses of action and into states of feeling which they and not we have determined. As Handke says about his first full-length play: "In *Kaspar* history is conceived of as a story of sentences."

Kaspar is derived from the bizarre true story of one Kaspar Hauser, a youth in his late teens who was discovered wandering the streets of Nuremberg in May of 1828. Emaciated, terrified, and able to speak only one sentence to the effect that he wanted to be a cavalry officer like his father had once been, he refused all sustenance except bread and water. Imprisoned for vagrancy, he was turned over after a while to a guardian and died five years later under mysterious circumstances.

His story aroused intense interest in literary and educated circles, and he became the subject of a number of imaginative works and scientific studies during the period and beyond. Verlaine, Hofmannsthal, and Trakl all used him as a figure for the poet, the person who, as Verlaine wrote, "does not know what he is to do in this world," and one origin of Brecht's famous poem "Of Poor B.B." has been traced to Verlaine's *Pauvre Gaspard*. Both for these writers and for others, the chief factual speculation about Kaspar Hauser was that he had been kept prisoner all his life, perhaps by demented parents, most likely in total isolation, and had thus failed to grow into speech or most other human attributes. In this he resembled the famous "wolf-boy" who had fascinated French literary and medical circles in the previous century and who was the subject of Truffaut's film *The Wild Child*.

What made Kaspar Hauser and the wolf-boy so interesting to both literary and scientific minds was their social and psychological status, their position outside culture and even civilization. Their existence as monsters or avatars provided troubling reminders to the humanist thinker of our nearness to savagery and to the poet of our suffering in the isolation of "expression." (The poet, who helps make culture, is nevertheless a stranger to it, as Verlaine wrote, someone who has to invent a new language.) Kaspar and the wolf-boy became instigations to look into the mysteries of normal socialization and psychic maturation or to try to imagine what it must be like to have been deprived of them. And since speech has always been considered the pre-eminent human attribute and means of differentiation from the animal realm, it was their speechlessness that above all constituted their "tragedy" or violent disaffiliation or, from some romantic viewpoints, their symbolic wound.

For Handke, however, the interest lies elsewhere, in a region where philosophy and aesthetics mingle and where both humanist and romantic stances have no solidity. His play, he has said, is not a psychological or social study; it doesn't "show how it *really is* or *really was* with Kaspar Hauser. It shows what *is possible* with someone." Handke's Kaspar is not a symbolic figure, for the poet or anyone else: he is a creation.

Going further than the historical facts, Handke entirely strips down his character, making him at the beginning incapable even of purposeful and sequential movements and changing his one sentence to something more poignantly remote and unspecific: "I want to be a person like somebody else was once." The action of the play concerns his development into coordinated movement, speech, and consciousness, and so into ostensible humanity. Above all else, it is his growth into language and verbal capacity that constitutes his attainment of human being and, as we shall see, becomes at the same time the process of his destruction.

The play opens with Kaspar appearing on stage through a slit in the curtain, dressed in a highly theatrical style, his face a mask. He is "the incarnation of astonishment." He begins to move, learning the way a child does, learns then to speak, pronouncing at first the one sentence he knows but without any idea of its meaning. Three invisible "prompters" make him speak by speaking themselves, setting examples, the way a child is set them, and offering him precepts and arguments for verbal consciousness. "Already you have a sentence with which you can make yourself noticeable," they tell him. "With this sentence you can make yourself noticeable in the dark, so no one will think you are an animal . . . The sentence is more useful to you than a word. You can speak a sentence to the end . . . With the sentence you can compare one word with the other. Only with a sentence, not with a word, can you ask leave to speak."

The education goes on. The sentence, he is told, is useful for placing "between yourself and everything else," for exorcising disorder, for becoming "aware of yourself," for learning how to hesitate, for learning that "you were elsewhere the last time you uttered the sentence," learning, that is to say, about *elsewhere* as a concept. While the prompters speak, Kaspar begins to utter broken parts of the sentence, having been pushed back to the earliest phase: "I want . . . I want to be like once . . . Like a person else . . . Somebody . . . Was I . . . Be one . . . I want to be somebody like." Gradually he becomes able to speak the sentence again in its correct order and, as the first real triumph, to understand its principle, the principle of sentences, which is to make connections that imply the connectedness of the world. With this power he is able to move on in "the adventure of speech," until he is taught and absorbs "model sentences with which an orderly person struggles through life."

Power over words gives Kaspar power over objects too. By being able to name things he is able to manipulate reality, arranging its parts according to his ostensible needs. The point arrives when he is pronounced "fit" for existence, having been thoroughly trained in the logic by which we organize what we think of as the world. This logic, however, is the logic of language; it is of social derivation and while it may indeed conform at points to the physical world it can't by its nature conform to any individual's reality.

It is at this point that Kaspar's destruction by language begins. For once he has been trained in linguistic forms and been given verbal models of behavior, he becomes aware of his longing for specificity, individuality, freedom from the abstractions and coercive systematizing of the forms themselves. He conceives the wish to use language "creatively," to go out on his own with it, imagining that words and linguistic patterns will obey him, when the truth is that he, like every one of us, is compelled to obey them, for they have their own "life." His desire to be creative, unique, is mocked by the appearance on the stage of a proliferating number of other Kaspars, doubles whose presence establishes that he is just like everyone else. The play ends with his death, along with that of the doubles; almost his last words, as he comprehends his victimization by the prompters, who have socialized him and equipped him for life but not selfhood, are "I am only accidentally I."

A summary such as this may convey something of *Kaspar*'s intellectual vigor and sophistication but very little of its quality as drama, its existence as a stage piece of extraordinary originality and vivacity. Indeed, Handke's plays are all extremely resistant to conventional methods of criticism and critical reporting, and this of course is due to their radical lack of the usual elements of conflict between characters or, as a moral or psychic dilemma, within a protagonist. Instead, their tension and struggle rise from a sense of a stricken human condition beyond any immediate causes; the drama of their drama lies in the forcing upon our consciousness of this condition, against our resistance, the protective action of our formulas for experience and our systems for codifying it along emotional or moral lines and so making it manageable.

Like any great innovator in any art, Handke does not conceive of his medium as the container or expressive instrument of his ideas, but as the principle of their existence, the only way they can be alive. From the moment Kaspar is thrust before the audience through the curtain slit he exists entirely on the stage; his very appearance—a mask with heavy theatrical make-up, a costume like a clown or burlesque comedian—indicates at once that he is an artifact, a histrionic invention, and not an intellectual case history. And the play itself proceeds the way every sort of drama does, as the unfolding in time and in real physical space of *something imagined about human life*.

Though we often lose sight of it, the imagination is a

faculty that deals not so much with the actual as with the possible, with what doesn't yet exist, at least in the shape or location or relation to other phenomena that the mind finds desirable, but may be brought into being by invention. And this action of imagination is what makes us capable of seeing life differently. When Handke describes *Kaspar* as a play which "shows what *is possible* with someone," he is therefore saying something that defines his art (defines most subtly all literary art) as well as telling us about the play's particular theme or concern. And in fact his dramaturgy derives more radically in *Kaspar* from playing with possibilities, forcing things to become what they might become, than almost all drama we have known.

For Kaspar is placed on stage for just the purpose of demonstrating a patent "invention," a man being constructed and destroyed by language, and not to be part of a narrative fiction or personal drama. He is not a replica or representative of anyone we have known or heard about, not even of his historical instigation, the "real" Kaspar Hauser. For Handke the stage isn't the world, but something entirely separate, a contrived place, an "artifact," as he has called it. In such a place you do not gain surrogate emotional or moral experiences; the theater is not a means of imitation, representation, or, for that matter, transcription of events, values, meanings, or images existing outside it.

One basic idea behind his plays, Handke has said, is that of "making people aware of the world of the theater, not of the outside world." Objects on his stage have "an artificial function in the game I force them to play." Both objects and words participate in this game (once more the connection with Wittgenstein is significant; the philosopher used the word *Sprachspiel*, "language game," to describe the life of words) whose purpose on one level is to reveal the tyranny of organized verbal forms, of linguistic uses, functions, and implications, and on another to combat the theater as a place of illusion.

For Handke theater is the place where one can see what the world is really like only by being placed outside its ordinary actions and, most important, its self-definitions, which are of course our own. In this attitude he is not so very far from Ibsen, who also saw the theater as judging the world, who spoke of it as a place for "seeing," and who, when told that *Peer Gynt* wasn't poetry, replied that it would be, that the definition of dramatic poetry would have to change to conform to his work.

Handke is even closer, of course, to such immediate predecessors and contemporaries as Beckett, who revealed his attitude toward the inventedness of artistic works when he remarked of Joyce that "he is not writing about something, he is writing something," and Jerzy Grotowski, who believes that the theater ought not attempt to resemble life because it is a means precisely of "going against" life in order to reanimate it. The strange theatrical power of all Handke's plays springs, as has been said, from some of the same sources as Beckett's: the reduction of drama to non-contingent, non-historical elements; the setting free in this space cleared of anecdote of a primal awareness of consciousness itself; the pressure on language to dramatize itself; the involvement of the spectator in a process rather than a story. Like Beckett, too, Handke has felt the extreme difficulty of composing meaningful works out of language which is forever betraying our specific meanings, and the sentiment this gives rise to of mingled rage, despair, and crafty resolution is what animates these plays of language on exhibition.

If Handke has evidently absorbed and been much influenced by Beckett, he has necessarily gone on to something new; in the process of articulating his own vision, he has cut even more ties with the past than Beckett has. His first two plays contain no characters at all in any accepted dramatic sense. They are *Sprechstücke*, speech pieces or speak-ins, "spectacles without pictures," as Handke has called them.

"They point," he says, "to the world not by way of pictures but by way of words; the words of the speak-ins don't point at the world as something lying outside the words but to the world in the words themselves."

His first play, *Offending the Audience* (better translated, perhaps, as *Saying Mean Things to the Audience*), is spoken by four persons, two men and two women, who do nothing but speak and have no set parts, dividing up the lines of the text at the will of the director or whoever is staging the piece. The stage has no scenery or props but, as the directions insist, the "usual theater atmosphere should prevail": attentive ushers, elaborate programs, lights dimming and rising, buzzers to signal the start of action, a curtain drawn at first to suggest the impending "story," then opened to reveal the empty boards. The speakers should utter their lines without coming into any sort of contact with the audience or indeed indicating any awareness of their presence.

The piece begins with one or more of the speakers saying, "You are welcome. This piece is a prologue." Then begins a litany, or rather a series of litanies, whose purpose is twofold: to drive out of the audience the expectations it unquestionably has of witnessing some theatrical work which reflects both the world and other theatrical works (of experiencing, that is to say, the traditional action of drama as the communication of emotion in stylized ways); and to create, out of nothing but language, a drama in which words are used to expose themselves, to strip themselves, as it were, of their habitual function as surrogate experience.

"You will hear nothing you have not heard here [in any theater] before," a speaker intones.

You will see nothing you have not seen here before. You will see nothing of what you have always seen here. You will hear nothing of what you have always heard here. You will hear what you usually see. You will hear what you usually don't see.

You will see no spectacle . . . You will see no play. There will
be no playing here tonight . . . You expected something . . .
[but] This is no play . . . We show you nothing. We are playing
no destinies. We are playing no dreams . . . This is no slice of
life. We don't tell you a story . . . We don't simulate any actions. We don't represent anything . . . We only speak . . .
Here you don't receive your due. Your curiosity is not satisfied.
No spark will leap across from us to you . . . These boards don't
signify a world . . . [they] exist for us to stand on . . . The possibilities of the theater are not exploited here . . . We are not
theatrical . . . This room does not make believe it is a room
. . . This is no drama. No action that has occurred elsewhere is
re-enacted here. Only a now and a now and a now exist here.

The piece moves on to compose not dialogue but structures of speech in which the very facts of speaking and
listening become paramount and the sheer phenomenon of
language is laid bare in the very space where *some particular
use*, the telling of a story, the imparting of information about
physical or moral reality, had been expected. Handke's intention is artistic and not pedagogic (even on a "creative" level),
for he works at the heart of theatrical and dramatic traditions
and conventions, using them against themselves in a judo-like
action and doing this for the liberation of the form. It is the
conflict between the stage's ordinary uses and the playwright's
"nausea" over their ossification and complacency that gives his
works their tension and aesthetic truth, again in much the
same way that Beckett's plays subvert the theater's traditional
"movement" and emotive power by presenting static, emotionally neutral dramas in the teeth of contrary expectations.
The audience is at first puzzled, then bored or disappointed, perhaps angered. Depending on its sophistication and
openness, it will gradually come into the spirit of the piece,
begin to understand that its very presence, the phenomenon
of theatergoing and so, by extension, of *going to culture* as to

some external source of constructed truth, is what is being examined and "dramatized" here.

A speaker says:

> Because we speak to you, you can become conscious of yourself . . . You become aware that you are sitting. You become aware that you are sitting in a theater. You become aware of the size of your limbs . . . You become aware of your sex organs . . . You become aware of the flow of your saliva . . . You become aware of our words entering your ears . . . You are the topic . . . You are the occasion . . . This piece is a prologue. It is not the prologue to another piece but the prologue to what you did, what you are doing, and what you will do. You are the topic.

The audience knows now that it will not be wafted away to a world of dreams or fantasy; it knows itself to be physically in a theater; in the truest sense it is self-conscious, aware of what consciousness is. Now the speakers go on to fill its ears with a series of clichés, honorifics, and insults, in a swelling lexicon of words converted into actions, a spectacle of utterance, a violent exposure of how language leaves us far behind its own intensities, how its contrarieties cancel each other out, how it fills the world with names and putative qualities in place of things and beings. It is an exposure of utterance that has the effect of making us sick and yet at the same time of reviving, through this unshielded experience of words, the peculiar, all-but-forgotten awareness that, for better or worse, words are how we are human:

> You windbags . . . you gargoyles . . . you milquetoasts . . . you chicken-shits . . . you wrong numbers . . . you cardboard figures . . . you hucksters . . . you would-be revolutionaries, you reactionaries, you draft-card burners, you ivory-tower artists, you defeatists, you massive retaliators . . . you Communists, you

vigilantes . . . you ofays . . . you abortions, you bitches and bas-
tards . . . You phonies. You milestones in the history of the
theater . . . You positive heroes . . . You anti-heroes. You everyday heroes. You luminaries of science . . . You educated gasbags
. . . You wretches. You congressmen . . . You chairmen of this
and that . . . You Excellencies . . . You crowned heads. You
pushers. You architects of the future. You builders of a better
world. You mafiosis . . . You who embrace life. You who detest
life. You who have no feeling about life . . . you brothers and
sisters you, you comrades you . . . you fellow humans you.

You were welcome here. We thank you. Good night.

Handke's next play, *Self-Accusation,* is a work which
foreshadows *Kaspar.* In it a male and a female speaker who are
never seen (and who may divide up the lines as the director
sees fit) recite a progress similar to Kaspar's, the tale of a
person's acquisition of language, which is simultaneously a tale
of how language erects the world, steers us through it, forces
us into adaptation, and compels us through its logic to believe
in it and in our coherence with its designs. Out of clichés,
received ideas and their received expressions, logic and anti-
logic, Handke builds a funny and terrifying, if narrow, work of
dramatic imagination which is not so much a self-accusation as
an indictment of the action of language in creating false
selves.

I came into the world [a speaker says]. I became. I was begot-
ten. I originated. I grew. I was born. I was entered in the birth
register. I grew old. I moved . . .

I learned. I learned the words. I learned the verbs. I learned the
difference between being and having been. I learned the nouns.
I learned the difference between singular and plural. I learned
the adverbs. I learned the difference between here and there
. . . this and that . . . good and evil . . . mine and yours . . .

I became the object of sentences . . . I became the object and supplement of principle and subordinate clauses. I became the movement of a mouth. I became a sequence of letters of the alphabet . . .

I did. I failed to do. I let do. I expressed myself. I expressed myself through ideas. I expressed myself through expressions . . . I expressed myself before the impersonal power of the law and of good conduct . . .

I signified . . . With each of my expressions I signified the fulfillment or disregard of rules . . .

I played. I misplayed. I played according to rules which, according to existing rules, were against convention. I played at times and places where it was asocial and ingenuous to play . . . I played with myself when it would have been humane to play with others . . . I failed to play seriously . . . I played with fire . . . I played with marked cards . . . I played with the thought of suicide . . . I played with my sex organ. I played with words . . .

I crossed on the red . . . I failed to move to the rear in streetcars . . . I used the toilet while the train was stopped in the station . . . I exceeded the load limit in elevators . . . I did not remain calm in accidents . . . I put up unauthorized resistance . . . I did not aim at the legs . . . I failed to save women and children first . . .

I did not regard the movement of my shadow as proof of the movement of the earth . . . I did not regard the demands of reason for immortality as proof of life after death . . . I did not regard my lust for life as proof that time stands still.

I am not what I was. I was not what I should have been. I did not become what I should have become. I did not keep what I should have kept.

I went to the theater. I heard this piece. I spoke this piece . . .

For all their originality and revelatory force, the plays of
Handke that have been discussed so far remain within the
category of the experimental. That is to say, they are attempts,
stabs into a resistant body, probes for openings toward a
renewal of theater, not indestructible, permanent additions to
the theatrical repertoire. With the possible and partial exception of *Kaspar*, their interest is rather quickly exhaustible, once
their procedural principle has been grasped and once the
spectator or reader has had his eyes opened to what Handke is
doing with language on the one hand and the idea of theater
on the other. Astonishing as they are, it's difficult to imagine
wanting to see *Self-Accusation* or *Offending the Audience*
more than once.

This is not to derogate them but to place them: they are
preliminary to Handke's assumption of full dramaturgical
powers and continue to underpin all his methods. After he
had finished his play *The Ride Across Lake Constance*,
Handke told an interviewer that he was dissatisfied with all his
earlier works, calling them plays of "statement" instead of, as
he felt the new play to be, "presentment." Yet the difference
isn't so complete or so invidious as he seems to think. *The
Ride Across Lake Constance*, unquestionably a much larger
and more complex work than any of the others, a full "drama"
in any conceivable terms, has the relationship to its predecessors of a portrait to a sketch or a flower to a seed, not of a
proof to an assertion.

There has always been something disingenuous in
Handke's public comments on his work. He has strenuously
denied any intention of being an innovator and, as has been
said, has refused to admit his evident connections to Wittgenstein. When an interviewer observed that *The Ride Across
Lake Constance* was a very "complicated" play which had
thoroughly confused both the actors and the audiences during

its production in New York, he expressed surprise and sorrow, saying that he had "imagined that it was an unusually obvious play and immediately so. It's not my intention to confuse people," he went on, "but at most to estrange them—and I consider estrangement a positive thing."

Doubtless it is, aesthetically: Brecht (whose work Handke has said he dislikes, probably because of its didactic side) built his dramaturgy on just such an assumption. But Handke is playing the naïf in refusing to see that for most audiences estrangement *is* confusing, that in being ousted from familiar grounds and deprived of guideposts the spectator in the theater finds himself suddenly in a whirl, blinking at unheard-of connections and dismayed at the absence of what the characters on the stage *ought to be doing*. In any case, *The Ride Across Lake Constance* is an extremely difficult play on a first encounter, requiring, as does any work outside the conventions, the shedding of expectations, though in fact making the existence of such expectations one of its dramatic elements.

The title, Handke's translator Michael Roloff tells us, comes from a German legend about a horseman who one snowy winter day attempts to find a boat to take him to a village on the other side of Lake Constance, loses his way, and after many hours comes to a town where he inquires about the boat. He is greeted with astonishment, for this is the place he was seeking and the people cannot understand how he could have made it across the ice, which is only an inch thick. On hearing this, the horseman slowly sinks from the saddle and dies. This gave rise to a folk expression in southern Germany: someone who has been in danger without being aware of it has taken "a ride across Lake Constance."

At first Handke's use of the expression is completely enigmatic, for nothing in the play seems to indicate physical or moral danger to any of its characters. There are eight of them, five women and three men, who, Handke says in a stage direction, should have the same names as the actors who take their roles; his original text uses the names of well-known German-speaking performers: Erich von Stroheim, Emil Jannings, Elisabeth Bergner, and so on. The play's action unfolds in a large, heterogeneously furnished room with a double staircase leading to an unseen upper floor, a setting which reminds one of some old resort hotel.

From the outset there is a strong sense of displacement from ordinary reality, something that is heightened by the very matter-of-factness of the scene. The entire atmosphere seems drugged; in a stage direction Handke writes that "all objects are positioned so that it would be difficult to imagine them elsewhere; it is as if they could not bear to be moved ever so slightly." The first conversations of the characters, who move onto the stage without fanfare or preliminaries—as though *fitting into* an arrangement—are on the surface commonplace, even banal, but one quickly becomes aware that extremely strange passions, unaccountable furies, and mysterious sufferings underlie almost every sentence. At the same time, nearly every physical action seems to be undertaken against a powerful counterpressure, as though from some presence attempting to prevent it.

Jannings and another actor, Heinrich George, engage in a dialogue which, one senses, is really an attempt at dialogue, an effort to connect words both to objects or actions and, as communication, to a listener. "Didn't you notice how silly everything suddenly became when we began to talk about 'kidneys flambé'?" George asks, and then says: ". . . because we spoke about something that wasn't visible at the same time." A moment later he asks Jannings, "Have you ever heard people talk about a 'born loser'?" and goes on to ask him about "born troublemakers" and "born criminals" and finally about "scurrying snakes" and "fiery Eskimos." The implication is that the former expressions refer to nothing more real than the latter. Suddenly the conversation ends when both break into laughter and slap *each other's* thighs.

Everything proceeds in a dream-like state of missed connections, reversals of expected connections, non sequiturs ("It takes a trained mind to relish a non sequitur," the British playwright N. F. Simpson has said), and sudden irruptions of nonsense which make up a parody of expected dramatic action that resembles Ionesco's early plays yet is much more complex because of its greater appearance of normality. The characters search for a "play" to enact, trying to feel connected to their speech and gestures. At one point Jannings says, "The sun has come up," to which George replies, "Why? I mean why do you say that?" Jannings answers (*snapping at him*, the directions say): "Those are *my* words! (*as if exhausted*) I don't know why." Another time Elisabeth Bergner, who has been asleep, wakes, looks around, and screams, "Who are you? What do you want? Why am I here?" *During these questions,* Handke's directions state, *she has quieted down again and finishes them only for form's sake.*

For form's sake . . . or for the sake of a form. After a while it becomes clear that *The Ride Across Lake Constance* is working, as all Handke's plays do, on two levels: the one a mockery of traditional drama's orderliness, logic, and meaningfulness, the other a perceptiveness about life's mistaking itself for drama. The idea that nature imitates art is of course an old one, but what Handke does is to make an artwork which displays the process: *The Ride Across Lake Constance* is a play about the way people in "real" life act as though they were cast in plays. In this light, Bergner's asking of her questions is an act of self-dramatization that is purely formal; halfway through, she loses interest but continues to the end because as a "character" she has a role to fill.

In the same way, the fumblings and incapacities during physical actions make up both a satire on the absurdly realistic detail in conventional plays and a subtle, disturbing enactment of the way the physical world sometimes seems to us inimical in its functioning, a place of stuck doors, unopenable bottles, and slippery silverware—a drama in which the props refuse to be docilely used.

More than this, physical objects are invested in the play with an almost occult and exaggerated significance. At one point Jannings finds a pin. (*They all look at it as though surprised.*) Von Stroheim says, "A pin? You don't mean 'the pin'?" Jannings: "The very one." An actress named Henny Porten: "And it really exists? It isn't merely a figure of speech?" "Please convince yourself," Jannings says, and hands it to her, upon which she exclaims, "It has all turned out to be true . . . It has all come true." The inappropriateness of the response as well as the discrepancy between the largeness of the expressions and the minuteness of the event are at the heart of Handke's vision: we are forever struggling to find meanings and to make objects meaningful—we find ourselves under the obligations of characters in a drama.

The gulf between language and reality, between actions and the meanings we give to them through language, is given its most Wittgensteinian expression in the following exchange:

PORTEN: Someone keeps looking over his shoulder while he's walking—does he have a bad conscience?

BERGNER: No, he's simply looking over his shoulder from time to time.

PORTEN: Someone is sitting there with lowered head—is he sad?

BERGNER: No, he's simply sitting there with lowered head.

PORTEN: Two people sit there, don't look at each other and are silent—are they angry with one another?

BERGNER: No, they simply sit there, don't look at each other and are silent.

PORTEN: Someone is banging on the table—to get his way?

BERGNER: Couldn't he simply be banging on the table?

The stage directions read: *They run toward each other with a little yelp of joy, embrace, and separate at once, looking at one another tensely.*

In *Philosophical Investigations*, Wittgenstein had written: "The aspects of things that are most important to us are hidden because of their simplicity and familiarity . . . we fail to be struck by what, once seen, is most striking and powerful." Like philosophy of Wittgenstein's kind, imaginative literature—plays, novels, poems—has the power not so much of uncovering new phenomena as of curing our blindness and so restoring us to what was present but shrouded. Peter Handke's plays, by refusing to surrender to received wisdom, by taking the most ordinary words and gestures as deeply problematic, and by exposing our "artificiality" through their own, make up the aesthetic counterpart of Wittgenstein's thought. They show us, as Shaw said of Ibsen's dramas, "ourselves in our own situations."

INDEX

289